Mountain Movers

The products of mining are everywhere – if it wasn't grown, it was mined or drilled. But the mining industry has a chequered past. Pollution, human rights abuses and corruption have tarnished the reputation of the industry across the globe. Over a decade ago the major mining companies embraced the concept of sustainable and equitable development and embarked on an explicit process of reform – but has the industry actually changed?

This book explores the dynamics of change-making for sustainable development in the resources sector, specifically the mining of mineral and energy resources. The author recounts the stories and insights of over 40 change-makers both inside and outside the industry, from anti-mining activists to the professionals charged with the task of reform, introducing the people who are moving an industry that moves mountains. The book takes stock of what has worked and what has not, analysing the relative influence and dynamics of the key corporate, civil society and government actors with a view to developing new approaches for improving environmental and social outcomes from mineral and energy development.

Illustrated with case studies from Angola, Australia, Brazil, Canada, Chile, Colombia, El Salvador, Guinea, Peru, the Philippines, Romania, Sierra Leone, South Africa, and the United States of America, and brimming with the backstories to the major sustainability initiatives, *Mountain Movers* reveals where progress has been made and where reform is still needed towards a more sustainable and equitable mining industry.

Daniel M. Franks is Deputy Director at the Centre for Social Responsibility of Mining at the University of Queensland's Sustainable Minerals Institute, Australia, and serves as Co-Chair for Social Impact Assessment at the International Association for Impact Assessment.

Routledge Studies of the Extractive Industries and Sustainable Development

African Artisanal Mining from the Inside Out
Access, norms and power in Congo's gold sector
Sarah Geenan

Mountain Movers
Mining, sustainability and the agents of change
Daniel M. Franks

Mountain Movers

Mining, sustainability and the agents of change

Daniel M. Franks

Routledge
Taylor & Francis Group
LONDON AND NEW YORK

from Routledge

First published 2015
by Routledge
2 Park Square, Milton Park, Abingdon, Oxon OX14 4RN

and by Routledge
711 Third Avenue, New York, NY 10017

Routledge is an imprint of the Taylor & Francis Group, an informa business

© 2015 Daniel M. Franks

British Library Cataloguing-in-Publication Data
A catalogue record for this book is available from the British Library

Library of Congress Cataloging in Publication Data
Franks, Daniel M.
Mountain movers : mining, sustainability and the agents of change /
Daniel M. Franks.
    pages cm – (Routledge studies of the extractive industries and
    sustainable development)
Includes bibliographical references and index.
1. Mining engineering. 2. Mines and mineral resources –
Environmental aspects. 3. Mineral industries – Social aspects.
I. Title.
TN146.F77 2015
333.8–dc23   2015012647

ISBN: 978-0-415-71170-8 (hbk)
ISBN: 978-0-415-71171-5 (pbk)
ISBN: 978-1-315-88440-0 (ebk)

Typeset in Goudy
by HWA Text and Data Management, London

Printed and bound in the United States of America by Edwards Brothers Malloy
on sustainably sourced paper.

Contents

Figures

Tables

Preface

If it wasn't grown

The stark reality of modern society is, that of all of the material we use in our daily lives, if it wasn't grown, it was mined or drilled. We are all incredibly reliant on the mining industry. Much of this reliance is hidden. Packaged into products or embedded within the value chain. But for an industry that is so fundamental to most of our lives, it certainly has a bad reputation. With every transaction society affirms its reliance (its lust) for the products of the mineral sector, but with every word it restates its displeasure at the way that these products were produced. There are few professions in the world as maligned as a politician, but being a mining executive may just be one of them. At the same time, there are few easier things to do than to abdicate our own responsibility and blame others for the consequences of our own consumption.

I was made to confront the paradox of a 'resented provider' early in my life. My father spent his career in the gas industry, and while I cheered on the Greenpeace activists who buzzed around the tankers that had fouled the oceans with spilt oil, he was quick to point out the composition of the activists' petroleum-derived wetsuits and inflatable dinghies. At university, while studying geology I was active in Friends of the Earth. I never viewed this as a contradiction. My grandfather was a fossicker, my father a petroleum engineer, and my mother imparted to me a progressive consciousness. I felt entirely comfortable inhabiting both worlds. But to the students of the engineering society, who wore on their shirt: 'Ban mining. Let the bastards freeze in the dark', my position was too contingent. I would ask to blank stares, 'Surely there are circumstances whereby mining should, and should not, exist?'

Navigating the paradox of our reliance on an industry in need of dramatic reform is a complex and delicate task. There are indeed executives in the mining industry who fit the caricature. There are also those who take their responsibilities very seriously. What looks like a monolith from afar, up close is a contest of ideas and visions of the future as reformers and activists are now counted among the industry's ranks.

In the late 1990s the global mining industry chose, under pressure from civil society, to embrace the concept of sustainable and equitable development and embark on an explicit process of change. In this book I ask: How far has the industry come? Has the process of change been authentic? Where has change occurred? And what were the key drivers? I chose to answer these questions by meeting the people, both inside and outside of the industry, who have demanded or delivered on change. Have they found success? Where? How did they do it? Formally I have interviewed more than 40 people. Over the past 15 years, in my research and practice on sustainable development in the extractive industries, I have learnt from hundreds more. Importantly, I have tried to capture a diversity of voices, from anti-mining activists to industry professionals. People who are moving an industry that moves the mountains.

Addressing the 'oxymoron'

In the same way that I never thought it a contradiction to be interested in rocks *and* the fate of the planet I have never thought of mining as inherently unsustainable. Where many insist *sustainable mining* to be an oxymoron, to my mind sustainable development was always about the integrity of earth's ecosystems and the human development of its people. That minerals are replenished so slowly seemed to me to be largely irrelevant. It is the ecosystems and social systems on the surface of the earth that needed sustaining, not the rocks deep below it. Before they are unearthed, ore bodies are mostly divorced from the surface environment, encapsulated by the impermeability of layers of rock. What to me mattered was not whether minerals were renewable, but whether they could be extracted in a way that did not disturb or degrade the environments and societies above them, and whether we had developed the economic and social systems to equitably distribute those resources, recycle them, and adapt to new resources as stocks waxed and waned. As my geology professor would often state, every sample of rock will have 92 elements within it, it is just a matter of their proportion. Minerals will never run out – they just become increasingly expensive (in environmental as well as economic terms) to extract as lower ore grades are pursued. As society changes, so too will our patterns of resource consumption. With new technologies, a green economy will demand its fair share of unique minerals and metals.

This is not to say that the current practices of mineral extraction are compatible with sustainable development or that the depletion of ore is not of immense economic importance at local, national or even international scales. It is just to say that the debate about sustainability and mining being an oxymoron tends to prematurely shut down discussion of what is a rather complex topic.

The mines are they a-changin'?

The commodities unearthed at mine sites are transported, processed, manufactured and consumed by society; they are recycled and they are disposed. Each of these stages in the lifecycle of metals and minerals has important implications for sustainability, but in this book I focus on the people and the initiatives that are influencing sustainability outcomes at the locality of the mine.

Similarly, no one book could profile all of the different companies that make up the mining industry. In fact, the 'mining industry' is somewhat of a misnomer – it is actually made up of a number of sub-industries with a variety of different types of company. There are service companies, construction companies, exploration companies, mineral processing, mineral extraction and refining companies. There are juniors, mid-sized and major mining companies that operate industrial mines. And there are artisanal and small-scale miners who often operate informally. Some mining companies are diversified. Some are focused on a single commodity. Most mining companies are publicly listed, or privately owned. Only a handful mining companies are owned by a state. All of these different organisations respond to slightly different drivers, with different cultures and histories and slightly different operating contexts. In this book I predominantly focus on the large-scale, multi-national mining companies that dominate production in the sector.

The stories written in this book are not definitive histories. They were not written to capture all of the events, or all of the people involved. In telling these stories my motivation was to understand the dynamics of change. Inevitably key individuals or important events may have been omitted or obscured from view, and many of people I spoke with were quick to point out the contributions of others. Any errors in facts or emphasis are entirely my own.

We start the book by seeking to understand the imperative of change and the events that led the mining industry to embark on explicit process of reform through the Global Mining Initiative (GMI), and a public dialogue called the Mining, Minerals and Sustainable Development Project (MMSD). In Chapters 2 through 6 we look at markers of change across five key areas: rights, environment, development, conflict and transparency. Key initiatives are profiled, including: the Voluntary Principles on Security and Human Rights; the International Finance Corporation's Performance Standards on Environmental and Social Sustainability; The International Cyanide Management Code; The Africa Mining Vision; the Fatal Transactions campaign; the Kimberley Process Certification Scheme; the Publish What You Pay coalition; The Extractive Industries Transparency Initiative; and The Natural Resource Charter. In the final chapter (Chapter 7) we look at the agents of change and the interactions between them, before finally, we look back on the MMSD to see how far the industry has come, and what the future might hold for the sustainable development agenda.

A little help from my friends

I am incredibly indebted to David Brereton, Deanna Kemp, Chris Moran, Peter Erskine, Saleem Ali, Mansour Edraki, Warwick Browne and Julia Keenan; and many other colleagues, past and present, from the Sustainable Minerals Institute at the University of Queensland. If there is originality in the pages to follow, it is likely that the idea was sparked from being around one of them. Their knowledge of the sector is amazing and I have benefited greatly from their advice. I am thankful to the staff and students at the Centre for Social Responsibility in

Mining, of which there are too many of you to name – your work has made a real difference. I must also thank the wonderful colleagues with whom I have undertaken collaborative research, which is referenced in this book, including, Rachel Davis, Diana Arbeláez-Ruiz, Jo-Anne Everingham, Frank Vanclay, Anthony Bebbington and Martin Scurrah.

Gillian Cornish, Armando de la Flor Olavide and Vladimir Pacheco assisted with interviews, translation and research assistance. Cristian Parra compiled the first version of the data on corporate social investment spending. The irrepressible Gavin Mudd from Monash University shared with me his data store and has been the best of colleagues for over a decade and a half. Abbi Buxton from IIED provided the download data on the MMSD final report. My dear friend James Davidson offered the use of his architecture studio as an occasional writing refuge.

To my family, especially my wife Marion, and sons, Finn and Luka, thank you always and for everything. Thanks must also go to Marni Stuart for turning the cover idea into reality; Germán Hevia Martini for kindly lending his photographic talents and his incredible photo of Los Bronces; Tim Hardwick and Ashley Wright at Earthscan/Routledge for their patience and confidence; and the University of Queensland Foundation Research Excellence Awards for essential funding support. Lastly, and most importantly, I am grateful to the change-makers who shared with me their stories of hope and resilience.

Credits

Lyrics of 'Beds Are Burning' published with permission, written and composed by James Moginie, Martin Rotsey, Peter Garrett, Peter Gifford and Robert Hirst, published by Sony/ATV Music Publishing Australia.

Abbreviations

AfDB	African Development Bank
AMD	acid and metaliferous drainage
AMV	Africa Mining Vision
ANC	African National Congress
AO	Officer of the Order of Australia
ASM	artisanal and small-scale mining
ASMP	Advanced Social Management Program
ASX200	Australian Stock Exchange – 200 largest companies
AUD	Australian dollar
BHP	Broken Hill Proprietary Company Limited
BP	British Petroleum
BSGR	Beny Steinmetz Group Resources
CAN	Canadian dollar
CAO	Office of the Compliance Advisor Ombudsman
CEO	chief executive officer
CODELCO	*Corporación Nacional del Cobre de Chile*
Comalco	Commonwealth Aluminium Corporation
CRA	Conzinc Rio Tinto of Australia
CSIRO	Commonwealth Scientific and Industrial Research Organisation
CSRM	Centre for Social Responsibility in Mining
DfID	Department for International Development, United Kingdom
ECA	United Nations Economic Commission for Africa
EITI	Extractive Industries Transparency Initiative
EO	Executive Outcomes
ERM	Environmental Resources Management
ESG	Environmental, Social & Governance
EU	European Union
FPIC	free, prior and informed consent
G8	Group of Eight
GABB	*Grupo de Accion por el Bío-Bío*
GAO	General Accounting Office, United States
GDP	gross domestic product
GFN	good faith negotiation

GMI	Global Mining Initiative
GPs	Guiding Principles on Business and Human Rights
HIV	Human Immunodeficiency Virus
ICME	International Council on Metals and the Environment
ICMI	International Cyanide Management Institute
ICMM	International Council on Mining and Metals
ICP	informed consultation and participation
IFC	International Finance Corporation
IIED	International Institute for Environment and Development
ILO	International Labour Organization
IMF	International Monetary Fund
IPIECA	International Petroleum Industry Environmental Conservation Association
IRMA	Initiative for Responsible Mining Assurance
ISG	International Study Group on Africa's Mineral Regimes
ISO	International Standards Organization
IUCN	International Union for Conservation of Nature
JATAM	*Jaringan Advokasi Tambang*
km	kilometres
KP	Kimberley Process Certification Scheme
MAC	Mines and Communities network
MCEP	Mining Certification Evaluation Project
MDGs	millennium development goals
MMSD	Mining, Minerals and Sustainable Development Project
MPLA	Popular Movement for the Liberation of Angola
Nabalco	North Australian Bauxite and Alumina Company
NEPAD	New Partnership for Africa's Development
NGO	non-governmental organisation
NPRC	National Provisional Ruling Council
NPV	net present value
NRC	Natural Resource Charter
NRGI	Natural Resource Governance Institute
NT	Northern Territory
OECD	Organisation for Economic Co-operation and Development
PGMs	Platinum Group Metals
PNG	Papua New Guinea
PS	Environmental and Social Performance Standards
PS7	Performance Standard on Indigenous Peoples
PWYP	Publish What You Pay
QRC	Queensland Resources Council
Rio +10	World Summit on Sustainable Development
Rio +20	United Nations Conference on Sustainable Development
RJC	Responsible Jewellery Council
RTZ	Rio Tinto-Zinc Corporation
RUF	Revolutionary United Front

RWI	Revenue Watch Institute
SDGs	sustainable development goals
SEAT	Socio-Economic Assessment Toolbox
SEC	Securities and Exchange Commission, United States
SIMP	Social Impact Management Plan
SIMS	State Intervention in the Minerals Sector
SL-EPA	Sierra Leone Environmental Protection Agency
SLST	De Beers Sierra Leone Selection Trust
SLTRC	Sierra Leone Truth and Reconciliation Commission
UK	United Kingdom
UN	United Nations
UNCTAD	United Nations Commission on Trade and Development
UNDP	United Nations Development Programme
UNDRIP	United Nations Declaration on the Rights of Indigenous Peoples
UNEP	United Nations Environment Programme
UNITA	National Union for the Total Independence of Angola
UNSC	United Nations Security Council
UNSDSN	United Nations Sustainable Development Solutions Network
US	United States
USGS	United States Geological Survey
VPs	Voluntary Principles on Security and Human Rights
WACAM	The Wassa Association of Communities Affected by Mining
WALHI	*Wahana Lingkungan Hidup Indonesia*
WB	The World Bank
WBCSD	World Business Council on Sustainable Development
WCCCA	Western Cape Communities Co-Existence Agreement
WCED	World Commission on Environment and Development
WCMC	World Conservation Monitoring Centre
WH	World Heritage
WMC	Western Mining Corporation
WWF	World Wide Fund for Nature / World Wildlife Fund

1   Breaking new ground

The 'long petal of sea, wine and snow'

The story that I will tell across the pages to follow begins in Chile on the Western flank of the South American Andes. This 'long petal of sea, wine and snow', as Chilean poet Pablo Neruda famously described his homeland, is also the world's principal source of copper. Chile accounts for around 32% of world copper production and 27% of world copper reserves.[1] Copper is a commodity central to our daily lives. It carries energy to our homes, and our voices across the telephone. Copper is used in our coins, our plumbing, the wiring of our electronics and even as building product in our hospitals to prevent infection. The copper deposits of the Chilean Andes have been mined for millennia, but industrial mining found its way to the continent in 1915, with breakthroughs in low-grade oxide mineral processing and the opening of the Chuquicamata mine.

I have chosen to start the story here for two reasons. The first is a personal one. Chile is the place where my own involvement with mining industry reform began. I arrived in Chile, an aspiring geologist in the late 1990s. I visited the copper mines of northern Chile and the tin and silver mines of Potosí in neighbouring Bolivia and I was confronted with the striking disparities that seem to typify many parts of Latin America, and indeed the world. In Potosí, the mines, and the forced labourers that once worked them, contributed thousands of tonnes of silver to the Spanish Monarchy during colonialism and are still worked today using the backbreaking methods of centuries past. Potosí is a marvel of inequity. It is the ordinariness of the town that is so striking given the riches that have been unearthed. In Antofagasta, Chile's mining capital, I stayed with an acquaintance who was an expatriate mining professional. We were stationed in a separate luxury suburb, an enclave of the developed world far removed from the circumstances of ordinary Chileans. While I lugged my baggage toward the enclave, which at the time was not connected by the normal public transport system, I wondered whether the disparities of the present were the children of historic injustices in Chile as they had been in Bolivia. I have since returned many times to the region and witnessed the transformations that have accompanied mining development over the past decade and a half. I have worked with communities, companies and governments globally in the pursuit of better environmental and social outcomes from mining and I will share some of these experiences in this book.

The second reason for starting this story of mining industry change in Chile is that one thread of reform can be traced to events that happened here just a few years before my first visit to the region. A controversial hydroelectric project constructed between 1993 and 1996 triggered a chain of events that led to new standards for private sector investment globally and sustainability reform within the mining industry. That dam was the Pangue Hydroelectric Project.

Pangue, the Bío-Bío and the Performance Standards

Originating in the Andes of south-central Chile, the Bío-Bío River flows eastward, falling around 1100m on its 380km journey to the Pacific coast. Fed at its origin by both lakes and glaciers, the river descends through evergreen Araucaria forests, vestiges of the ancient Gondwana super-continent, and passes by cinder cone volcanoes before meeting the Pacific in the city of Concepción. Prior to the dam the river was one of the last major free-flowing, white-water rivers in the world. The name Bío-Bío comes from the language of the Mapuche, and the river itself marked the borderline, or '*La Frontera*', between the foothold of the Spanish colony to the north and the Mapuche indigenous resistance to the south. It was not until the 1880s that the Chilean State firmly established its presence here following the 'Pacification of Araucanía' military campaigns. Still today there is a timeless quality to both the people and the landscapes of this captivating region.

The river, and the controversy over its damming, is an unlikely setting for a story about change in the mining sector, but change tends to meander an unlikely course. The Pangue Hydroelectric Project was proposed following the privatisation of Chile's state owned electric utility, ENDESA, by the Pinochet dictatorship in 1989. The 467 MW dam secured part funding from the International Finance Corporation (IFC), the private sector lending arm of the World Bank. Where the World Bank lends to governments, the IFC lends to the private sector with the stated goal to attract private capital into developing countries to foster development. The IFC was created in 1956, more than a decade after the International Monetary Fund and the World Bank, which were both created at the United Nations Monetary and Financial Conference in the resort town of Bretton Woods, New Hampshire, in 1944.[2] The rationale for the IFC's creation was that government-to-government lending was argued to be an insufficient source of development spending and that what was needed to mobilise development was private capital.

The World Bank has funded hundreds of dam-building projects since the 1950s. The Bank committed around US$1 billion per year up until the 1970s, rising to around US$2 billion per year until the late 1990s when investment began to tail off.[3] Over the course of the 1960s and 1970s hydro-power projects attracted significant opposition from environmental and affected peoples' groups. Many were also beginning to question whether the model of economic development implicit in large-scale lending to governments and companies for infrastructure projects was indeed leading to widespread improvements in social development.[4] The World Commission on Dams estimated that the construction of large dams has been responsible for the displacement of between 40 million and 80 million people with many people not receiving resettlement support or adequate compensation.[5]

Under pressure from social movements, the World Bank adopted a series of reforms during the 1980s and early 1990s, including policies on involuntary resettlement (1980), tribal peoples (1982), environmental assessment (1988), and the introduction of an independent complaints-handling body known as the Inspection Panel (1993). Environmental and social policies were progressively strengthened under the banner of Operational Directives (1987) and Operational Policies (1992), and then Safeguard Policies in 1998.[6]

Pangue was a controversial project from the beginning. The project was conceived in a politically charged environment. The Pinochet dictatorship was in its last days and the privatisation of key assets, such as ENDESA, were viewed by many Chileans as a 'closing down sale' where allies of the dictatorship lined up to buy public assets at discount rates.[7] The hydroelectric project itself posed significant risks to the environment and local communities and was thus designated as a Category A project by the IFC (that is, a project with a high potential for significant negative impacts). In November 1995, after the dam was built, a Chilean non-government organisation, the *Grupo de Accion por el Bío-Bío* (GABB), lodged a claim with World Bank President, James Wolfensohn, alleging that the Pangue project had not followed World Bank safeguard policies or the provisions of the investment agreement, and requesting that the World Bank's Inspection Panel review the case. The claim was also supported by a large coalition of forty-seven other NGOs, demonstrating the breadth of civil society concern about the matter.[8] In fact, the claim was just the latest phase of a large civil society campaign that had petitioned the IFC not to fund the project in the first instance.[9]

James Wolfensohn took up the position as World Bank Group President in July of 1995, so he came to the controversy with the energy of a fresh mandate. As an IFC-funded project, Pangue was technically not subject to the same environmental and social safeguards that were applicable to World Bank-funded projects where lending is directly to governments. The IFC evaluated World Bank policies to determine what was relevant to IFC projects, but no clear guidance was available to IFC staff or their clients on what this actually entailed. Critics of the IFC argued that on the one hand the IFC was trading on their association with the World Bank and the safeguards that applied to World Bank projects, but on the other hand those very same policies were not applied consistently to the IFC, because the IFC argued that it was different to the World Bank and could only apply the policies to the extent that they made sense in the private sector context.

In light of this complexity, James Wolfensohn informed the complainants that IFC-funded projects were not within the mandate of the Inspection Panel and he designated an Independent Advisor to undertake an audit of the project. The audit was a first of its kind for the IFC. In May of 1996, Wolfensohn appointed Dr Jay Hair, the immediate past president of the World Conservation Union (IUCN) to the role of Independent Advisor. Jay Hair was accompanied by two other audit team members, Luke Danielson and Benjamin Dysart, as well as a research assistant, Avra Rubalcava.

The auditors reported their findings in April 1997. In a hard-hitting report the audit team identified some commendable aspects of the project, in particular the standard by which eight non-indigenous families were involuntarily resettled, but the report also highlighted serious shortcomings. The report found that: significant project-induced impacts on 12 indigenous *Pehuenche* families adjacent to the reservoir had not been properly addressed; the cumulative impacts of the project, in light of five other proposed dams in the same catchment, had not been adequately considered by the IFC during decisions about whether to invest; the governance arrangements of a project-supported indigenous social development foundation were questionable; and the IFC had not developed project specific environmental and social standards or criteria that were acceptable.[10]

The key conclusion of the report, however, did not relate to the oversight of the Pangue project per se, but to the capability of the IFC as an institution to achieve its stated mandate to foster development. The report concluded that:

> There is no indication at this time (April 1997) that IFC has in place the necessary institutional operating systems, or clarity in its policy and procedural mandate, to manage complicated projects such as Pangue in a manner that complies consistently with World Bank Group environmental and social requirements and recognized best practices.[11]

The audit team recommended that: appropriate management systems and performance standards be established; that a process akin to the World Bank's Inspection Panel be developed by the IFC; and that environmental and social oversight of projects should be handled by an independent body with direct reporting to the Office of the President. Looking in retrospect, it is clear that each of these recommendations have found their way into the institutional sustainability architecture of the IFC and beyond. In subsequent years the IFC created an Environmental and Social Development Department; adopted Safeguard Policies for IFC projects (and later developed a comprehensive set of Performance Standards on Environmental and Social Sustainability); and established the Office of the Compliance Advisor Ombudsman, a dedicated recourse mechanism to receive and investigate complaints from people negatively impacted by IFC projects.[12]

According to the IFC 'no other project in the history of IFC has led to such... far-reaching institutional change'.[13] Pangue is indeed an unlikely candidate for this mantle. The project is one of the lowest impact hydro-electric projects in the world when measured by the amount of land inundated and persons displaced per mega-watt hour of power produced.[14] So why is it that the project attracted so much controversy? And perhaps more interestingly, why was Pangue the catalyst that led to a wave of reform that spread well beyond the IFC. In one answer to the first question, Pangue typifies the underappreciated truism: context matters. Just because a development project looks comparatively low impact does not necessarily mean that it will be accepted in its environmental, social, political and historical context. And as for the second question of why Pangue was the catalyst for wider reform, Pangue reminds us that change is not steady, but is replete with tipping points and recidivism, deep disappointment and deep elation. Change is connected. The ripeness of any one moment is bound to the multitude of other moments.

In the coming chapters I will attempt to answer questions such as this, using as my entry point the people that have involved themselves in driving change in the mining industry. The advocates and campaigners, the institutional reformers and the sustainability professionals working for change from within and from without. It is through the stories of these 'change-agents' that I hope to uncover the details of how change is really won (and perhaps lost). What looks on paper like a logical process of 'complaint-review-recommendation-adoption' is often far from the reality in practice. When I spoke to Luke Danielson, now President of Sustainable Development Strategies Group, he described the course of the Pangue Independent Review as extraordinarily tense and difficult:

> I came home from a week in the Bío-Bío and [the] landlord of my office said, 'You have to get out of here, I got a call from the electric company and they want you out of here.' And I said, 'Well it's late in the day, I'll come back in the morning.' 'No, you have to be out of here today.' [So] I went in my office and somebody had been through every piece of paper in my office and tossed it all over the floor and rattled through everything I owned. It was distressing and very stressful.

Change is rarely easily won. When established norms and the power of institutions and individuals are threatened, ugliness and resistance are ever the companions. In the case of Pangue, hundreds of passages of the final report of the Independent Review were redacted. The IFC, under the threat of a liable suit, felt obliged to remove any passage that could be construed as critical of their client, while leaving those passages that dealt directly with the conduct of the IFC. To this day the full report has never been released to the public.

It is true that the findings of the Pangue Independent Review led to 'far-reaching institutional change' within the IFC but that doesn't mean that the IFC welcomed that change at that point. Similarly, with the passage of time and the growth of sustainability professionals within organisations like the IFC, new norms have been established and events like Pangue take on a different meaning. While the full report of the Pangue Independent Review has never been released, the IFC did more recently release a précis of the key lessons learned,[15] which proudly reflected on the role that the Pangue Independent Review played in catalysing the reforms that led to the IFC Performance Standards on Environmental and Social Sustainability.

The IFC Performance Standards (PS) are now the international benchmark for sustainability due diligence and risk management for private sector projects. First adopted in 2006, they replaced the World Bank's Safeguard Policies for IFC investments. The Office of the Compliance Advisor Ombudsman, helmed by Dame Meg Taylor, was responsible for leading the transition from the Safeguard Policies into the PS. Rachel Kyte, now World Bank Group Vice President and Special Envoy for Climate Change was the key driver of this process.[16] The way the PS work is to require recipients of project finance to adopt a set of environmental and social management practices as a condition of the loan. The periodic revision of the PS has become an important space for innovation and contestation in environmental and social practice in the proceeding years. As we shall see in Chapter 2, the 2012 revision of the standards catalysed mining industry acceptance of key norms on Indigenous rights, even while some people have criticised the PS for their lack of enforceability and accountability.

The PS and the Safeguard Policies before them have, over time, won much farther reach than simply those projects funded by the IFC. In 2003 the private banking sector adopted a parallel set of standards called the Equator Principles. Seventy-nine financial institutions in 34 countries are now signatories of the Equator Principles, covering around 70% of project finance debt in emerging markets.[17]

'Change begets more change. Nothing propagates so fast.' We saw that civil society pressure at the site of one hydro-electric project in Southern Chile combined with the detailed and incisive critiques of the Pangue Independent Review to win important reforms to established institutional norms. As one event leads to another change-agents adapt their practice and sometimes go on to spur new ventures, in new arenas.

In 1999 Luke Danielson received a call from Richard Sandbrook. Richard was a founding member of Friends of the Earth and the Executive Director of the International Institute for Environment and Development (IIED). Richard was tasked with leading the Mining, Minerals and Sustainable Development Project (MMSD), a new industry initiative to confront the sustainable development challenges posed by the sector. The MMSD was one component of the broader Global Mining Initiative (GMI). Luke was appointed the Project Director of MMSD and Jay was later asked to chair the multi-stakeholder assurance group to oversee the independence of the process. The MMSD would itself lead to larger things, including the formation of the International Council on Mining and Metals (ICMM), the peak mining industry body charged with advancing sustainable development in the sector. Jay Hair was ICMM's first Secretary General.[18]

This book is about these stories. In the chapters to follow we will meet the people and initiatives that have driven change and the limits, dynamics and implications of that change. In the following section we will look at the events that led the mining industry to front its critics and shift from a position of rejection to adopt the language of sustainable development.

The Global Mining Initiative

In the late 1990s the mining industry was in crisis. Commodity prices were low, market capitalisation was low, and the environmental legacies of a number of major mining projects had spurned a significant, and increasingly global, environmental movement against mining. The campaigns were largely coordinated by international environmental NGOs[19] and more specialist mining-focused organisations,[20] and they were given legitimacy by local civil society groups the world over. They highlighted the environmental legacy at operating mine sites to characterise the industry as out of touch with the times. The legacies included: the tailings dam failure at BHP's Ok Tedi mine and subsequent disposal of tailings (waste from mineral processing) into the Fly River in Papua New Guinea; the tailings dam failure and direct discharge of tailings into the ocean at Placer Dome's Marcopper mine on the island of Marinduque in the Philippines; and the civil conflict in Bougainville, which eventually led to around 20,000 conflict deaths, and was sparked by Conzinc Rio Tinto of Australia's mine and again, its disposal of mine tailings into the Jaba River.

Research was also published at this time on the relationship between economic dependence on natural resources and GDP by authors such as Richard Auty, Jeffrey Sachs and Andrew Warner, and Michael Ross.[21] This research showed that ore bodies and oil fields were not always the boon that many countries had been led to believe. This negative correlation became known as the 'Resource Curse', and has since framed much of the discourse of the industry's critics.

The industry felt, and indeed was, under siege by this wave of activism, which was turning the broader public against the industry, putting at risk the access to capital necessary for production and project development, and pitting miners against politicians in the race for the title of most disreputable profession. Of course the industry itself viewed its cause as more noble, in providing the resources for all of the things that we take for granted in modern society.

In mid-1998, Hugh Morgan, the then-CEO of Western Mining Corporation (WMC), and Doug Yearly, CEO of Placer Dome, reached out to a number of the other mining CEOs, including Sir Robert Wilson of Rio Tinto, to explore whether a more proactive and collective response from the industry was necessary. Hugh Morgan was a tough-minded mining boss but he read very well that a new approach was needed. Hugh was the Chairman of the International Council on Metals and the Environment (ICME), the body tasked with coordinating the industry's response to environmental issues:

> I used to go to [ICME meetings] and you'd look pretty thin on the ground, representing the whole industry saying, 'Our life is at stake.' They'd say, 'Well, mmm, there's not many of your colleagues here, it can't be that desperate' … It's not as if the CEOs were disinterested. They were under huge competing demands for their time and attention. What I think was necessary was to make it more enabling for the CEOs to get engaged. If you look at the mining industry their engineering task is to remove this mountain, down this railway line, out of this port, at price x. That's their business, it's an engineering culture. Here we were dealing with the soft tissue issue of community concerns…it wasn't something that naturally came to the top of their emotional judgment, of saying what's important.[22]

Hugh sounded out Sir Robert Wilson at a lunch meeting at Rio's headquarters at St James's Square, London. The proposition that he and Doug Yearly put to Wilson at that meeting was that ICME's headquarters be moved from Canada to Europe as part of a larger industry response to raise the profile of sustainable development issues in the industry. Morgan and Yearly also hoped that Wilson would chair the new venture. Wilson was agreeable to the concept of a new organisation but more cautious on the proposition of being President, in part due to the risk that it be seen as a Rio Tinto takeover of the association. Wilson agreed to study the proposal further. Discussions were then held between Chris Leptos (WMC), Andy Vickerman (Rio Tinto) and George Littlewood (Rio Tinto) in July 1998, before a larger meeting of CEOs in October.[23] The invitation for the meeting stated that the goal was to discuss reputational issues and 'to stem the regulatory and other pressures which are relentlessly constricting access to end markets for metals and limiting growth opportunities in other ways'.[24]

After agreement had been reached that *something* needed to be done, the question turned to the more practical, *what?* Across the industry two distinct camps had formed about what should be done to regain the support of the public – the view of the first was that the mining industry needed to better sell its message. The solution proposed by this group was better public relations to counter the negative press the industry was receiving with stories about the benefits of mining. The second camp had a quite different perspective. They viewed the problem as more fundamental: that environmental and social performance had indeed been problematic and, instead, what was needed was a period of reflection and dialogue between the industry and its critics. It was this second perspective that this group of CEOs led by Hugh Morgan and Sir Robert Wilson advocated. I joined George Littlewood in his Melbourne apartment to recount the formative events that lead to the establishment of the Global Mining Initiative (GMI). George was one of the nine *sherpas* who became the link between each of the CEOs and the GMI as it took shape:[25]

> We were our own worst enemies. My environmental friends used to say, 'Well of course everybody understands you're important for Australia's future, but you're just about the worst advocates for your own case. You come across as bolshy and not listening to anybody else.' The [Global Mining Initiative] was seen as an exercise of analysis, of understanding what was going on, what behavioural changes were necessary, an educative process. We set out from the beginning to involve as best we could, and we never got nearly as far as we wanted to, the NGO movements and inter-governmental organisations. We wanted to bring people in to this process.

Danielson shares this view that the industry that was struggling to deal with criticism:

> There were really a lot of people in the industry who thought that anybody who criticised them had no right to criticise them, was ignorant, was some

kind of a communist, [but] at the same time there were a lot of people in the environmental movement that were so angry at mining that they had no vision at all of how a mining industry could operate in a way that could be acceptable to them and there was a lot of talk in some quarters of just abolishing mining.

The mining industry had not engaged deeply in the sustainability debate to this point. The territory was unfamiliar, but engagement was now unavoidable. According to Aidan Davy, the Deputy President of the International Council for Mining and Metals:

> In the latter part of the 1990s what struck me very forcibly is that the locus of global leadership on corporate responsibility in the extractive sector was not in mining. It was in oil and gas. And even within oil and gas, it was a fairly shallow pool of companies. Then the [GMI] process came about ... You got a sense that some of the companies involved in that were incredibly serious about changing the way that they did business.

The potential of the Global Mining Initiative was that it offered an opportunity to flesh out the core of the debate and fill the voids between polarised perspectives with considered possibilities. This alluring prospect was, however, tempered by the sobering reality that distrust was not only an emotional state or political position, but something on which both sides depended. According to Danielson, 'It was bitter. It was brutal. And it was personal.' The 'arrival of the marauding miner' was as powerful a rallying cry (and fundraising tool) for some non-governmental organisations as 'here come the barbarians' was in some quarters of the industry.

Tom Burke, a Rio Tinto consultant, was part of developing the strategy for the Global Mining Initiative. Tom was the former Executive Director of Friends of the Earth in the United Kingdom, and like a number of other key figures in this story had been recruited from civil society into the industry. Tom proposed a three-track process. Track one would be a global dialogue process and collaborative research study that became known as the MMSD – the Mining, Minerals and Sustainable Development Project. The MMSD was to be undertaken in partnership with the World Business Council on Sustainable Development (WBCSD) and be led by an independent body. Richard Sandbrook, Executive Director of the International Institute for Environment and Development was asked to lead this component. Richard also had a pedigree in the environmental movement as a founding member of Friends of the Earth (and former Executive Director), and he recruited Luke Danielson as the Project Director and Caroline Digby as the Research Manager.

Track two was to consist of a concerted effort to engage within the industry, culminating in a global conference. The conference was held in May 2002, in Toronto, attracting more than 500 participants. It was timed to contribute to the Rio +10 event in Johannesburg later that year. Track three was the formation of a new industry association to implement what was learnt from Tracks one and two. The International Council on Mining and Metals was headquartered in London and replaced the ICME as the peak mining industry body tasked with addressing the issues of sustainable development.

The Mining, Minerals and Sustainable Development Project

Undertaking a global dialogue process on the performance of a controversial and contested industry was a difficult task. Some NGOs were sceptical of the industry's motives and stayed out of the process, particularly in the beginning. The depth of distrust was reflected by the parallel launch of a 'Global Mining Campaign' by a coalition of NGOs,[26] and a meeting of 27 community and civil society representatives from 13 countries in London in May 2001 that issued the 'London Mining Declaration', denouncing the GMI as a part of a 'corporate-led propaganda offensive' and catalysing the formation of the Mines and Communities network.[27] Other representatives of civil society such as Steven D'Esposito from the Mineral Policy Center (now known as Earthworks), and Alan Young from the Environmental Mining Council of British Columbia (a coalition of conservation groups) approached the MMSD cautiously and viewed it as an opportunity to build common purpose among mining-focused environmental NGOs.[28]

The MMSD Work Group, led by Luke Danielson and Caroline Digby took advice from the coordinators of other contemporaneous dialogue processes to design a process cognisant of the importance of independence. Advice was sought from Achim Steiner, Director of the World Commission on Dams, which was coming to an end at the time the MMSD was ramping up. The team also benefited from the experience of an earlier study the IIED undertook with the WBCSD on paper and pulp mills. Even so, the final report of the MMSD, *Breaking New Ground*, acknowledged the difficulty of building trust in the process:

> The project has not been without controversy for the report challenges all sides in the debate … The project has had considerable success in engaging with stakeholders in some parts of the globe, but has fallen short of a deep involvement with every interest group. Indeed it has been explicitly rejected by some special interest groups, sometimes before there was anything concrete to judge [it] by.[29]

At its peak, the Work Group consisted of 17 people based in London. The project was further grounded by four regional partnerships (Australia, North America, South America and Southern Africa), each having its own governance structure. Coordinators were appointed for each of the regional partnerships to facilitate the dialogue process.[30] Through these partnerships and beyond, national efforts were undertaken in 20 countries, 700 people were engaged in 23 global workshops, 175 individual pieces of research were commissioned, and 21 project bulletins were distributed to a list of more than 5,000 people.[31] An Assurance Group was formed to provide oversight with 25 individual members drawn from civil society, government, labour unions, indigenous groups, industry associations and the mining industry. A charter guided the activities of the Assurance Group and a Sponsors Group from which funding was drawn.[32] As momentum built so did the industry outreach, with corporate participation growing from the nine initial companies to 25.

Cristina Echavarría was one of the coordinators of the South American component of MMSD. Five countries were the focus of the engagement (Chile, Peru, Bolivia, Brazil and Ecuador) and a national coordinator was appointed in each of these countries. I spoke to Cristina from her home in Colombia. Cristina describes herself as both a 'hard questioner' of industry and governments and a 'practitioner', willing to roll up her sleeves and do things on the ground. She explained to me the process: 'The methodology was to build an agenda from the bottom up, working through specific groups of stakeholders (governments, NGOs, indigenous people, small scale miners and the large scale mining industry). We held focus groups, building up to national meetings for national agendas, and then to a regional agenda based on those national agendas.' The South American regional partnership galvanised the involvement of more than 700 people in 50 workshops, surveyed a further 354 people from 15 countries and published five national reports. 'One of the things I value most about MMSD,' said Cristina, 'is that it put on the table a multi-stakeholder discussion about issues that were not even talked about – that were taboo.'

Breaking New Ground was ground-breaking. It is remarkable when reading the report, now more than a decade on, how relevant the issues and recommendations remain (see Table 1). The report was frank in its findings. It acknowledged that the 'negative social and environmental legacy of the sector is a major obstacle to building trust and moving forward';[33] that there is a 'legacy of abuse';[34] and that the industry 'is falling far short of meeting [sustainable development] objectives, it is seen as failing in its obligations and is increasingly unwelcome'.[35] The study found that corporate performance was variable, with some good companies improving, while the performance of others was 'inexcusable, and the past record is even worse'.[36]

The initial industry reaction to *Breaking New Ground* was mixed. Richard Morgan, editor of the *Mining Journal*, wrote in a piece for one of the ICMM's first newsletters following the release of the draft that he had concerns that the report adopted the language of environmentalism. He argued that the MMSD was a significant and brave step forward for the industry but asked: 'Who on earth would have time to read it?'[37] If downloads of the report are anything to go by then Morgan's fear has proved to be dramatically unfounded. Thousands of copies of the report have been downloaded from the IIED website, and it is still today one of the IIED's most downloaded items.[38]

In the period since the release of the report, some within civil society who had viewed the project as an exercise in 'green wash' have also begun to re-evaluate their views on the process and its outcomes, though detractors of the process do remain.[39] In speaking to key figures within civil society and the industry in the writing of this book, many now regard the MMSD as a process that changed the

Table 1 Summary of actions to support sustainable development in the minerals industry from the Mining, Minerals and Sustainable Development project

Summary of actions recommended by Breaking New Ground

- Greater research and education to better understand the implications of mining and minerals production on sustainable development.
- Development of corporate policies and management systems to embed sustainable development commitments.
- Adoption of a global declaration by the minerals industry and a protocol to ensure industry-wide implementation (including independent auditing).
- Development of national industry codes of conduct.
- Drafting of a collective statement of principles by civil society outlining their expectations.
- Improved government policy and regulation, including the avoidance of riverine disposal of tailings, and the wider adoption of financial surety to ensure rehabilitation after mine closure.
- Better integration within impact assessment
- Integrated planning for the closure of operations.

- Creation of project level and industry wide grievance handling and dispute resolution mechanisms.
- Respect for the principle of free prior and informed consent from Indigenous Peoples.
- Wider use of agreement making processes with communities and indigenous peoples.
- Establishment of an international and public register of all payments by mining companies to governments at all levels to address corruption.
- Harmonization of reporting guidelines.
- Development of clear criteria between the mining industry and key actors like the IUCN on mining and protected areas.
- Establishment of a global financial facility to remediate abandoned mines and a global initiative to address mining legacies.
- Creation of an ongoing multi-stakeholder forum on mining, minerals and sustainable development.

Source: IIED and WBCSD, 2002, *Breaking New Ground*

conversation around mining and sustainable development and made it acceptable within the industry to discuss, reflect and respond to these challenges.

Keith Slack is the Global Program Manager of Oxfam America's Extractive Industries team. 'At the time, we were, as NGOs, pretty critical of the process for not involving civil society more directly, being industry driven and not being independent,' said Keith when I spoke to him from his base in Washington, DC, 'but I think the end result, at least in terms of the report, has quite a lot of good recommendations in it that we would agree with. I think where it fell down in the end,' said Keith 'was any kind of real lasting commitment to take forward the recommendations.'

There was initial disappointment within civil society circles that MMSD didn't produce much more in terms of tangible commitments on the part of companies, based on the recommendations. The lack of binding commitments fed into the fears about whether the process was indeed an authentic exercise in change. Keith relayed to me a scene from the Global Mining Initiative Conference, 'Resourcing the Future', held in Toronto in May 2002:

I remember the final session of the Toronto conference, they had four or five of the big mining companies' CEOs up on stage, and the panel moderator asked Brian Gilbertson, the CEO of BHP Billiton, 'Okay, so now it's the final day of this conference, we've had this multi-stakeholder process, what are you all going to put on the table in terms of commitments?' And there was this deafening silence, and then [the moderator] said, 'What about this issue of riverine tailings disposal, will you all commit to not using that anymore?' And the CEOs wouldn't even go there. So that, to me, was symptomatic of – at the time, a bit of a distancing of the mining industry from the actual results and product of MMSD, which I think, over time, has reduced to some extent, at least amongst some of the larger companies in terms of the rhetoric and some of the policies.[40]

Members of the ICCM did adopt the 'Toronto Declaration'[41] following the GMI Conference (see Table 2) but Keith Slack argues it is only now more than a decade on that a solid link can be made between where the MMSD left off and the areas where the ICMM is now advancing reform. George Littlewood also lamented that momentum was lost in the early days after to process to press the implications of the analysis and operationalise the findings internally. 'Ownership for the findings should have been more deeply embedded in the participant organisations,' said George. Perhaps one of the downsides of ICMM taking on this responsibility was that individual companies did not take as great an ownership of the MMSD outcomes.

Catherine Coumans is Research Coordinator and Asia Pacific Program Coordinator of MiningWatch Canada. MiningWatch Canada is an advocacy

Table 2 Commitments made by members of ICMM following the Global Mining Initiative Conference

ICMM *Toronto Declaration Commitments*

- Expand the current ICMM Sustainable Development Charter to include appropriate areas recommended in the MMSD Report.
- Develop best-practice protocols that encourage third-party verification and public reporting.
- Engage in constructive dialogue with key constituencies.
- Assist Members in understanding the concepts and application of sustainable development.
- Together with the World Bank and others, seek to enhance effective community development management tools and systems.

- Promote the concept of integrated materials management throughout the minerals value chain wherever relevant.
- Promote sound science-based regulatory and material-choice decisions that encourage market access and the safe use, reuse and recycling of metals and minerals.
- Create an emergency response regional register for the global mining, metals and minerals industry.
- In partnership with IUCN, The World Conservation Union and others seek to resolve the questions associated with protected areas and mining.

Source: International Council on Mining and Metals, 2002, 'ICMM Toronto Declaration'

organisation that supports affected communities in Canada and overseas and was one of the organisations that chose to stay outside of the MMSD process. According to Catherine, MMSD 'opened up wide the whole arena for the mining industry to get more comfortable with actually talking about its problems … almost every conversation you have now starts with, yes, there are many problems but the conversation quickly turns to a debate about the solutions, what are the right solutions.' Catherine was very careful to note that not all of this shift could be attributed to MMSD as there were many efforts outside of MMSD that were pushing in a similar direction. 'I do think there's sort of a pre-MMSD and a post-MMSD,' said Catherine, but 'I would still say that there is great resistance to change on some really key areas where I think the harm is great, but where also probably profits are most intimately tied into these areas.'

In the post-MMSD period the response of the industry was to: professionalise sustainability and community relations roles; develop corporate policies and processes; strengthen monitoring and reporting; and institute internal management systems.[42] A very large pool of good practice guidance has also been developed across a very wide array of topics. ICMM now has 22 mining company members and 33 members from national and regional mining associations. Their members represent around 40–50% of global production (depending on the commodity) from 1200 sites in 70 countries.[43]

Professor Anthony Hodge, former coordinator of MMSD North America, is now President of the ICMM. He reflected in 2006 on the outcomes of the MMSD as part of *Architecture for change*, an historical account of the MMSD process written by Danielson:

> Seen from a birds eye view, the change in the culture and values of the mining industry (and society) that we are witnessing at this time is without precedent. Within that change, MMSD has played an important role as a change agent, contributing a small but significant push along a very long road the end of which is nowhere in sight. The very inception and completion of MMSD itself is an indicator of this change.[44]

But, has *practice* really changed? And if so, is it enough? How long is that road to which Tony refers. And given the enormous consequences should we not expect reform to be more rapid? In the chapters to follow I will search for some answers to these questions. I will wear the mantle of a 'hard questioner' and talk to the people working to bring about change in key areas such as rights, environment, development, conflict and transparency. In the next chapter we explore the intertwined issues of human rights and Indigenous rights, and consider the extent to which the mining industry has engaged with this agenda.

Notes

1 United States Geological Survey (USGS) (2014), 'Copper. Mineral commodity summaries.' February, pp. 48–49.

2 At this time the World Bank simply consisted of the International Bank for Reconstruction and Development.

3 World Commission on Dams (2000), *Dams and Development: A new framework for decision-making*. The report of the World Commission on Dams. November. London: Earthscan.

4 See for example: Payer, C. (1974), *The Debt Trap: The IMF and the Third World*. Penguin, Harmondsworth; Payer, C. (1982), *The World Bank: A critical analysis*. New York: Monthly Review Press.

5 World Commission on Dams (2000), *Dams and Development*, pp. 16–17.

6 The ten Safeguard Policies include: Environmental Assessment; Cultural Property; Disputed Areas; Forestry; Indigenous Peoples; International Waterways; Involuntary Resettlement; Natural Habitats; Pest Management; and Safety of Dams. For an analysis of the development of the safeguards see: Wade, R. (1997), 'Greening the bank: The struggle over the environment, 1970–1995.' In D. Kapur, J.P. Lewis and R. Webb (eds) *The World Bank: Its first half century*, The Brookings Institution, Washington DC, Vol. 2, Chapter 13, pp. 611–734; and Freestone, D. (2013), *The World Bank and Sustainable Development: Legal essays*. Leiden, The Netherlands: Martinus Nijhoff Publishers.

7 For an analysis of the terms of these sales see for example: Marcel, M. (1989), 'Privatización y finanzas públicas: el caso de Chile 1985–88.' In Colección Estudios Cieplan no. 26, June, pp. 5–60. Online resource: http://www.cieplan.org/media/publicaciones/archivos/88/Capitulo_1.pdf Accessed: 16 June 2014.

8 Hair, J., Dysart, B., Danielson, L. and A.O. Rubalcava (1997), 'Pangue Hydroelectric Project (Chile): An independent review of the International Finance Corporation's compliance with applicable World Bank Group environmental and social requirements.' April, Santiago, Chile.

9 International Finance Corporation (2008), 'Lessons learned: Pangue hydroelectric. Summary.' Environment and Social Development Department. Online resource: http://www.ifc.org/wps/wcm/connect/85ce100048865954b8dafa6a6515bb18/pangue_summary.pdf?MOD=AJPERES&CACHEID=85ce100048865954b8dafa6a6515bb18 Accessed: 23 June 2014.

10 Hair et al. (1997), 'Pangue Hydroelectric Project.'

11 Hair et al. (1997), 'Pangue Hydroelectric Project.' p. 4.

12 IFC (2008), 'Lessons learned.'

13 IFC (2008), 'Lessons learned.'

14 IFC (2008), 'Lessons learned.'

15 IFC (2008), 'Lessons learned.'

16 Rachel Kyte previously served as WB Vice President for Sustainable Development and held various roles in the IFC. Before joining the IFC she was a member of the management team of the World Conservation Union – IUCN. The 2006 and 2012 versions of the performance standards can be found as: International Finance Corporation (IFC) (2006), 'IFC Performance Standards on Environmental and Social Sustainability.' April, Washington; International Finance Corporation (IFC; 2012), 'IFC Performance Standards on Environmental and Social Sustainability.' January, Washington.

17 The Equator Principles are periodically revised in line with the PS. The third version of the principles came into force in June 2013 following the revision of the PS in January 2012; Equator Principles (2014), 'About the Equator Principles.' Online resource: http://www.equator-principles.com/index.php/about-ep/about-ep Accessed: 23 June 2014.

18 Sadly Jay Hair died of cancer soon after taking up the post.

19 For example: Friends of the Earth International, Greenpeace, World Wide Fund for Nature, the Australian Conservation Foundation and WALHI (Indonesia).

20 For example: Project Underground (United States), Mineral Policy Centre (United States), Mineral Policy Institute (Australia), Partizans (United Kingdom), Minewatch

(Asia Pacific, United Kingdom), MiningWatch Canada, Wassa Association of Communities Affected by Mining (Ghana), Jaringan Advokasi Tambang (JATAM; Indonesia) and Cooperaccion (Peru).

21 Auty, R. (1993), *Sustaining Development in Mineral Economies: The resource curse thesis.* London and New York: Routledge; Sachs, J. and A. Warner (1995), 'Natural resource abundance and economic growth.' Development Discussion Paper no. 517a. Harvard Institute for International Development, Cambridge, MA; Ross, M. (1999), 'The political economy of the resource curse.' *World Politics*, 51(2): 297–322.

22 The ICME was founded in 1991 out of an initiative of the Mining Association of Canada. Gary Nash was the founding Secretary General of the ICME. Based in Ottawa the council found it difficult to motivate the attendance of a quorum of CEOs at the very time when greater engagement was needed on sustainable development issues.

23 Attendees of the London event included: Hugh Morgan (WMC Resources); Doug Yearly (Phelps Dodge); Robert Wilson (Rio Tinto); Richard Osborne (Asarco; which later dropped out of the GMI process); John Wilson (Placer Dome); and Hans Slack (Minorco; Anglo American subsidiary but later integrated). Others accepted but cancelled at the last minute (sending messages of support), including: Ron McNeilly (BHP); David Kerr (Noranda); Marcos Lima (CODELCO); and Jyrki Juusela (Outokumpu). Julian Ogilvie-Thompson (Anglo American) also sent a message of support. Ron Cambre (Newmont) and Alain Belda (Alcoa) joined for the second scheduled meeting at the World Economic Forum in Davos in February 1999.

24 Global Mining Initiative (GMI), undated, 'Chronology of Events of ICMM Significance.'

25 The core group of *sherpas* consisted of: Andrew Vickerman (Rio Tinto); George Littlewood (ex-Rio Tinto consulting to WMC Resources); David Colton (Phelps Dodge); John Groom (Anglo American); Dave Rodier (Noranda); Bob Muth (Asarco, which later dropped out of the GMI process); Tony Wells (BHP); Santiago Torres (CODELCO) and Dave Baker (Newmont).

26 Knight, D. (2002), 'Global groups seek action on mining industry.' Inter Press Service News Agency, 28 May. Online resource: http://www.ipsnews.net/2002/05/environment-global-groups-seek-action-on-mining-industry/ Accessed: 13 June 2014.

27 For more information on the London Mining Declaration, see: Mines and Communities (2001), 'The London Mining Declaration.' Online resource: http://www.minesandcommunities.org/article.php?a=8245 Accessed: 13 June 2014; Details of the Mines and Communities network can be found in: Whitmore, A. (2006), 'The Emperor's new clothes: Sustainable mining?' *Journal of Cleaner Production*, 14: 309–314.

28 Danielson, L. (2006), 'Architecture for change: An account of the Mining, Minerals and Sustainable Development Project.' Global Public Policy Institute, Berlin, Germany.

29 International Institute on Environment and Development (IIED) and World Business Council for Sustainable Development (WBCSD; 2002), *Breaking New Ground; Mining minerals and sustainable development. The report of the MMSD project.* London: Earthscan, p. v.

30 The regional coordinators were: Chris Burnup (Australia); Anthony Hodge (North America); Hernán Blanco and Cristina Echavarría (South America); and Alex Weaver (Southern Africa).

31 IIED and WBCSD (2002), *Breaking New Ground*.

32 The total bill of the GMI exercise was in the vicinity of US$9 million (Groom, 2003).

33 IIED and WBCSD (2002), *Breaking New Ground*, p. xxiv.

34 IIED and WBCSD (2002), *Breaking New Ground*, p. xx.

35 IIED and WBCSD (2002), *Breaking New Ground*, p. xiv.
36 IIED and WBCSD (2002), *Breaking New Ground*, p. xxiv.
37 Morgan, R. (2002), 'Communicating change.' International Council on Mining and Metals Newsletter, 1(3): 5.
38 The full report was downloaded 8933 times between October 2008 and June 2014, averaging around 2000 unique downloads per year; International Institute for Environment and Development (2014), 'PDF downloads tracking: Breaking new ground'. Accessed: 23 June 2014.
39 For critiques of the MMSD from a civil society perspective see, for example: Moody, R. (2002), 'Sustainable development unsustained: A critique of the MMSD project.' Nostromo Research and Society of St Columban, April, London; and Whitmore (2006), 'The emperor's new clothes.' For a corporate perspective on the MMSD see: Groom, J. (2003), 'Mining and the environment: Challenges and opportunities.' Proceedings of the 19th World Mining Congress, 1–5 November, 2003, New Delhi, pp. 111–122.
40 Brian Gilbertson, alone among his peers, had earlier in the conference reiterated BHP's commitment to no longer invest in new projects that dispose of tailings into rivers. He also rather boldly asserted that the existing BHP Billiton Charter and HSEC Policy would 'require only limited, if any, modification to accommodate the MMSD recommendations'; see Gilbertson, B. (2002), BHP Billiton Statement at Global Mining Initiative Conference, 15 May 2002, Toronto. Online resource: http://www.bhpbilliton.com/home/investors/reports/Documents/BrianGilbertsonSpeechGMIConf.pdf Accessed: 23 June 2014.
41 International Council on Mining and Metals (2002), ICMM Toronto Declaration, 15 May. Online resource: http://www.icmm.com/document/31 Accessed: 13 June 2014.
42 Buxton, A. (2012), MMSD +10: Reflecting on a decade of mining and sustainable development. International Institute for Environment and Development, June, London.
43 International Council on Mining and Metals (2014), Our members. Online resource: http://www.icmm.com/members Accessed: 19 June 2014.
44 Tony Hodge in Danielson (2006), 'Architecture for change', p. 90.

2 Rights

People and their place

The environmental and social challenges that confront the mining sector, are routinely expressed by civil society and some members of the broader public in the language of human rights. Alleged 'rights' transgressions are among the most controversial legacies of the mining industry. Human rights are sometimes thought to be peripheral to the sustainable development debate. For some, the concerns of sustainable development are strictly biophysical. However, at the core of the concept of sustainable development is the reconciliation of society and the natural world: the promotion of harmony between people, and between people and their environment.

In her foreword to 'Our common future', Gro Harlem Brundtland argues that concerns over 'rights' to a healthy and productive environment in the 1970s played a key role in the establishment of the World Commission on Environment and Development and the evolution of the sustainable development agenda. She argued against isolating the environment from human challenges:

> The environment does not exist as a sphere separate from human actions, ambitions, and needs … the 'environment' is where we all live; and 'development' is what we all do in attempting to improve our lot within that abode. The two are inseparable.[1]

In this chapter we will look at the extent to which the mining sector has reconciled with the rights agenda. The chapter addresses both individual (human) and collective (Indigenous) rights. First, we trace the story of how one of the major mining companies has confronted its past, and the dispossession of Indigenous land for mining. The chapter then introduces the Voluntary Principles on Security and Human Rights, the issue of business and human rights and the evolving international rights framework. Finally, we return to the issue of Indigenous rights and the recent acceptance of the concept of Free, Prior and Informed Consent (FPIC) within key mining industry standards.

Saltwater, freshwater

Garma is a word for the melding of saltwater and freshwater. It is also a place where Indigenous and non-Indigenous Australians can meld, learn from each other and be enriched by the diversity of their perspectives. The *Garma Festival of Traditional Culture* is the premier Aboriginal cultural festival in Australia. It is held on the lands of the Yolngu people in Northeast Arnhem Land, in the Northern Territory. The Yolngu have been custodians of this land for at least 50,000 years.[2] Rio Tinto has a strong presence at the event. They purchased the nearby Gove alumina refinery and bauxite mine from Alcan in mid-2007 and the company is a major sponsor of the festival.

At the 2014 Garma Festival, Rio Tinto Alcan and the Gumatj Corporation announced a partnership to deliver a AUD$2.4 million mining training centre to help fulfil Yolngu ambitions to create a bauxite mining operation to be run by the Gumatj clan at the Dhupuma Plateau.[3] The cultural shift implicit in such an announcement is extraordinary. Historically, relationships between mining companies and indigenous peoples in Australia have been fraught. Rio Tinto, and its predecessor company, Conzinc Rio Tinto of Australia (CRA), was singled out for particular criticism until a change in culture within the company in the mid-1990s.[4] The historical distrust indigenous peoples felt toward mining companies in Australia was epitomised by a bumper sticker campaign in the early 1980s by the Aboriginal Mining Information Centre, which colourfully read: 'Don't CRAp on our land!'[5]

The Gove mine began production in 1972, instituted by an Act of Parliament,[6] which gifted unfettered access to Yolngu land to the then project owners, Swiss–Australian consortium Nabalco (North Australian Bauxite and Alumina Company). The Yolngu resisted the mine, the refinery and the deceit implicit in this original sin for four decades. So how was it possible for relations between the Yolngu and the Gove mine to have so quickly improved from discord to partnership, where Indigenous companies are now looking to become operators of the mine? What caused such an abrupt change, when for decades the pace of change was glacial?

Gove holds a very special place in the history of the Indigenous land rights movement in Australia. Indeed, it holds a very special place in the history of Australia. In the late 1950s Yolngu elders became aware of interest in the mining of bauxite, the mineral ore of aluminium, on their land. In March of 1963, the Australian Government excised around 300 square kilometres of land from the Arnhem Land reserve to facilitate mining access. After deep consultation, the Yolngu at Yirrkala sent to the Australian House of Representatives in August of 1963 two petitions, delicately and beautifully painted on bark.[7] The Yirrkala Bark Petitions read:

1   That nearly 500 people of the above tribes are residents of the land excised from the Aboriginal Reserve in Arnhem Land.
2   That the procedures of the excision of this land and the fate of the people on it were never explained to them beforehand, and were kept secret from them.

3   That when Welfare Officers and Government officials came to inform them of decisions taken without them and against them, they did not undertake to convey to the Government in Canberra the views and feelings of the Yirrkala aboriginal people.

4   That the land in question has been hunting and food gathering land for the Yirrkala tribes from time immemorial: we were all born here.

5   That places sacred to the Yirrkala people, as well as vital to their livelihood are in the excised land, especially Melville Bay.

6   That the people of this area fear that their needs and interests will be completely ignored as they have been ignored in the past, and they fear that the fate which has overtaken the Larrakeah tribe will overtake them.

7   And they humbly pray that the Honourable the House of Representatives will appoint a Committee, accompanied by competent interpreters, to hear the views of the people of Yirrkala before permitting the excision of this land.

8   They humbly pray that no arrangements be entered into with any company which will destroy the livelihood and independence of the Yirrkala people.[8]

The petitions captured the attention of the world and the imagination of other First Peoples in Australia. They formally asserted Indigenous rights to country; were the first Indigenous documents to be recognised by the Australian parliament; and spurred a wider land rights movement in Australia.

The committee requested by the Yolngu failed and litigation followed. The litigation failed and injustice continued. The unsuccessful case against the company, *Milirrpum v. Nabalco Pty Ltd (1971)*, was the first litigation about land rights in Australia, however it was not the last. With each case the fiction of *terra nullias*, the legal doctrine describing pre-colonial Australia as 'land belonging to no-one' inched closer to being exposed. Following the Milirrpum case Justice Edward Woodward, who was previously legal counsel for the Yolngu, was asked to chair the Aboriginal Land Rights Commission.[9] The establishment of Indigenous-run land councils and the recognition of Indigenous Rights in the Northern Territory, through the Aboriginal Land Rights (Northern Territory) Act of 1976, soon followed. Disappointingly, for the Yolngu, the Act did not negate the Gove Peninsula Nabalco Agreement that had already established the Gove project.

In the intervening years, other cases inspired by the excision of Indigenous land for the purpose of mining were lodged in Australian courts and as a result of these and other non-mining related cases Indigenous rights eventually found recognition in the Australian Commonwealth in the early 1990s. In 2011, four years after Rio Tinto took ownership of the Gove project, the long-running dispute with the Yolngu was brought to a close with the signing of the Rio Tinto Alcan Gove Traditional Owners Agreement. This partnership agreement includes royalties of between AUD$15m and AUD$18m a year for 42 years, as well as employment and business opportunities, and protocols on cultural heritage and other matters.[10] To understand how Indigenous rights found recognition across Australia and how mining companies such as Rio Tinto came to pursue partnership agreements with Indigenous communities, we must follow a parallel mining struggle, also a bauxite mine, on the Western tip of Cape York Peninsula.

Beds are burning

Rio Tinto was a latecomer to the affairs at Gove, but the company had its own historical legacies to confront. At another nearby bauxite deposit, Weipa, located on Cape York Peninsula in Northern Queensland, Australia, the Commonwealth Aluminium Corporation was given an 84-year lease on thousands of square kilometres of Aboriginal land for large-scale mining development. The red pisolitic cliffs that frame the Western beaches of Cape York Peninsula were identified as bauxite in 1955 by a Consolidated Zinc Corporation geologist, Harry Evans, in the company of Aboriginal elder Matthew (Wakmatha) of the Linngithig people.[11] In haste the Queensland Government passed the Commonwealth Aluminium Corporation Pty Ltd Agreement Act in 1957. The Act gave the company secure title over Aboriginal land, including over the former Aboriginal reserves of Weipa and Mapoon. According to Queensland Premier Frank Nicklin, it was hoped that the Act would also create an economic driver for 'white' settlement of the North.[12] The Consolidated Zinc Corporation Ltd entered into a partnership with Kaiser Aluminum and Chemical Corporation in 1960, and was from then on known as Comalco. Consolidated Zinc merged in 1962 with the Rio Tinto Corporation to form Rio Tinto-Zinc Corporation (RTZ), and its subsidiary, Conzinc Riotinto of Australia (CRA).[13] The first shipment of bauxite was dispatched in 1963.

On 15 and 16 November 1963, the Queensland Police, acting on instruction of the Director of Native Affairs forcibly removed residents of the Aboriginal community from the Presbyterian Mission at Mapoon, within the bauxite mining lease, and demolished and burnt their houses to prevent them from returning. This event left an 'indelible stain' on Indigenous relationships in the region. The closure of the mission was slated as early as 1953, prior to the discovery of bauxite in the region, but equally Comalco was the beneficiary of the dispossession of Indigenous land; declined requests for financial assistance from the struggling mission, thus contributing to the decision by the Mission to give into government pressure to close; and remained silent in the aftermath, when the homes of the Aboriginal custodians were left to smoulder.[14]

A number of commentators over the years have asserted that Comalco and Alcan (another mining company who was exploring nearby) were active participants in these events but a recent academic study could not find evidence of direct mining company involvement.[15] Government motivations were to promote mineral development in the region, and while Consolidated Zinc had floated the idea of moving the mission they also stated that they would only do so at a time when the land was needed.[16] In the end, neither mining nor harbour development proceeded in the immediate vicinity of the mission. Whatever the involvement of the company in this notorious event it dogged CRA's reputation for decades.

In the 1980s the land rights movement started to gather momentum in Australia. Proposals for national land rights legislation by the centre-left Labor Government, which came to power at the Federal level in Australia in 1983, met fierce and organised resistance from the mining industry, in particular the Chamber of Mines of Western Australia and the Australian Mining Industry Council. The campaign against the proposals was the first major political campaign by the mining industry in Australia.[17] The industry was concerned that recognition of land rights in national legislation would restrict access for exploration and mining, especially if the legislation included rights for indigenous peoples to veto proposals. The Western Australian Chamber of Mines spent as much as a million dollars in newspaper and television advertisements to pressure the government to abandon the laws or accommodate the industry's concerns. One advertisement depicted the state of Western Australia, divided by a wall. A sign in front of the wall read 'Keep Out, this land is under Aboriginal Claim', with an Aboriginal hand laying the final brick. By late 1984 the proposals were watered down and in 1986 they were withdrawn.[18]

The 1987 rock anthem, 'Bed's Are Burning', by Australian band Midnight Oil carried the theme of land rights to an international audience and kept the pressure on action at home. Ostensibly about the Pintupi people of the Western Desert of central Australia, the song is about a country wrestling with its history:

> The time has come
> To say fair's fair
> To pay the rent
> To pay our share
> The time has come
> A fact's a fact
> It belongs to them
> Let's give it back
> How can we dance when our earth is turning
> How do we sleep while our beds are burning
> How can we dance when our earth is turning
> How do we sleep while our beds are burning.

The title lyric, 'beds are burning', has sometimes been attributed by residents of Mapoon to the burning down of the Mission. I asked Midnight Oil member, Rob Hirst, about the lyric. He said any similarity is by coincidence. The lyric speaks to inaction in the face of urgency.

In 1992 a landmark legal ruling changed the landscape for recognition of land rights in Australia. Eddie Koiki Mabo, an Indigenous Australian from the Torres Straight Islands initiated legal proceedings in 1982 that challenged the absence of Aboriginal title in Australian common law. The case was decided in his favour in the High Court of Australia in 1992, overruling the *Milirrpum v. Nabalco Pty Ltd* (1971) case that was lost by the Yolngu against the bauxite mining operations at Gove. The Mabo case was the foundation for recognition of Indigenous land rights in Australia and Eddie Mabbo was posthumously awarded the Australian Human Rights Medal. In 1993, following the Mabo ruling, the Wik peoples brought a case against the excision of the Aboriginal reserve for bauxite mining at Weipa and the granting of pastoral leases. The Wik challenged the legality of Comalco's operations, and had done so since the 1970s with limited success. In 1996 when the Federal court ruled that the granting of mining and pastoral leases extinguished native title it looked as though the status quo would continue. In late 1996, however, on appeal, the High Court of Australia overturned the original ruling, affirming the co-existence of native title with other forms of title, but also sparking another round of divisive political debate.

The Mabo case provided the impetus for the Federal Labor Government to finally legislate a system of native title in Australia. The Native Title Act of 1993 established a process to hear claims and determine Indigenous land title, which on the most part coexists with other land uses. Native title rights are recognised unless extinguished by law, such as the granting of freehold (private) land title (but not lease-hold land) and where there is a loss of connection to land by indigenous people. The Act also established a process for agreement making between Aboriginal groups and other parties about land use (Indigenous Land Use Agreements). There were practical challenges to the implementation of the Act, such as the slow pace of recognition of title and inter-community conflicts about recognition. Many mining companies chose to negotiate with Aboriginal people assuming that those claiming title would eventually be recognised once their claims were processed.

The Native Title Act loosely mirrored some of the key provisions of the International Labour Organization Indigenous and Tribal Peoples Convention (ILO 169), which was concluded in 1989 and came into force in 1991. Article 6 of the ILO convention states that: 'Consultations carried out in application of this Convention shall be undertaken, in good faith and in a form appropriate to the circumstances, with the objective of achieving agreement or consent to the proposed measures.'[19] That is, the convention, like the Native Title Act in Australia, affords an opportunity for consultation and negotiation about proposals on Indigenous land, but not the right to block developments, when consent has not been achieved. 'There is no right of veto, but a seat at the table,' said University of Melbourne Professor Marcia Langton, in her Boyer lectures. 'These newly won native title rights have placed [Aboriginal people] in a key position in the market economy with companies seeking land access.'[20]

The senior leadership of the Australian mining industry, almost to a man, viewed native title with alarm. Hugh Morgan, CEO of Western Mining Corporation, said in June of 1993:

> The economic and political future of Australia has been put at risk and our territorial integrity is under threat. They don't tell us that our freehold titles

will slump in value if the earning capacity of our mining, pastoral, tourist, fishing and forestry industries is wound down as a result of the consequences of Mabo.[21]

John Ralph, the CEO of Conzinc Rio Tinto of Australia, expressed similar sentiments. Ralph asserted in a television interview in 1993 that the Federal Court claim made by the Wik people of Cape York threatened more than a billion dollars in investments that CRA was making in its downstream alumina processing at the port of Gladstone.[22] Noel Pearson, at the time Director of the Cape York Land Council and spokesman for the Wik claimants, described the threat as 'absolutely shallow'. 'The spectre of disinvestment that has been thrown up by irresponsible parties,' said Pearson, 'has no foundation whatsoever.'[23]

The strident opposition to Native Title within CRA, however, retreated with the appointment of new leadership in 1995. Leon Davis, shortly after his appointment to the role of Managing Director and CEO, gave a speech to the Securities Institute of Australia. Davis addressed the room of investors, listing the fundamentals of the CRA business that he argued positioned CRA for growth. Fresh in his mind were the consequences of the adversarial position CRA had taken with Aboriginal opposition to the Marandoo iron ore project in Western Australia, which had caused a two-year delay. Towards the end of the speech, Leon reflected on contemporary Australian politics, and uttered a handful of words that shifted the foundations of the industry:

> As someone keenly interested in getting access to Australia's mineral and energy resources, I am glad to see that the vexed question of whether or not native title can still exist has been settled in principle. Translating principle into law is another matter and a vitally important one for states such as Western Australia, whose economy depends upon a clearly defined and efficient system of mineral rights.
>
> Let me say this bluntly. CRA is satisfied with the central tenet of the Native Title Act. In CRA we believe that there are major opportunities for growth in outback Australia, which will only be realized with the full cooperation of interested parties. This government initiative has laid the basis for better exploration access and thus increased the probability that the next decade will see a series of CRA operations developed in active partnership with Aboriginal people.[24]

With these two seemingly innocuous paragraphs, Leon Davis re-positioned CRA, and by implication its parent company and future namesake Rio Tinto, strongly in opposition to the hostile stance that the broader mining industry was taking on Native Title. Davis signalled to Australia's First Peoples that Conzinc Rio Tinto of Australia was now a company apart, willing to recognise land rights and work in partnership with Aboriginal people. The reaction was immediate and the major newspapers editorialised the significance of the shift. One cartoon in *The Australian* newspaper pictured Davis arm in arm with an indigenous elder under the caption 'sensitive new-age miner'. Bruce Harvey, who at the time was Chief Geologist for CRA in northern Australia and was strongly supportive of the changed position, said to me, 'If you read it at face value, he really doesn't say much that's not just common sense, but at the time it was like a declaration of a treaty between Rio Tinto and the people's republic of Aboriginal Australia!'

Under Davis's leadership CRA matched the change in rhetoric with new competencies. Employees were recruited with the skills to build relationships with indigenous people and communities, more generally. Paul Wand was appointed to the position of Vice President Aboriginal Relations. The company was also asked by its leadership to reconcile with its past attitudes. When I spoke to George Littlewood, who was Vice President of External Affairs for CRA during the period, he described the change as follows:

> I think we broke a lot of ground, we put in place a lot of partnerships [with Indigenous and environmental groups] … and it paid handsome dividends because people in those organisations, who like all of us have to go out the door and do an advocacy job sometimes, came to see and to learn that our commitment was more than skin deep.
>
> One of the proudest aspects of my working life, although [Paul Wand was the] key driver of this, was the extent to which we worked with the Aboriginal leadership and forged sustainable partnerships with them. We got the Aboriginal and environmental leadership into our organisation right from the Executive Committee, down to our Manager level. You've got Noel Pearson [Cape York Land Council], Marcia Langton [Cape York Land Council], Michael Rae [WWF Australia] and Trish Caswell [Australian Conservation Foundation] in to talk to these people about where they were coming from and it was a revelation.
>
> I mean you might believe you understand some these issues from the other side of the fence as it were, but until you see people arguing as strongly and expertly as those people could do, you don't really have a glimpse of where others are coming from and vice versa. There must have been 60 or 70 of those programmes run through the company over a year or so and I think that that had a major impact and change of thinking. Of course, all this had to be led. It won't happen unless there is leadership and Leon in particular was very dedicated to making it happen.

An enthusiastic effort followed to reach negotiated outcomes with the Native Title holders of the land on which CRA was mining and exploring. The first two agreements under the Native Title Act were for CRA exploration projects.[25] Longstanding employees, like Bruce Harvey, were now enabled to 'push the envelope a bit'. Within six weeks of Leon's announcement, Harvey and colleagues, including Ron Levi at the Northern Land Council, negotiated the Walgundu agreement for exploration adjacent to Arnhem land in the Northern Territory. Harvey reflected:

Of course it takes longer than six weeks to negotiate an agreement, but we'd been working on it for two years. The policy was we couldn't make agreements with Aboriginal people, but the policy didn't say we couldn't talk to them. We'd been preparing the ground such that we could seize the moment ... Although Leon had made those statements and we had the imprimatur, we would continually run up against reasons why we couldn't do this or why we couldn't do that. Lots of the changes we made were by, kind of, subterfuge. We didn't set out to – they were minor issues in isolation – but they accumulated over time into a continuous shift. For example, we couldn't use the word 'royalty' for Aboriginal benefits. So we just used 'benefits receiving accounts linked to the enterprise of the operations' instead.

Negotiating in brownfields contexts, where mines were already built and running, proved more difficult and took some time. At Weipa, a memorandum of understanding was signed between Comalco and the Cape York Land Council in 1995.[26] It took until 14 March 2001 to reach an agreement with the 11 indigenous groups of the Western Cape; the Councils of Aurukun, Mapoon, Napranum and New Mapoon; the Cape York Land Council; and the Queensland Government. The Western Cape Communities Co-Existence Agreement (WCCCA) provides for a minimum of AUD$2.5 million/year in royalties from Comalco and a further AUD$1.5 million/year from the Queensland Government. The funds, which currently total around AUD$6 million/year, are directed to the Western Cape Communities Trust where 60% are invested in long-term secure investments and the remainder distributed to sub-regional trusts.[27]

Keith Johnson, the Acting CEO of Comalco, faced up to Comalco's past at the signing ceremony of the WCCA:

We have not always been good listeners... When the Lease was granted to Comalco in 1958, the Native Title of the indigenous people of the Western Cape was unrecognised and unacknowledged. Comalco must, and does now, in this Agreement, face up to that unfinished business. Comalco is sorry that it has taken more than 40 years to get here.

The closure of Mapoon by the Director of Native Affairs and the forced removal of people in 1963, although not at the instigation of Comalco, was a particularly sad chapter in the history of the Western Cape. There are Elders amongst us today, and others from the Communities, for whom the years have done little to dull the pain of that memory. I want to acknowledge the pain still felt by those Mapoon families affected by removal and relocation against their wishes ... on behalf of Comalco I want to say sorry to the people of the Western Cape; sorry that it has taken 40 years to come to a clear understanding on how we can co-exist in a way that will meet all our aspirations; and so work together to create a better future for us all.[28]

Leon Davis moved on to became CEO of Rio Tinto, based in London, and held the position from 1997 to 2000. One of his final directives as CEO was to increase aboriginal employment in Australia.[29] At Weipa 24% of employees are now Aboriginal, with 12% representing local traditional owner groups.[30] Paul Wand, Rio Tinto Vice President of Aboriginal Relations between 1995–2000, and Bruce Harvey, by then Rio Tinto Global Practice Leader for Communities and Social Performance, reflected on the period of change inspired by Davis within Rio Tinto in their paper for the 10th anniversary of the Mabo decision. They argued that, 'the dire predictions that *Mabo* was a death rattle for industry have not come to pass, the sky has not fallen in and Australia's minerals and metals industry remains in rude good health'. Rio Tinto, according to Wand and Harvey, 'simply had to catch up' to new norms. The company 'inexorably shifted to match the evolving post-*Mabo* norms, often with hiatus but with very few reversals'.[31]

The events at Gove and Weipa played very prominent roles in the recognition of Indigenous rights in Australia and forced one of the majors of the mining industry to reconcile with its terrible history of dispossession and rights transgressions. In later parts of the chapter we will look at how the recognition of Indigenous rights has started to infiltrate the mining sector globally, but first we look at the issue of human rights.

The Voluntary Principles on Security and Human Rights

John Browne was the CEO of BP between 1995 and 2007. He was a progressive figure in the oil establishment, a physicist by background and one of the few oil industry leaders that believed in the science behind human induced climate change. John was the first major industry leader to stake a public position accepting climate change and from the late 1990s he attempted, with mixed success, to reposition BP 'beyond petroleum'. As Director of BP's Policy Unit, David Rice was a key advisor to John Browne. Climate change, indigenous peoples, biodiversity and human rights were building as issues of corporate concern in the 1990s and David corralled these issues into a broader sustainability policy. David was also one of the instigators of the Voluntary Principles on Security and Human Rights (VPs), the first industry-wide initiative in the extractive industries aimed at embedding human rights into corporate practice. Now a Fellow at University of Cambridge Institute for Sustainability Leadership, David shared with me the background to the establishment of the VPs:

> Something happened while I was working as the Exploration Manager for BP in China. When I arrived it was just after Tiananmen Square, so it was a very sensitive time. I was told that the offices of some of the international companies in Beijing had been used to photocopy leaflets, which were distributed by the students and the protesters. I started to think about this connection between business and society. I found myself in conversations with Chinese officials curious about human rights. A few years later, I joined the Government and Public Affairs team at BP headquarters. We got a letter from Amnesty International in the UK asking about our policies and raising

the fact that we were working in places like China and Colombia. At a breakfast meeting, one Monday morning, I remember this letter appeared and nobody knew what to do with it, and I said, 'Well I'm a member of Amnesty International, shall I deal with it?' It was one of those moments when everyone around the table looks at you as if you are mad. I wrote back to the author of the letter, Sir Geoffrey Chandler, and said 'Well come and have a talk.' Geoffrey instigated a lot of what became the business and human rights movement. Some years later Geoffrey told me that he wrote that letter to a huge number of companies. Very few replied and only one, BP, invited them into have a conversation. BP then got itself into trouble with human rights in Colombia, due to its association with the security forces, and I got involved in trying to sort some of that out.

BP started exploring in the Casanare province of Colombia in 1987. By 1991 it was clear that Cusiana field represented more than a billion barrels of oil and a nearby discovery at the Cupiagua field in 1993 almost doubled these reserves.[32] BP was entering a society in civil strife. The *Fuerzas Armadas Revolucionarias de Colombia* and the *Ejército de Liberación Nacional* guerrilla movements, on the left, and the *Autodefensas Unidas de Colombia* paramilitary group and Colombian military, on the right, wrestled for control of the country. BP was not a neutral player. Their oil discoveries in the Llanos foothills of the Andean cordillera replenished the Colombian treasury and military campaign, and the coffers of BP itself.

Barbed wire, armoured cars and armed bodyguards did little to insulate the company from its context. More than 30 BP contractors were kidnapped, and special military units were deployed to guard the oil infrastructure, indirectly financed by the company. In 1995 the company was accused of involvement in the assassination of a local community leader, Carlos Arrigui, who the year before led a blockade of the only road to the Cuisana production facility. An international media storm ensued.[33]

David realised that the efficiency and oversight that the company applied to other areas of its work was not being applied to the security departments. Moreover, security was thought of as a function of the company's ability to mobilise force rather than as a function of the relationship the company held with its local community. To help manage BP's exposure to these risks they worked up a set of rules about how to organise security. These new rules had the potential to lift standards at BP sites, but David and others in the company knew that the public did not differentiate between the practices of companies like BP, Shell, Chevron or Exxon. When one oil company opens fire on a village somewhere, the reputation of the whole industry takes a hit. David approached Arvind Ganesan at Human Rights Watch and Bennett Freeman, Deputy Assistant Secretary for Democracy, Human Rights and Labor in the Clinton administration. The proposition was to set up an industry wide voluntary standard to reduce, and hopefully eliminate, instances where people were being hurt by abusive private and public security forces. Together, they were successful in enlisting the British

Foreign Office; civil society organisations, including Amnesty International, International Alert and Human Rights Watch; and a core group of companies that included Shell, Chevron, Texaco, Conoco, and BP from the oil sector, and Rio Tinto and Freeport McMoran, who were involved in mining.[34] The involvement of civil society was crucial to the integrity of the initiative. At least one prominent company, however, was critical of the initiative fearing that it dragged the industry into a 'regulated' space.

On 19 December 2000, Madeleine Albright, United States Secretary of State, and Robin Cook, British Foreign Secretary, announced the formation of the VPs. The VPs were developed in around 18 months, a remarkably short period of time for an initiative of such scope. There was some mislaid concern that if the Clinton administration lost office that the incoming Bush administration would withdraw US government support for the scheme, so the founders moved quickly. At the time of writing there were nine governments, ten civil society organisations and 26 companies participating in the scheme, around half of which are mining companies. Colombia and Ghana are the only governments representing the developing world. The ICMM and the International Petroleum Industry Environmental Conservation Association (IPIECA) participate as observers.

The VPs commit participant companies to undertake comprehensive human rights assessments; screen and train public and private security forces; institute procedures to ensure proportionate use of force and to report and investigate allegations of human rights abuse.[35] Companies must submit an action plan upon acceptance as a participant of the VPs, commit to practically implement the plan, and report on progress to the Annual Plenary Meeting. Companies must also respond to requests for information or concerns from other participants. While there is not a formal assurance process, participants can be expelled from the VPs following a structured dialogue process if concerns are not resolved.[36]

The VPs have brought greater oversight, control, and scrutiny to an area of corporate practice that was capricious and of substantial concern to civil society and local communities. While some authors have been critical about the voluntary nature of the scheme, as well as other deficiencies,[37] the multi-stakeholder forum created by the initiative does build pressure on extractive companies for improved human rights performance. The VPs were also a precursor for wider initiatives in the sector, including the business and human rights mandate of Professor John Ruggie.

Protect, respect, remedy

In 2005, UN Secretary General, Kofi Annan, appointed Professor John Ruggie as his Special Representative on the issue of human rights and transnational corporations and other business enterprises. After more than 30 years of failed attempts to regulate corporations by international treaty his appointment was cautiously welcomed by both business and civil society alike. Professor Ruggie's mandate was to research the issue of business and human rights and clarify the responsibilities of corporate actors vis-à-vis the responsibilities of states.

Professor Ruggie's appointment as Special Representative was his second significant role within the UN system. He served as United Nations Assistant Secretary-General and Chief Advisor for Strategic Planning during Kofi Annan's first term as UN Secretary-General and played a founding role in two important UN initiatives. When Kofi Annan was invited to speak at the World Economic Forum in Davos, Switzerland, in 1999, the Secretary General was reluctant to attend unless he could set a meaningful challenge to the business community. 'Kofi Annan realised that the UN was fundamentally constrained by being a state based entity and it couldn't possibly solve the various issues that governments asked it to solve without help from the private sector,' explained Professor Ruggie during our interview. 'To Annan, beyond an object of regulation, the business community was a potential ally in achieving UN goals from poverty reduction, to dealing with the HIV Aids crisis.'

Professor Ruggie, and UN Deputy Secretary-General, Georg Kell, drafted Annan's speech for the Davos forum. The speech called on global business to embrace a set of principles representing a 'global compact'. It wasn't intended as a programme, simply a call to action. After a strong response to the speech, Ruggie and Kell designed the Global Compact, a voluntary framework for mobilising business to adopt human rights and sustainable development standards. The programme emerged a year later in July 2000. Georg Kell was its Executive Director. The programme now has more than 8,000 corporate participants.

As Assistant Secretary-General, Ruggie also played a principal role in preparing the UN Millennium Summit in 2000, and drafted the summit's final declaration, which adopted the Millennium Development Goals. The idea was to re-energise the field of development by mobilising the international community around indicators of development progress.

What Ruggie learnt from these engagements, and his prior academic work, is that ideas matter and can have influence beyond their codification in law. Legal reform is slow, especially at the international level, and there is much that can be achieved in the absence of the perfect legal instrument. Furthermore, the process of legal reform often engenders a defensive position from the constituency with whom the law is hoping to influence. Ideas that can captivate and engage, on the other hand, can disseminate norms, complement legal reform and bring change as ideas are incrementally embedded into the myriad of soft forms of regulation that can influence behaviour. It is this philosophy of 'principled pragmatism' that John took to the business and human rights mandate.

The origins of the mandate stem from a UN Human Rights Council vote in 2005 that decided against adopting a binding instrument on business and human rights, known as the norms on trans-national corporations and other business enterprises. There was support within the council to progress the issue further, despite the failed vote, and a research mandate was designed to help to bridge the impasse that had developed. Over the course of the mandate John Ruggie was supported by a team of legal and business specialists, including Caroline Rees, Rachel Davis, John Sherman, Christine Bader, Gerald Pachoud, Andrea Shemberg, Lene Wendland and Vanessa Zimmerman.

One of the first outputs was the development of a framework to clarify the responsibilities of actors with regard to human rights. The Protect, Respect, Remedy, framework recognises that States have an obligation to protect, respect and fulfil the human rights of their citizens; businesses have a responsibility to respect human rights and comply with applicable laws; and citizens are entitled to appropriate and effective remedy when rights have been breached.[38]

In 2008 the Human Rights Council extended the term of the mandate for a further three years. The goal was to implement the framework. A set of Guiding Principles on Business and Human Rights (GPs) was developed. Two aspects in particular were emphasised: prevention, through human rights due diligence; and remedy, through mechanisms to track and handle grievances. The logic was that the presence of preventative and remedial measures would reduce the incidence of human rights harm.

The team realised early in the mandate, that whatever the UN agreed to would not necessarily mean anything to the corporations they were hoping to influence. 'The United Nations has relatively little direct influence over the business community,' explained John. 'Treaties apply to states, they don't apply directly to companies, so if you're going to make any progress in this area, you have to engage the business community.' They set out to learn from business about how to translate human rights policy into practice, and engaged them in running pilot projects of human rights due diligence processes. They also engaged other standard setting bodies to make sure that whatever policies they were developing were closely aligned with what was happening at the UN.

The GPs have been adopted, in whole or in part, by a variety of national and international standard setting bodies. They have been incorporated into the IFC Performance Standards, the International Standards Organization's guidance on social responsibility (ISO 26000), and the OECD Guidelines for Multinational Enterprises, among others. The European Union has endorsed the GPs and the European Commission has asked its governments to develop national implementation strategies. Companies have also aligned their policies and practices to the GPs. BHP Billiton, for example now requires all sites to conduct a human rights assessment. Grievance handling mechanisms are also more commonplace across the sector (discussed in more detail in Chapter 5). 'The world is littered with small initiatives that can never reach scale, because they don't amplify one another,' said John. 'Achieving a scale effect was an objective of the mandate.'

In 2011 the GPs were presented to the Human Rights Council, and in a first for a normative text that was not negotiated by governments, the GPs were 'endorsed' by the council in resolution number 17/4 on 16 June.[39] The Ruggie mandate demonstrated the power of coordinated policy development in the absence of international consensus. There are, however, many human rights advocates, who are holding out hope for an elusive treaty at the international level to regulate corporate behaviour with respect to human rights and in June of 2014, the UN Human Rights Council narrowly voted to establish an open-ended intergovernmental working group to, again, begin negotiations for a binding international treaty.[40]

Free, prior and informed consent

One possible cause for optimism about the potential for protracted international negotiations to find conclusion is the fate of the United Nations Declaration on the Rights of Indigenous Peoples (UNDRIP).[41] After more than 25 years of negotiation, the United Nations General Assembly voted in September of 2007 to adopt the declaration. The vote was not unanimous but it was overwhelming. One hundred and forty-four countries voted in favour of the declaration, four countries voted against and eleven countries abstained. Only Australia, Canada, New Zealand, and the United States declined to support the declaration, though each has since retracted its earlier opposition.

UNDRIP is an historic international instrument. The first draft of UNDRIP was prepared in the early 1980s by the Working Group on Indigenous Populations, within the Sub-Commission for Prevention of Discrimination and Protection of Minorities of the United Nations Economic and Social Council.[42] Although it is not legally binding on States, as we shall see in the remainder of this Chapter, the influence of UNDRIP is projected vicariously through other non-legal instruments. Article 32 (2) of UNDRIP, firmly establishes indigenous rights with respect to mineral development:

> States shall consult and cooperate in good faith with the indigenous peoples concerned through their own representative institutions in order to obtain their free and informed consent prior to the approval of any project affecting their lands or territories and other resources, particularly in connection with the development, utilization or exploitation of mineral, water or other resources.[43]

The provisions articulated within UNDRIP were not quickly adopted by the mining industry as some may have hoped. In May 2008 the ICMM finalised its first Position Statement on Mining and Indigenous Peoples. During the member consultations for the preparation of the statement it was clear that inclusion of a 'consent' provision was completely off the table, despite the adoption of UNDRIP the previous year. The opposition to UNDRIP by Australia, Canada and the United States, three important mining economies, contributed to the reluctance by ICMM members to embrace 'consent'. The position statement was a progressive set of commitments, in comparison to the prior industry position on the issue, and while the statement did not subscribe to Free, Prior and Informed Consent (FPIC), it came close, and committed the ICMM membership to continue to engage in debates about the concept.[44] This was a subtle but important element. The industry recognised that the external pressure to adopt FPIC was not going to ease, and therefore wanted to continue to be part of the evolving conversation. ICMM during this time played an important role in preparing a very reluctant industry for further movement on the subject.

In 2009, the IFC began the revision of their Performance Standards. The 2006 version of Performance Standard on Indigenous Peoples (PS7) appropriated the rather clumsy, World Bank-coined term, Free, Prior and Informed *Consultation*. PS7 required participation by indigenous peoples in decision-making about projects that may affect them, or that are developed on their land, but did not explicitly endorse indigenous peoples' right to withhold their consent.[45] The Guidance Note that accompanied the standard did, however, state:

> In cases involving good faith negotiation, IFC will both review the client's documentation for the negotiation process and its outcomes and verify that the affected communities of Indigenous Peoples are broadly in support of the project.[46]

The IFC knew that inclusion of FPIC in PS7 would be controversial; industry would be opposed or hesitant; some of the states that are shareholders of the IFC, who were opposed to UNDRIP, were likely to continue to hold reservations about FPIC; and that FPIC was an article of faith for indigenous peoples and civil society organisations. The IFC chose to approach the topic conservatively and in the first consultation draft, released in May of 2010, the concept of 'Free, Prior and Informed *Consultation*' remained.[47]

Following the negotiation of UNDRIP, and in the context of the Ruggie mandate, the IFC understood that politically some aspect of reform was needed, but because any change was a fairly significant change, they felt they didn't have to indicate that right away. They could continue to consult until such time as they felt completely comfortable with the policy change and its wording, as well as what it would mean for implementation.

In late July of 2010, the IFC convened a consultation workshop in Washington with indigenous peoples representatives. In her opening remarks, Rachel Kyte, IFC Vice President for Business Advisory Services, strongly hinted that the IFC was open to full inclusion of FPIC. She acknowledged the global trend toward the 'consent' criterion and the precedent set by other International Finance Institutions, such as the European Bank for Reconstruction and Development and the Asian Development Bank, who had embraced the concept, but noted the need to address questions of implementation and to define, who does consent apply to? what does it mean? and who decides what consent means?[48] The formal speakers at the consultation, James Anaya, United Nations Special Rapporteur on the Situation of Human Rights and Fundamental Freedoms of Indigenous People; Jose Carlos Morales, Chairperson of the United Nations Expert Mechanism on the Rights of Indigenous Peoples; and Carlos Mamani, Chairperson of the United Nations Permanent Forum on Indigenous Peoples Issues all strongly endorsed the adoption of FPIC in PS7.[49] A joint civil society submission on the first consultation draft, signed by 70 organisations, echoed these views.[50]

The second consultation draft was publicly released in December of 2010. To the surprise of the mining industry, the second draft included a full-throated endorsement of FPIC.[51] The IFC had, even after all of the consultation meetings that followed the first consultation draft, given the impression to the industry that 'we are getting a lot of pressure, but we will live with it'. Typically the way policy reform is conducted, if you're open to change, is to stake a challenging position at the outset and then negotiate back to something closer to 'consensus'. The staged approach to public consultation afforded the IFC the opportunity to meander its way to a final position. In the first consultation draft, they gauged the Indigenous and civil society reaction to the continued absence of FPIC and bought themselves time to work out how to include a consent provision. In the second draft, they used the civil society pressure to justify a shift to include consent, leaving room to temper the requirements in the final standards.

Once FPIC made its way into the draft, it was never going to make its way out. The industry was left to try to position the PS to a more qualified commitment that recognised the practical operating challenges that they believed were absent from the draft. The place for such qualification was the 'Guidance Note' that accompanied the standard. The indigenous 'lobby' was less concerned about how the implementation of FPIC was defined within the Guidance Note and was broadly open to positioning the revision in such a way that would bring industry constituencies aboard. As long as the PS endorsed FPIC this strengthened the hand of Indigenous representatives in future revisions of The World Bank Safeguard policies that, to them, were more consequential.

The ICMM, and its membership, engaged directly with the IFC to have the standard and the Guidance Note more explicitly recognise the implementation challenges, in particular how companies interfaced with the responsibilities of states; what to do if indigenous representatives refused to participate in good faith negotiations; and how the standard might be applied to projects that were already underway. When the IFC Board approved the revision of the PS it was on the proviso that the guidance note for PS7 accommodate industry concerns about implementation. The ICMM membership was engaged closely during the preparation of the Guidance Note. The IFC position was that what made consent different to consultation was that it implied some kind of a documented process *and* a consequence or an outcome from that process.

The final revised versions of the IFC Performance Standards and Guidance Notes were released on 1 January 2012. PS7 states:

> The client will document: (i) the mutually accepted process between the client and Affected Communities of Indigenous Peoples, and (ii) evidence of agreement between the parties as the outcome of the negotiations. FPIC does not necessarily require unanimity and may be achieved even when individuals or groups within the community explicitly disagree.[52]

The Guidance Notes articulate a significant number of qualifications; however, FPIC is defined as both a process and an outcome:

> The process builds upon the requirements for ICP [Informed Consultation and Participation] (which include requirements for free, prior and informed consultation and participation) and additionally requires Good Faith

Negotiation (GFN) between the client and Affected Communities of Indigenous Peoples. GFN involves on the part of all parties: (i) willingness to engage in a process and availability to meet at reasonable times and frequency; (ii) provision of information necessary for informed negotiation; (iii) exploration of key issues of importance; (iv) use of mutually acceptable procedures for negotiation; (v) willingness to change initial position and modify offers where possible; and (vi) provision of sufficient time for decision making. The outcome, where the GFN process is successful, is an agreement and evidence thereof.[53]

The adoption of FPIC in the 2012 IFC PS was a significant advancement on the mining industry position as articulated in the 2008 ICMM Position Statement on Mining and Indigenous Peoples. ICMM members now faced a decision. They could continue to subscribe to 'consultation' rather than 'consent'. In doing so, they would have risked being seen to subscribe to a standard that was no longer regarded as best practice and invited ongoing public criticism. Or, they could bridge the policy gap. The ICMM membership chose the latter and in their 2013 Position Statement on Indigenous Peoples and Mining they endorsed FPIC and its formulation as both a process and an outcome.[54] 'The outcome', according to the Position Statement 'is that Indigenous Peoples can give or withhold their consent to a project, through a process that strives to be consistent with their traditional decision-making processes while respecting internationally recognised human rights and is based on good faith negotiation'.[55] The decision ICMM members made to endorse FPIC, was not simply about political calculations. An unexpected consequence of ICMM membership engagement during the revision of the IFC PS was that members found a level of comfort with FPIC that was previously absent. They realised FPIC was now a settled norm and that it was implementable in a way that did not undermine their core interests. In short, it was possible to respect Indigenous rights, and extract minerals at the same time.

In this chapter we have traversed half a century of policy on indigenous and human rights in the mining industry. The chasm that separated Indigenous and mining industry perspectives in the 1960s, in Australia, and elsewhere to be sure, has progressively filled as stronger policy has developed. The pace of change has been slow, and despite the policy reform, practice within some parts of the mining industry has lagged. Rights abuses still remain all too common place. But there is no doubt that through the advocacy of Indigenous Peoples and civil society; legal reform at the national level; international diplomacy within the framework of the United Nations; standards reform within financial institutions, like the IFC; and the efforts of insiders within the mining industry, and its associations, have combined to achieve tangible improvements. Those in the mining industry, ahead of the reform curve, accrued a very real competitive advantage. According to Paul Wand and Bruce Harvey:

> far from being an aberration [the Mabo-inspired native title reforms in Australia were] at the forefront of an emerging global innovation in land

rights and resource development consent. Like many innovations in history, a leap of advantage can accrue to early movers who, finding themselves in the right place at the right time, respond in the right way. Viewed in this light, the journey Rio Tinto commenced through Mabo has taught it how to make agreements with host Indigenous communities and gain a unique competence and competitive advantage along the way. It looks remarkably prescient in this globally connected world.[56]

In the next chapter we look at the environmental performance of the mining industry across three broad areas: waste, spills and hazardous chemicals; climate, energy and water; and biodiversity and rehabilitation.

Notes

1 Brundtland, G.H. (1987), 'Our common future: Chairman's foreword.' In Report of the World Commission on Environment and Development: Our Common Future. United Nations, A/42/427.
2 Roberts, R.G., Jones, R. and M.A. Smith (1990), 'Thermoluminescence dating of a 50,000-year-old human occupation site in Northern Australia.' *Nature*, 345(10 May): 153–156.
3 Yothu Yindi Foundation (2014), 'Mining training centre to generate economic development for Yolngu people.' Press release: 2 August 2014. Online resource: http://www.yyf.com.au/news/detail.aspx?SubjectID=1&ArticleID=38 Accessed: 5 August 2014.
4 Wand, P. and B. Harvey (2012), 'The sky did not fall in! Rio Tinto after Mabo.' In T. Bauman and L. Glick, *The Limits of Change: Mabo and native title 20 years on*. AIATSIS, Canberra. pp. 289–309; Wand, P. and B. Harvey (2012), 'The sky did not fall in! Rio Tinto after Mabo.' Extended unpublished manuscript.
5 Moody, R. (1992), *The Gulliver File. Mines, People and Land: A global battleground*. London: Minewatch, p. 234.
6 The Mining (Gove Peninsula Nabalco Agreement) Ordinance 1968 (NT).
7 Museum of Australian Democracy (2005), 'Yirrkala bark petitions 1963.' Online resource: http://foundingdocs.gov.au/item-did-104.html Accessed: 8 August 2014.
8 Australian Government (2008), 'Bark Petition (transcript) tabled in the House of Representatives 14 and 28 August, 1963.' Online resource: http://australia.gov.au/about-australia/australian-story/bark-petition-1963 Accessed: 8 August 2014.
9 Geordan Graetz writes about the Woodward Royal Commission in his history of the Ranger Uranium mine, including Justice Woodward's role in the Yolngu case; Graetz, G. (2015), 'Ranger Uranium Mine and the Mirarr (Part 1), 1970–2000: The risks of "riding roughshod".' *The Extractive Industries and Society*, 2(1): 132–141; the two reports of the Woodward Royal Commission are: Woodward, A.E. (1973), *Aboriginal Land Rights Commission First Report*. Australian Government Publishing Service, Canberra. July; Woodward, A.E. (1974), *Aboriginal Land Rights Commission Second Report*. The Government Printer of Australia. Parliamentary Paper no. 69, April, Canberra.
10 Agreements, Treaties and Negotiated Settlements Project (ATNS) (2011), 'Rio Tinto Alcan Gove Traditional Owners Agreement.' Online resource: http://www.atns.net.au/agreement.asp?EntityID=5599 Accessed: 8 August 2014.
11 Courtenay, P.P. (1982), *Northern Australia: Patterns and problems of tropical development in an advanced country*. Melbourne: Longman Cheshire; Wharton, G. (1996), 'The day they burned Mapoon: A study of the closure of a Queensland Presbyterian Mission.' BA (Hons) thesis, University of Queensland.

12 Courier Mail (1957), 'Bauxite will "open" Gulf, says Nicklin.' 17 December 1957, p. 3.
13 Rio Tinto (2010), History. Online resource: http://www.riotinto.com/aboutus/history-4705.aspx Accessed: 8 August 2014.
14 Wharton (1996), 'The day they burned Mapoon.'
15 See for example: Roberts, J. (1978), *From Massacres to Mining: The colonization of Aboriginal Australia.* London: Colonialism and Indigenous Minorities Research and Action, and War on Want; Roberts, J. (1981), *Massacres to Mining: The colonization of Aboriginal Australia.* Melbourne: Dove Communications; and Moody (1992), *The Gulliver File.* Detailed archival research by Wharton (1996) does not back these claims; Wharton (1996), 'The day they burned Mapoon.'
16 Wharton (1996), 'The day they burned Mapoon.'
17 Libby, R.T. (1989), *Hawke's Law: The politics of mining and Aboriginal land rights in Australia.* Nedlands: University of Western Australia Press.
18 Libby (1989), *Hawke's Law.*
19 International Labour Organisation (1989), 'Convention concerning Indigenous and Tribal Peoples in independent countries.' No. 169. Online resource: http://www.ilo.org/dyn/normlex/en/f?p=NORMLEXPUB:12100:0::NO:12100:P12100_INSTRUMENT_ID:312314:NO Accessed: 8 August 2014.
20 Langton, M. (2012), '2012 Boyer Lectures. Lecture 1 – Changing the paradigm: Mining Companies, Native Title and Aboriginal Australians.' Sunday 18 November 2012. Online resource: http://www.abc.net.au/radionational/programs/boyerlectures/boyers-ep1/4305610 Accessed: 12 September 2014.
21 Ferguson, S. 2010. 'What's yours is mine.' *Four Corners*, 7 June, Australian Broadcasting Corporation. Online resource: http://www.abc.net.au/4corners/special_eds/20100607/mining/ Accessed: 5 February 2015.
22 Tickner, R. (2001), *Taking a Stand: Land rights to reconciliation.* Crows Nest, New South Wales: Allen & Unwin, p. 142.
23 Koori Mail (1993), 'Mabo style claim held to ransom by mining giant.' Wednesday 28 July, p. 1.
24 Davis, L. (1995), 'New directions for CRA.' Speech to the Securities Institute of Australia, Melbourne/Sydney, March.
25 Wand and Harvey (2012), 'The sky did not fall in!'
26 Keenan, J.C. and D.L. Kemp (2014), 'Mining and local-level development: Examining the gender dimensions of agreements between companies and communities.' Centre for Social Responsibility in Mining, The University of Queensland, Brisbane, Australia.
27 Johnson, K. (2001), 'Signing of the Western Cape communities co-existence agreement.' Comalco. 14 March 2001. Online resource: http://www.riotinto.com/documents/ReportsPublications/MDG_Western_Cape_Communities_Coexistence_Agreement.pdf Accessed: 22 August 2014; Keenan and Kemp (2012), 'Mining and local-level development.'
28 Johnson (2001), 'Signing of the Western Cape agreement.'
29 Wand and Harvey (2012), 'The sky did not fall in!
30 Employment figures from 2012; Keenan and Kemp (2012), 'Mining and local-level development.'
31 Wand and Harvey (2012), 'The sky did not fall in!'
32 Browne, J. (2010), *Beyond Business.* London: Phoenix.
33 Browne (2010), *Beyond Business.*
34 Voluntary Principles on Security and Human Rights (2000), Statement by the Governments of the United States of America and the United Kingdom. Online resource: https://www.unglobalcompact.org/issues/conflict_prevention/meetings_and_workshops/volsupport.html Accessed: 26 September 2014.
35 Smith, G. (2014), Participants in the Voluntary Principles Initiative gather for discussions on outreach and implementation and welcome five new participants and one new observer. Press statement: 28 March. Online resource: http://www.

voluntaryprinciples.org/wp-content/uploads/2014/03/Press-Release-March-28-2014. pdf Accessed: 26 September 2014.

36 Voluntary Principles on Security and Human Rights (2013), Participation criteria. Online resource: http://www.voluntaryprinciples.org/wp-content/uploads/2013/03/ VPs_Participation_Criteria_Final_-_127000_v1_FHE-DC.pdf   Accessed: 26 September 2014.

37 See for example: Simons, P. and A. Macklin (2013), *The Governance Gap: Extractive industries, human rights, and the home state advantage*. London: Routledge.

38 United Nations Office of the High Commissioner for Human Rights (2011), 'Guiding principles on business and human rights: Implementing the United Nations "Protect, respect and remedy" framework.' New York and Geneva. HR/ PUB/11/04.   Online   resource: http://www.ohchr.org/Documents/Publications/ GuidingPrinciplesBusinessHR_EN.pdf?v=1392752313000/_/jcr:system/jcr:versi onstorage/12/52/13/125213a0-e4bc-4a15-bb96-9930bb8fb6a1/1.3/jcr:frozennode Accessed: 5 February 2015.

39 UNOHCHR (2011), 'Guiding principles on business and human rights.'

40 Ruggie, J. (2014), 'The past as prologue? A moment of truth for UN Business and Human Rights Treaty.' Institute for Human Rights and Business, 14 June. Online resource: http://www.ihrb.org/commentary/past-as-prologue.html   Accessed: 29 September 2014.

41 United Nations (2008), 'United Nations Declaration on the Rights of Indigenous Peoples.' A/61/L.67 and Add.1. Online resource: http://www.un.org/esa/socdev/ unpfii/documents/DRIPS_en.pdf Accessed: 5 February 2015.

42 Willemsen-Diaz, A (2009), 'How Indigenous Peoples' rights reached the UN.' In C. Charters and R. Stavenhagen (eds) *Making the Declaration Work: The United Nations Declaration on the Rights of Indigenous Peoples*. International Work Group for Indigenous Affairs, Document no. 127. Copenhagen, pp. 16–31; For a detailed history of the quarter-century of negotiations written by some of the principal protagonists see: Charters and Stavenhagen (2009), *Making the Declaration Work*.

43 United Nations (2008), 'UNDRIP.'

44 International Council on Mining and Metals (ICMM) (2008), 'Mining and Indigenous Peoples Position Statement.' May. Online resource: http://www.icmm. com/document/293 Accessed: 21 September 2014.

45 International Finance Corporation (IFC) (2006), 'Performance Standard 7. Indigenous Peoples.' 30 April. Online resource: http://www.ifc.org/wps/wcm/connect/ a6b1b6804885565ab9bcfb6a6515bb18/PS_7_IndigenousPeoples.pdf?MOD=AJPER ES&attachment=true&id=1322818661604 Accessed: 21 September 2014.

46 International Finance Corporation (IFC) (2007), 'Guidance Note 7. Indigenous Peoples.' 31 July. Online resource: http://www.ifc.org/wps/wcm/connect/707761004 885582bbf24ff6a6515bb18/2007%2BUpdated%2BGuidance%2BNote_7.pdf?MOD =AJPERES&attachment=true&id=1322818940215 Accessed: 21 September 2014.

47 International Finance Corporation (IFC) (2010), 'Performance Standard 7 – Rev-0.1 Indigenous Peoples. Mark up of draft Policy and Performance Standards on Social and Environmental Sustainability (Against April 30, 2006 Version).' 14 April. Online resource: http://www.ifc.org/wps/wcm/connect/345b950049800a0ba8ebfa336 b93d75f/CODE_Progress%2BReport_AnnexB_PS7.pdf?MOD=AJPERES Accessed: 21 September 2014.

48 International Finance Corporation (IFC) (2010), 'Review and update of the Policy and Performance Standards on Social and Environmental Sustainability and Policy on Disclosure of Information.' Indigenous Peoples Thematic Consultation Summary, Thursday 29 July. Washington, DC. Online resource: http://www.ifc.org/wps/wcm/ connect/6268c58049800a5baa5bfa336b93d75f/IFCConsultationIndigenousPeoples. pdf?MOD=AJPERES Accessed: 21 September 2014.

49 IFC (2010), 'Review and update of the Policy.'

50 Accountability Counsel et al. (2010) 'Comments on IFC's consultation drafts of the IFC Sustainability Policy and Performance Standards and Disclosure Policy.' 27 August. Online resource: http://www.ciel.org/Publications/CSO_Submission_IFC_27Aug10.pdf Accessed: 21 September 2014.

51 International Finance Corporation (IFC) (2010), 'Performance Standard 7 – V2. Indigenous Peoples. Draft Sustainability Framework – Tracked Changes (Against April 14, 2010 Version (V1).' 1 December. Online resource: http://www.ifc.org/wps/wcm/connect/1f59e880498007f6a1e7f3336b93d75f/Phase3_PS7_V1_Vs_V2.pdf?MOD=AJPERES Accessed: 21 September 2014.

52 International Finance Corporation (IFC) (2012) 'Guidance Note 7. Indigenous Peoples.' 1 January 2012. Online resource: http://www.ifc.org/wps/wcm/connect/50eed180498009f9a89bfa336b93d75f/Updated_GN7-2012.pdf?MOD=AJPERES Accessed: 21 September 2014.

53 IFC (2012), 'Guidance Note 7.'

54 International Council on Mining and Metals (ICMM) (2013), 'Indigenous Peoples and Mining Position Statement.' May. Online resource: http://www.icmm.com/document/5433 Accessed: 21 September 2014.

55 ICMM (2013), 'Indigenous Peoples and Mining Position Statement.'

56 Wand and Harvey (2012), 'The sky did not fall in!'

3 Environment

Sirloin and sausages

A mountain of rock must be moved to make a mere molehill of metal. The target minerals within an ore body make up but a minor proportion of the rock, and mining commonly requires the removal of tonnes of un-mineralised rock overlying the deposit. As a consequence, the mining industry is the largest producer of solid wastes by orders of magnitude. Gavin Mudd and David Boger have estimated annual global mine waste generation for 2011, finding that the industry produced approximately 7.1 billion tonnes of tailings – the ground up residue that remains after processing – and 55.9 billion tonnes of waste rock – rock that is mined but does not contain economic concentrations of ore.[1] That's the equivalent of more than nine tonnes of mine waste per human, per year. The water and energy inputs needed for extraction are also linked to the concentration of the target mineral within the rock (known as the ore-grade), as are emissions, such as greenhouse gases, and the consumption of process chemicals, such as cyanide. Everything in mining links to the ore body.

For nearly 20 years Bernhard Dold has been a scholar of geochemistry, sharing his knowledge to improve georesource management in the mining industry. During his time as Professor at the University of Chile and now Director of an applied research consulting company, SUMIRCO, he has worked with scores of companies to better characterise their ore and waste streams. Where others see ore bodies as a mass of rock, he sees the ore's character, and the full potential of its natural diversity.

'At the moment the target for the mining industry is the high-grade part of the ore,' said Bernhard when I spoke to him from his base in Concepción, Chile. 'But an ore body is not like a cake that is evenly mixed, it is more like a side of meat. What miners currently go for is the sirloin. A lot of the rest of the cow,' he said, 'they are throwing away (into the river, lake, or the sea), where it oxidizes and contaminates water.' Bernhard believes that low-grade ore can bring economic value, if it is properly characterised from the beginning. 'We need to stop talking about "ore" and "waste",' he said. 'Low-grade ore is not waste. It is a resource. We have to learn to improve. Every part of an ore body should be exploited. We need to start making money from sausages.'

As a butcher understands the cuts of meat and a chef understands how to cook them, so too must a miner. Sausages can be just as good a meal as steak, and waste dumps can be optimised for future extraction, but it does take a change in perspective. Bernhard believes the industry has changed. 'When I started nearly 20 years ago one geologist said to me that the 0.3% copper in their tailings would never be economic; today the exact same geologist is in charge of the study to recover copper from these tailings.' It is far easier now to make a convincing case to the geologists and engineers that fill the ranks of senior management. The translation to operational decision-making, however, Bernhard believes is still missing.

In this chapter we will track the environmental performance of mining and investigate how far environmental perspectives have infiltrated the industry. Now more than a decade after the completion of MMSD, it is worth taking stock and looking in detail at key indicators of environmental performance. Three broad areas are reviewed: waste, spills and hazardous chemicals; climate, energy and water; and biodiversity and rehabilitation. The chapter will reveal that ore grades are in decline for most mineral commodities, meaning more rock must be mined to produce the same amount of resource. These trends are placing pressure on water, energy, greenhouse gas intensity and chemical inputs, and increasing the risks associated with spills of solid and liquid wastes. Successes, however, are evident. Improved engineering practice and environmental management have led to a decline in tailings dam failures, even while the number of tailings failure incidents remains unacceptably high. Water recycling has become standard practice and initiatives like The International Cyanide Management Code have reduced major pollution events. We begin the chapter by looking at the fallout of one of the environmental incidents that, in the mid-1990s, shocked the industry into action on sustainable development.

Marinduque and Marcopper

Marinduque is a small island in the geographic heart of the Philippines. The island is mountainous, owing to its volcanic origins. Hundreds of thousands of tonnes of copper were extracted from the Marcopper mine on Marinduque between 1969 and 1996.[2] A major pollution incident in 1996 ended the operation. The incident is still considered one of the worst environmental disasters in the history of The Philippines.

On 24 March 1996 a drainage tunnel at the base of the Tapian mine pit burst, spilling mine waste into the Makulapnit and Boac rivers. The pit was being used to store mine tailings and for four days and nights a total of 1.6 million m^3 of ground up rock escaped from the tunnel. Twelve hundred people were evacuated. Two deaths were linked to the incident. Criminal charges were filed, though later dropped, against senior Marcopper executives. The mine did not reopen.[3]

The disaster brought short-, and long-term, environmental consequences. A clean up was initiated but never completed. Dredging removed a portion of tailings from the river and the river mouth, and 26km of levee banks were constructed from sand bags to prevent the overflow of the river.[4] Around 180,000 to 260,000m³ of tailings remained in the near shore marine environment as a result of the spill. Heavy metals contaminated the river and the ocean.[5] A Marcopper flyer distributed to residents in response to the tragedy detailed the jobs, the foreign exchange earnings and the direct and indirect taxes contributed by the mine. 'Can anybody argue,' the flyer reasoned, 'that this is not a more than fair return for the change in the environment that our mining operations had caused?'[6]

While this incident was one of the more notorious afflictions of the mining industry in the 1990s, it wasn't the first controversy to befall Marcopper. Placer Dome, headquartered in Vancouver, Canada, was a key partner in the mine. Under Philippine foreign ownership laws Placer was only permitted to own 39.9% of Marcopper, but they influenced management and mine design decisions through the secondment of managers to Marcopper (including the Mine Manager), and by having three members of the eight-member Marcopper board (including the Board Chair). Philippine President and dictator Ferdinand Marcos held 49.9% of Marcopper's shares through a front company, Performance Investment Corp. A fact undisclosed until his overthrow in 1986. Several attempts, by the National Pollution Control Commission of the Philippine Government, to enforce operational changes for improved environmental performance were overruled by President Marcos. Following the overthrow of the Marcos regime, the Philippine Government assumed his stake in Marcopper.[7]

From 1975 to 1991 the Marcopper mine disposed of 200–300 million tonnes of the tailings waste into the ocean at Calancan Bay, north of the deposit.[8] The original mine plan called for discharge of tailings into the submarine environment but after the disposal system failed the waste was instead discharged at the ocean surface, a practice well known for producing serious contamination. Lead poisoning of the children of Calancan Bay prompted Philippine President Fidel Ramos to declare a 'state of calamity' in 1998.[9]

In another Marcopper incident, a dam built on the Maguila-Guila creek, at the headwaters of the Mogpog river, failed in 1993 during one of the region's many typhoons. The dam was to collect and retain silt eroding from the waste dump of the San Antonio mine pit. The failure of the dam flooded downstream villages. Two children were killed and 70 families displaced. In 1997 Pacer Dome divested from Marcopper to a holding company in the Cayman Islands. In 2001 Placer personnel left the Philippines. A series of legal cases were filed. Placer Dome was acquired by Barrick Gold in 2006.[10]

Marinduque is at the headwaters of a number of stories of mining industry change. Catherine Coumans is the Research Coordinator and Asia Pacific Program Coordinator of MiningWatch Canada, a Canadian advocacy NGO. MiningWatch Canada supports communities in the vicinity of Canadian mining projects worldwide and advocates for policy reform in Canada. Catherine has worked at MiningWatch Canada since it began in 1999. It was Marcopper that drew Catherine into the orbit of the mining industry. 'None of this is what I thought I was going to be doing with my life. I started out just doing anthropological field work on a small island in the Philippines,' said Catherine during our conversation. A personal commitment to colleagues and friends that she met in Marinduque in the late 1980s prompted Catherine to seek out the skills of advocacy.

In 1996 when the Tapian pit drainage tunnel burst Catherine helped her Filipino colleagues to find a voice in Canada. Local action on the issue was coordinated by the Roman Catholic Church, through its umbrella organisation, the Marinduque Council for Environmental Concerns. With Filipino Congressmen Edmund Reyes, Catherine later organised for the United States Geological Survey to undertake scientific studies of the pollution around the mine and supported legal action by the Provincial Government of Marinduque in the United States. 'In 2005 when we found some lawyers and the case went to court,' said Catherine, 'my husband looked at me and said "Phew, you're done, you can now quit MiningWatch and go back to being an anthropologist." I thought, "Well it's too late now, there are all these other people that I am working with."'

The Marcopper experience also prompted deep reflection within Placer Dome and impetus for executives, like Jim Cooney and Henry Brehaut, who were already pushing for change internally. Cooney held positions at Placer Dome from 1982 to 2006, retiring as Vice President, International Government Affairs following the Barrick Gold acquisition. He now holds Adjunct positions at the Beedie School of Business, Simon Fraser University and the Norman B. Keevil Institute of Mining Engineering, University of British Columbia. Brehaut was at the time Senior Vice President, Environment. They both argued that Placer Dome and the wider industry should frame their activities around the concept of sustainable development, a concept that was still under challenge within the mining industry. In the lead up to the 1996 Marcopper disaster Placer Dome was preparing its first sustainable development strategy. In the aftermath, while the incident was still fresh, Cooney was invited to present at a World Bank workshop in Washington in early 1997. He spoke about how mining companies should manage political risk in developing countries. Cooney was involved in managing political and social issues at two of Placer's newest projects, Porgera in Papua New Guinea, and La Cristina in Venezuela. At La Cristina local communities were raising Placer's record at Marinduque as an issue of concern during consultations. It was at this World Bank meeting that Cooney first observed that companies require a two track approval process for major projects: a formal legal licence to operate from government; and an informal 'social license to operate' from the communities who live in the vicinity of projects.[11]

For Cooney, a social licence is constantly in flux and requires regular and continuous dialogue and joint project planning with community such that the impacts, risks and concerns of local communities are proactively addressed and the project wins their support. The term caught on at The World Bank and is now widely used across the mining industry and beyond. Through the concepts of 'sustainable development' and 'social license', environmental and social issues were now beginning to get some traction within the mining industry.[12]

Collapse

The generation of solid and liquid wastes and the release of these wastes onto land and into waterways are arguably the greatest impacts to the environment associated with mining. Tailings dam failures and direct discharge of mining wastes into rivers and oceans, can result in extensive environmental damage. There are two principle types of solid mining wastes: waste rock and tailings. Waste rock is rock removed during mining that does not contain economic concentrations of ore. This waste is usually stored in a waste rock dump. Waste rock may contain sulphide minerals that break down when exposed to water and oxygen at the surface and generate acid and metaliferous drainage (AMD), which can contaminate surface and ground water systems. AMD can present long-term, even perpetual, water management challenges.[13] Roman mine workings in the Rio Tinto estuary of south-western Spain, for example, still produce AMD today, more than 2000 years hence.[14] Tailings refers to the ground-up rock that remains after the processing of ore. Tailings are commonly stored in a Tailings Storage Facility, colloquially known as a tailings dam. Tailings, too, can generate AMD; however, the most significant pollution incidents associated with tailings dams result from the failure of the dam and the dispersal of tailings into nearby ecosystems.

Tailings dam failures are relatively uncommon, but they are a feature of the contemporary global mining industry. As we saw in Marinduque, the catastrophic descent of liquid rock can have severe environmental and social consequences. Other major incidents in recent history include: Mount Polley, Canada (2014; 7.3 million m³ discharged into Polley Lake); Kolontár, Hungary (2010; 700,000 m³ of red mud flooding several towns; 10 fatalities); Cerro Negro, Chile (2003; 50,000 tonnes of tails discharged, with tails flowing 20km downstream in the Rio La Ligua); Baia Mare, Romania (2000; 100,000m³ of cyanide contaminated liquid spilt into a tributary of the Somes, Tisza and Danube Rivers); Aznalcóllar, Spain (1998; 4–5 million m³ of liquid and slurry released); and Merriespruit, South Africa (1994; 600,000m³ of tails; 17 fatalities).[15]

Between 1990 and 2009, 39 tailings dam failure events were recorded, averaging 1.95 incidents per year.[16] More than 25% of the failure incidents involved a loss of life and this trend has continued in the period since 2000.[17] The rate of tailings dam failure has declined since a peak in the 1960s, 1970s and 1980s (see Figure 1). Mining production increased substantially after the Second World War and the increase in dam failures followed the trend of increased production. Advances in engineering and environmental management in the 1980s contributed to a subsequent reduction in tailings dam failures despite increases in production. While these trends are welcome, further reductions in the 2000s have not materialised against the improvement in the 1990s. The slow replacement of long-term infrastructure is one potential explanation, as is the cumulative presence of old tailings dams. A significant majority of contemporary dam failures are attributed to unusual weather and water management issues. Australia, North America and South America have reduced the incidence of

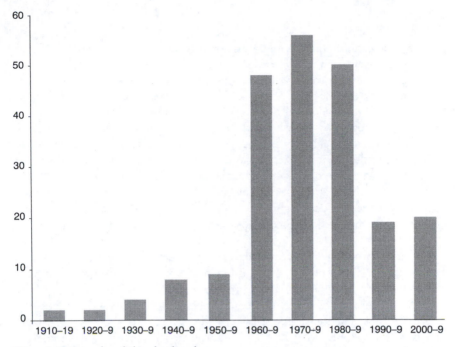

Figure 1 Tailings dam failure by decade

Source: Azam and Li, 2010, 'Tailings dam failures'; data compiled from UNEP; WISE; USCOLD; and USEPA

failures in contemporary times while Asia has increased and Europe and Africa have remained steady.[18]

Direct discharge of mine waste into waterways (lakes, rivers and oceans) is permitted at a small number of locations worldwide leading to some of the largest instances of industrial pollution. Three large-scale mines currently practise riverine tailings disposal (Grasberg, Indonesia; Ok Tedi, PNG; and Porgera, PNG). Gavin Mudd and colleagues report cumulative mine waste disposal into these three river systems to be 2.2 billion tonnes of tailings and 6 billion tonnes of waste rock.[19] Other historical examples include Panguna (PNG) and El Salvador (Chile). Over the past decade disposal of mine wastes into rivers has increased with production increases of existing mines; however, no new large-scale mines have opened using the technique. Marine tailings disposal has, however, undergone a renaissance of sorts with the opening of one recent large-scale mine using sub-marine tailings disposal (Simberi, PNG). Another mine using sub-marine tailings disposal has closed (Minahasa Raya, Indonesia), while three continue to operate (Lihir, PNG; Batu Hijau, Indonesia; and Çayeli Bakir, Turkey). Ocean surface tailings disposal, such as that at Marinduque (Philippines) and El Salvador (Chile), have left lasting environmental legacies with UNEP describing the pollution from El Salvador at Chañaral as one of the most serious examples of industrial marine pollution in the Pacific.[20]

Paste

Greater leadership in tailings management is needed at the international level. Tailings management was identified as a significant theme of the MMSD but the ICMM has not undertaken a major tailings initiative since its establishment. The final report of the MMSD called for: the ICMM and other appropriate conveners such as UNEP to develop guidance on the disposal of mine waste; the practice of riverine disposal to be ended; a collaborative programme of scientific research to be undertaken on marine disposal; and a source of technical expertise and advice to be made available to companies, communities and governments about mine waste management.[21] A step change in tailings management could come from mainstreaming of new technologies such as paste and thickened tailings, optimising mineral processing for tailings design outcomes and reform of mine accounting practices that discount long-term legacies (such as Net Present Value).[22]

Thickening tailings, simply put, refers to the removal of water from tailings before disposal. Paste and thickened tailings are a continuum of tailings with high solid concentration and greater fluid removal. Conventional tailings typically range between 30-50% solids, thickened tailings between 55–75% solids and paste over 75%. The thickening of tailings allows it to be stored in a more stable and inert form, contained in a smaller footprint, with greater water recycling and reduced potential for AMD generation and contamination. Transporting paste is a major challenge but recent technological innovations have made wider adoption possible.

David Boger is a fisherman and an enthusiast of healthy rivers. He is also a scientist of international standing and the namesake of a non-Newtonian, 'constant viscosity elastic fluid'. A Boger fluid. For this discovery Professor Boger was awarded the Prime Minister's Prize for Science, the Pol Eureka Prize for Environmental Research and he was elected as a Fellow to the Royal Society of London for Improving Natural Knowledge. A non-Newtonian fluid is a fluid that changes its viscosity depending on what you do to it. If you move it slowly it is a liquid. If you move it fast it behaves like a solid. Like other non-Newtonian fluids, a Boger fluid is elastic, but where Boger fluids differ is that they have a constant viscosity. You can control how they flow. Professor Boger has devoted his career to the application of rheology, the study of flow, to the mining industry. He has been a pioneer in the development and application of paste and thickened tailings technologies.

In 1974 Boger was approached by Alcoa of Australia to help them manage their 'red mud' waste, the residues of bauxite mined for the production of aluminium. Red mud is caustic, with a pH of 13, and typically stored as a suspension in a large pond. Boger and his students helped Alcoa to thicken red mud for transportation, drying and stacking. The dry stacking technique halved the footprint of Alcoa's waste. The innovation spread to bauxite production in Jamaica and other parts of the world. It wasn't until the 1990s, however, that other parts of the mining industry began to notice and in 1999 the first in a series of Paste and Thickened

Tailings Conferences was held in Edmonton, Canada. Richard Jewell and Andy Fourie from the Australian Centre for Geomechanics, at the University of Western Australia, have been key figures behind these events.[23]

'The technology has now matured to the extent that many tailings dams could be eliminated and reclamation could occur concurrently by using paste technology,' wrote David in a summary of his career contributions in the *Annual Review of Chemical and Biomolecular Engineering*.[24] Successful application in the Alumina industry has not been enough to spur widespread adoption in the other commodity sectors that produce waste in greater volumes and rates. The uptake of paste and thickened tailings technologies does contain an element of risk as new methods are adopted, as well as an increase in short-term cost. The ICMM could play a stronger role to support companies looking to transition to paste by providing guidance and creating fora for technical knowledge exchange. Another potential option for governments is to consider whether technology specification might be appropriate in some cases. While 'command and control' regulatory approaches are much maligned, there are some clear examples where specifying technology has led to dramatic improvements in industry performance.

In the oil industry large-scale marine pollution events arising from tanker spills were synonymous with the industry in the 1970s and 1980s. The annual frequency of oil spills from tankers, combined carriers and barges tracked seaborne oil trade up until the mid-1980s. The introduction of double hulled tankers, and the 1992 decision by the International Maritime Organization to mandatorily require double hulls for tankers above 5000 dead weight tonnage, contributed to a dramatic reduction in spill incidents and total oil spilt from tankers despite rising seaborne trade.[25]

There are differences between the two cases. Tailings infrastructure is designed to hold waste over very long time scales, while tankers only transport oil for a short period of time. Existing dams will not be replaced with new technology, and therefore specifying the use of tailings thickening will not reduce the risk of older tailings dams. Technology specification is also most successful when coordinated at an international scale, and by commanding the use of technologies it can have the side effect of stifling innovation and encouraging a one-size fits all approach. Nonetheless, the industry is currently not taking advantage of the full potential for improved environmental performance that can come from paste technologies. The status quo in mine waste management is not good enough.

One area where the mining industry can point to success is in the introduction of a voluntary code for the management of cyanide use in the gold mining industry.

The International Cyanide Management Code

On the evening of 30 January 2000, a tailings dam failed at a mine operated by the Aurul SA Company in Baia Mare, north-west Romania. Aural was half-owned by Australian junior mining company, Esmerelda Exploration. Poor design and bad weather conspired to fell the wall and 100,000m³ of slurry, laiden with 50–100 tonnes of cyanide, were released into a local waterway. Cyanide concentrations were recorded near the spill of 19,400 micrograms per litre, nearly 2,000 times the Romanian standard. Over the course of four weeks the plume fouled the Sasar, Lapus, Somes, Tisza and Danube rivers before discharging into the Black sea. More than 1,240 tons of fish were killed and 2,000km of the Danube catchment area were affected. Twenty-four municipalities were forced to interrupt their water supply.[26]

More than 90% of all gold produced is done using sodium cyanide as a process chemical. The use of cyanide in gold and silver mining has been a controversial topic.[27] Cyanide is an environmentally sensitive chemical compound that can cause acute toxicity. Thousands of bird mortalities were associated with cyanide use in the mining industry in the 1980s, particularly in the United States; however, reductions in concentration and physical covers on solution ponds have since reduced exposure and bird mortality.[28] Terry Mudder and colleagues reported on environmental incidents in the mining industry between 1965 and 2004 to identify major incidents involving cyanide.[29] Of the 67 total environmental incidents analysed over four decades (an average of 1.7 incidents per year) 12 of those incidents involved the presence of cyanide (an average of three major incidents per decade).

In the aftermath of the Baia Mare tragedy, UNEP and the International Council on Metals and the Environment (the precursor to the ICMM) co-hosted a workshop at the École des Mines in Paris in May, 2000, to consider a wider response to cyanide management in the gold mining industry. Thirty-eight people were invited to the event representing gold mining companies, The Gold Institute, the World Gold Council, the governments of Australia, United States, France, Romania and Hungary, suppliers of cyanide, the European Commission, the OECD, The World Bank, IFC, WWF, Mineral Policy Centre, Sierra Club, International Committee on Large Dams, experts and consultants. The group reached consensus on the need for a voluntary industry code of practice.[30]

Over the next 13 months a multi-stakeholder steering committee, auspiced by UNEP and ICME, developed the main components of what would become the International Cyanide Management Code for the Manufacture, Transport, and Use of Cyanide in the Production of Gold. Five steering committee meetings, and extensive stakeholder consultations were held. One-hundred and forty bodies were asked to review the draft code. Fifteen detailed presentations were made to the committee, with 68 written submissions received. The International Cyanide Management Institute was formed in 2003 to implement the certification process. The ICMI oversees a comprehensive audit process and independent third party certification to the code. Auditors are subject to strict criteria on experience and expertise. The summary reports of the audits are available online, and training workshops about the code are periodically held in regions around the world. ICMI has a multi-stakeholder board of directors and a dispute resolution mechanism.[31]

The first 14 signatories to the code were accepted in November of 2005. Forty gold companies, 20 cyanide producers and 109 transporters in 51 countries are now signatories to the code.[32]

Paul Bateman has been President of the ICMI since 2005. I talked to him about the effectiveness of the code and whether now, nearly a decade after the first companies became signatories, whether he believed progress had been made:

> The code is working and is making a difference in terms of protecting communities, employees, and the environment. In many instances, the code sets standards beyond those required by legislation, and the participating companies are taking the extra step of employing best practice. While the results are not easily quantified, there are key indicators of its impact. For example, before the advent of the code there was on average a significant incident involving cyanide in the gold mining industry every three years. Since implementation of the code began in late 2005 there have been no significant environmental incidents involving cyanide at any code-certified gold operation. We are seeing fewer incidents and the ones that do occur are smaller and are managed better, at least in part because of the programme's detailed emergency response planning requirements. We take some credit for that, but it's really the signatory companies implementing the programme at their operations that make the code work on-the-ground. We know from our discussions with companies that some have made significant investments to bring their operations into compliance with the code, and the recertification of operations shows a sustained commitment to responsible cyanide management.

As one of the most established certification schemes in the mining industry the Cyanide Code is now cross-referenced in an array of soft regulatory instruments. The IFC requires mine sites using cyanide to do so consistent with the Code as a condition of project financing.[33] The Responsible Jewellery Council Code of Practices and the draft standards of the Initiative for Responsible Mining Assurance also require performance consistent with the code.

Michael Rae was a member of the steering committee that developed the Cyanide Code. For almost 17 years he worked for WWF, leading its international work on mining. Michael's involvement in the Cyanide Code coincided with a three-year research programme, the Mining Certification Evaluation Project (2002–2005; MCEP), of which he was a key figure. The MCEP was led by WWF-Australia and the CSIRO (the Australian federal government agency for scientific research). The project investigated the feasibility of third party certification of environmental and social performance to the mining industry, and included mine site trials in Australia and Brazil.

As the concept of certification in the mining industry proved feasible, Rae, with colleagues Stephen D'Esposito from Earthworks (whom we met in Chapter 1), Ian Wood of BHP Billiton and Keith Ferguson of Placer Dome (and formerly of Environment Canada), began a dialogue process, unofficially known as the 'Vancouver Dialogue', between industry and civil society about the potential for additional certification schemes beyond the Cyanide Code. To foster collegiality, the first formative meeting of the dialogue coincided with a Robert Plant concert in Vancouver.

With time, and as the constituency expanded, the dialogue became the Initiative for Responsible Mining Assurance (IRMA), which officially formed in 2006. IRMA progressed slowly, and when the jewellery industry approached Rae to help establish a certification system for the sector, he accepted, holding the position of Chief Executive of the Responsible Jewellery Council from 2006 to 2013. Another key MCEP researcher, Fiona Solomon, took the position of RJC Director of Standards. The RJC Code of Practices has become the most established broad-based sustainability standard in the precious stones and metals industry.

IRMA released a draft standard in 2014 after eight long years of debate between NGOs such as Earthworks, mining companies like Anglo American, downstream users like Tiffany & Co, labour unions and affected communities. IRMA is a standard born of a true dialogue (albeit very slow) between the mining industry and civil society advocacy organisations focused on mining. Differing politics between the two schemes boiled over in 2013 with NGO backers of IRMA issuing a detailed critic of the RJC.[34] The IRMA standard is positioning itself as a stretch target for the industry. It will also apply to a wider set of commodities beyond precious stones and metals. Both standards have the potential to play important roles in improving sustainability practice across the sector.

The Cyanide Code and the MCEP proved to be the beginning of a proliferation of certification schemes applicable to the mining industry – a topic that we will return to in Chapter 5.

Climate, water and energy

Mine waste production is a growing challenge. Ore grades for most major commodities are in decline and the industry is producing more waste (tailings and waste rock) per unit of metal produced (Figures 2 and 3).[35] However, it is not just waste that is challenged by declining ore grades. Gavin Mudd, using historical data for Australia, demonstrated that declining grades, and the associated increase in waste rock (and its haulage) and ore milled per unit of metal is placing pressure on the water, process chemical (e.g. cyanide), energy and greenhouse gas intensity of mining per unit of production.[36] Improvements have been made, with water recycling and emissions reduction programmes; however, as mined ore grades continue to fall in the future some indicators of environmental performance are likely to decline on a global scale – all due of the declining quality of ore.

The increase in sustainability reporting associated with the Global Reporting Initiative now makes it possible to investigate these trends. Data from the global copper and platinum industries confirm that ore grade is having an influence on the environmental sustainability of mining. Stephen Northey, Nawshad Haque and Gavin Mudd have analysed energy, greenhouse and water intensity in the copper industry.[37] Global average ore grades are now less than 1% and

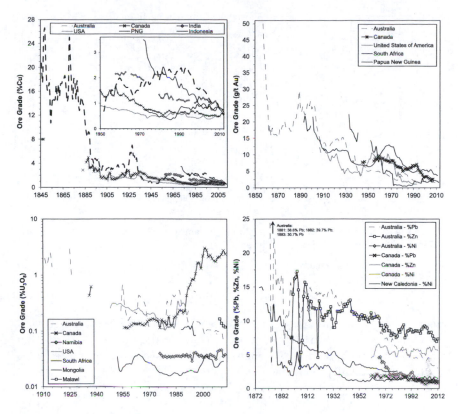

Figure 2 Average ore grades for selected metals and countries over time

(i) copper (top left); 216 (ii) gold (top right); (iii) uranium (bottom left); (iv) lead-zinc-nickel (bottom right)

Source: Data updated from: Mudd (2007, 2009, 2014); Mudd and Jowitt (2014); Mudd and colleagues (2013)

in decline, with the cut-off for profitability around 0.5%. For operations with only a mine and concentrator a clear correlation exists between ore grade and energy consumption. Smelting and refining adds more complexity as other variables influence the data. For greenhouse gas emissions the same general trend holds with increasing intensity following declining grades; however, there is some variability across geography depending on the sources of electricity. The relationship between water intensity and ore grade, however, shows significant variation across the sector, with variability across geography particularly important. Water intensity in arid regions is higher due to evaporation on site, requiring more external water input into the operation from an already water scarce environment.[38]

The data shows that efficiency programmes have reduced the water intensity of milled ore over the period 2004–2009.[39] The ICMM has released a compilation of case studies of water management in the mining industry to encourage best

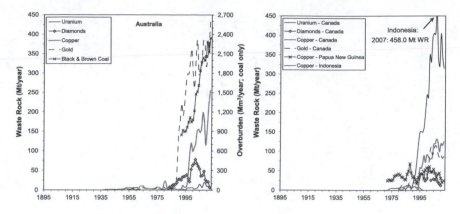

Figure 3 Minimum waste rock for Australia (left) and Canada, Papua New Guinea and Indonesia (right) for selected commodities

Source: Data updated from: Mudd (2007, 2009, 2014); Mudd and Jowitt (2014); Mudd and colleagues (2013)

practice.[40] In Australia, the Minerals Council of Australia, in association with the University of Queensland's Centre for Water in the Minerals Industry, has pioneered a water accounting system to assist water management and recycling in the mining industry.[41]

Gavin Mudd and Bonnie Glaister have reported on similar data for the platinum industry.[42] Platinum Group Metals (PGMs) are used in catalytic convertors for vehicle air pollution control, hydrogen fuel cells and increasingly in jewellery. The Bushveld Igneous Complex in the central Transvaal Province of South Africa dominates global production. Ten projects reported sufficient data for analysis. Ore grades are a significant factor for unit energy consumption, with declining grades increasing energy use. No mining project demonstrated long-term energy efficiency improvements over the period of analysis (2001–2011) and only one demonstrated a decline in greenhouse gas intensity (Figure 4). Ore grades do not appear to be a major factor in determining water efficiency in the platinum sector, though just one project demonstrated water efficiency improvements over the period of analysis.

Innovations in clean technology such as electric vehicles and solar power have been adopted at a handful of mining sites – for example, the use of photovoltaic power at Chuquicamata, Chile. But it is clear from the above data that energy efficiency improvements will need to overcome the challenge of declining ore grades across many commodities.

Biodiversity and rehabilitation

The mining industry is often argued to have a lower impact on biodiversity than other more extensive land-uses such as agriculture and urban development.

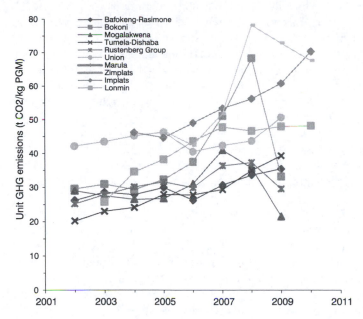

Figure 4 Greenhouse gas emissions per unit of production for the Platinum Group Metals industry

Source: Mudd, 2012, 'Sustainability reporting and the platinum group metals'

Mining and quarrying are estimated to have disturbed 0.3% of the Earth's ice-free land area in comparison to 13% for cropland and 23% for pastures.[43] While the global extent of land impacted is relatively low, the disturbance (and clearing) of land for mining can be locally and regionally very significant. The intensive nature of extraction, and persistence of associated wastes, can have an acute impact on biodiversity. Furthermore, the extent of land-use change that is driven by associated extraction and processing infrastructure, is often under-recognised. In Brazil's Iron Quadrangle, in the state of Minas Gerais, for example, global demand for steel has driven extensive land-use change through expansion of mining, increased charcoal production (for coking of iron) and associated plantation expansion.[44] Between 1990 and 2010, greater than 9,500ha (0.5%) of land transitioned to mining and 41,000ha (9%) transitioned to plantations to produce charcoal.[45]

The rehabilitation of mined land has proved problematic at many sites and few have been relinquished to government following successful rehabilitation. Peter Erskine is a Senior Fellow at the University of Queensland's Centre for Mined Land Rehabilitation, part of the larger Sustainable Minerals Institute. Peter works with companies to implement rehabilitation and closure programmes and after many years devoted to this work he is becoming increasingly concerned about the standard of mined land rehabilitation across the industry:

With closure costs heavily discounted under current accounting models mine rehabilitation legacies easily, and cheaply, change ownership during the life of a mine. Therefore, most existing mines have used a low cost engineering approach to ecosystem restoration and not invested in landform design, maintained soil quality nor created conditions that are appropriate for local flora and fauna to re-establish. [There are two solutions I would suggest] to remedy this failure: (1) the big stick approach, achieve short-term (<5 years) rehabilitation success or stop mining activities; (2) the carrot approach, invest a percentage of the commodity value or tonnage in biodiversity conservation and restoration in the broader landscape. Both approaches should improve on current outcomes and costs could be determined at the outset of a mining project.

Peter believes that the most effective use of resources may not be to attempt to rehabilitate and restore mining impacted landscapes to a pre-impact condition. Restoration to stable, non-polluting landforms, coupled with off-lease investment to restore biodiversity corridors may offer a better outcome from an environmental perspective.[46] An industry-sponsored scientific study of on- and off-lease biodiversity restoration programmes found that off-lease programmes could offer greater outcomes if coordinated across the sector.[47]

Rehabilitation challenges are not just confined to contemporary mines. Abandoned mines present ongoing environmental legacies and are an indicator of the historical performance of the sector. A recent inventory of abandoned mine sites in Australia, for example, identified 52,534 legacy mine sites.[48] In Canada, close to CAN$1 billion of public funds were spent between 2002 and 2012 on rehabilitation of abandoned and orphaned mines.[49] Much larger investments will be needed, with just one Canadian regional programme, the Northern Contaminated Sites Program, calculating a liability of around CAN$1.755 billion.[50]

A major achievement of the ICMM in the period since the MMSD is the partnership with the International Union for Conservation of Nature (IUCN), to commit ICMM members to respect designated protected areas and not explore or mine in World Heritage (WH) properties.[51] The confluence of mining development and the 217 properties of the World Heritage list was investigated by the United Nations Environment Programme World Conservation Monitoring Centre.[52] They found that of the 12,592 mining projects analysed, ten were inside a WH site (seven in exploration and three in production). Fifty-five producing mines were located within 10km of a WH site, 18 within 25km and four were located within less than a kilometre of a site.

A benchmarking of 30 mining, oil and gas companies undertaken by the Natural Value Initiative found 79% of mining companies had a policy commitment on biodiversity. However, only 21% of mining companies had developed biodiversity risk assessments for all sites, and only 29% of mining companies had piloted ecosystem services tools.[53] Only one company had committed to causing no net loss of biodiversity. The ICMM and IUCN undertook their own review of the performance of ICMM member companies in biodiversity management. They report a general increase in the sophistication of biodiversity management across the sector between 2003 and 2014 and a significant increase in the use of biodiversity action plans (from 21% to 63% of member companies for all sites in or near areas of high biodiversity).[54]

In 2013, IPIECA (the peak oil and gas industry association focused on environmental and social performance) in partnership with the ICMM, and the Equator Principles Association, launched a Cross Sector Biodiversity Initiative and charter to share good practices on biodiversity conservation. There is potential for effective management of biodiversity on mining leases, which are often much larger than the area needed for infrastructure and extraction, to lead to positive impacts on biodiversity. Evidence for this argument comes from programmes such as the Arid Recovery partnership on the Olympic Dam mining lease in remote South Australia, where a 123km^2 fenced reserve is restoring the arid ecosystem through the removal of feral foxes, rabbits and cats.[55] The extractive industries may also contribute to better knowledge about ecosystems through baseline flora and fauna surveys.

Quicksilver and the Virgin Mary

Perhaps of greater consequence within protected areas is the presence of Artisanal and Small-Scale Mining (ASM) – independent, often informal mining that provides a subsistence livelihood for millions of people. Cristina Villegas and colleagues found that ASM is occurring in at least seven WH sites, and 96 of the 147 protected areas evaluated in their study.[56] ASM is an important rural livelihood activity in many countries of the world, but it can present risks for biodiversity. ASM is estimated to directly involve 20–30 million people[57] and produce up to 25% of global minerals and metals production, for commodities such as gold, tin and tantalum.[58] An additional three to five times as many people are believed to indirectly support the sector.[59] Due to the very large numbers of people involved, ASM is simultaneously a significant source of development and a driver of environmental change. Water pollution, deforestation, community health, safety, child labour and in-migration have long been raised as issues of concern in the ASM sector.[60] ASM can generate up to five times of the income of other rural poverty driven vocations in agriculture and forestry,[61] and the role of the sector as a potential source of development is only slowly being realised.

The issues that have garnered the most attention within the scientific and development communities are the use of mercury in alluvial gold mining and deforestation associated with ASM extraction. Mercury, also known as quicksilver, is widely used as an amalgamation agent for the processing of alluvial ores. Kevin Telmer and Marcello Veiga estimate that one third of all mercury release to the environment can be attributed to ASM – approximately 1000 tonnes per year, from at least 70 countries.[62] The issue of mercury contamination has dominated the governance response to ASM; however, a lack of understanding and knowledge about the social dynamics of artisanal mining has hampered the success of education and alternative technology programmes designed to reduce mercury use.[63]

The Madre de Dios region of south-eastern Peru is estimated to host between 14,000 and 30,000 artisanal gold miners.[64] The region is named after its river, literally translated as 'Mother of God' – a reference to the Virgin Mary. Named by the Spanish colonists to the region, the river is a tributary of the Amazon. It snakes its way eastwards from Peru into Bolivia and eventually Brazil. ASM in the region represents roughly 70% of Peru's ASM gold production,[65] or about 14% of total gold production in Peru.[66] The miners operate a mixture of legal and illegal alluvial gold concessions predominantly along the Madre de Dios, Colorado, Inabari and Malinowski Rivers. Sixty-five percent of mining activity in the region occurs outside of permitted concessions.[67]

The Amazonian tropical forests of Madre de Dios are high in biodiversity. Mining has resulted in both deforestation and water pollution, with activities encroaching on protected areas such as the Tambopata National Reserve, the Amarakaeri Communal Reserve, the Los Amigos Conservation Concession and the World Heritage-listed Manu National Park.[68] Jennifer Swenson and colleagues found mining to be the fastest deforestation activity in Madre de Dios, showing a six-fold increase between 2003 and 2009 (to a rate of 1,915 hectares per year), with 6,600 hectares of wetlands and tropical forest cleared during the time period studied. The rate of deforestation was found to be closely associated with the price of gold.[69] The Peruvian Ministry of Environment reported in 2013 that deforestation associated with gold mining in the region was worse than previously thought, with the footprint increasing from less than 10,000 hectares in 1999 to more than 50,000 hectares in September of 2012. The study was undertaken in collaboration with the Carnegie Institution for Science, and combined satellite mapping, ground truthing and airborne surveys.[70]

Mercury is widely used as a process chemical by the miners. Between 45 and 50 tonnes of mercury are used each year in the region, with associated river pollution and health impacts, particularly as a result of fish consumption.[71] In 2011 and 2012 the Peruvian government issued decrees that established a 500,000 hectare 'Permissible Mining Corridor', and enforced the decree with military incursions, evictions and confiscation of equipment in operation outside of the mining zone. The government has also progressed formalisation of the sector, requiring all miners to register with the government.[72] The administrative process accompanying formalisation has proved difficult for a significant proportion of the miners and has been met with resistance. Negotiated access (through a mining corridor) and formalisation are commonly cited as best practice approaches to management of the sector; however, the case of Madre de Dios demonstrates the complexity and limitations of managing biodiversity and human development in the context of ASM.[73] Since a peak in mid-2011 the price of gold has declined more than 30%. While still high by historical standards, the decline in the value of gold may have the largest impact on the future extent of mining in the region.

Onto the agenda

The global sustainable development agenda has long been relevant to the mining industry, but prior to the MMSD the challenges of the industry did not find a place within the defining international agreements and texts. Neither the World Commission on Environment and Development (1987), the outcomes document of the United Nations Conference on Environment and Development (1992; Rio Earth Summit), nor the Millennium Declaration (2000), made significant mention of the mining industry's role in sustainable development or social development.

In Chapter 1 we saw that the finalisation of MMSD was timed to coincide with the Rio +10 event in Johannesburg. With greater engagement by the sector in sustainability, a greater awareness at the international level has followed. The potential role of mining in shaping a sustainable and equitable future is now recognised, as is the potential for mining to undermine these ambitions. The World Summit on Sustainable Development (2002; Rio +10) and UN Conference on Sustainable Development (2012; Rio +20) both made lengthy reference to mining and energy and the potential role of the extractives sector 'to catalyse broad-based economic development, reduce poverty and assist countries in meeting internationally agreed development goals, including the Millennium Development Goals, when managed effectively and properly'.[74] While some critics have argued that discussion of the role of mining in sustainable development within the forum of the United Nations legitimises unsustainable mining practices, exposing the challenges and the potential of the industry to a broader array of actors engaged in sustainability can help to consolidate reforms and drive further change.

The United Nations is currently debating the successor to the Millennium Development Goals (MDGs), which expire in 2015. The Post-2015 Development Agenda will seek to integrate the MDGs into the broader sustainable development agenda and adopt a set of universal Sustainable Development Goals (SDGs). The merging of the agendas places inclusive development and poverty eradication at the heart of global efforts to maintain the integrity of ecosystems. In June 2014 the 30-member Open Working Group released a draft set of SDGs to begin member negotiations. The draft goals call for the 'sustainable management and efficient use of natural resources'.[75] While mining is not explicitly mentioned there are many goals that are relevant to the sector. An effort to particularise the SDGs to mining will need to follow the adoption of the goals. Minerals and energy are the foundation of industrial production and global consumption. The relevance of the sector goes far beyond its impact during the extraction phase. The transition to a green economy, for example, will require commodities such as rare earth elements and lithium to drive low emissions technology. In the following chapter we look at the topic of development and ask whether mining can meet its potential to 'catalyse broad-based economic development, reduce poverty and assist countries in meeting internationally agreed development goals', as envisaged by the United Nations Conference on Sustainable Development.

Notes

1 Mudd, G.M. and D.V. Boger (2013), 'The ever growing case for paste and thickened tailings: Towards more sustainable mine waste management.' AusIMM Bulletin, April: 56–59.

2 Bulaong Jnr., O. (2004), 'A case study on Marcopper Mining Corporation and the tragedy of 1996.' Institute for Ethical Business Worldwide, University of Notre Dame, Consortium Case. April. Online resource: http://www.ethicalbusiness.nd.edu/researchScholarship/Consortium%20cases/Marcopper_CaseApril2.pdf Accessed: 4 January 2015.

3 United States Geological Survey (USGS) (1996), The mineral industry of the Philippines. Online resource: http://minerals.usgs.gov/minerals/pubs/country/1996/9326096.pdf Accessed: 4 January 2015; David, C.P. (2002), 'Heavy metal concentrations in marine sediments impacted by a mine-tailings spill, Marinduque Island, Philippines.' *Environmental Geology*, 42: 955–965; Bulaong (2004), 'A case study on Marcopper'; World Information Service on Energy (2014), 'Chronology of major tailings dam failures, 1960–2014.' Online resource: http://www.wise-uranium.org/mdaf.html Accessed: 7 November 2014.

4 Bulaong (2004), 'A case study on Marcopper.'

5 United States Geological Survey (USGS) (2000), 'An overview of mining-related environmental and human health issues, Marinduque Island, Philippines: Observations from a joint U.S. Geological Survey – Armed Forces Institute of Pathology Reconnaissance Field Evaluation.' 12–19 May 2000, U.S. Geological Survey Open-File Report 00-397; David (2002), 'Heavy metal concentrations in marine sediments'; Carr, R.S., Nipper, M. and G. Plumlee (2003), 'Survey of marine contamination from mining-related activities on Marinduque Island, Philippines: Porewater toxicity and chemistry.' *Aquatic Ecosystem Health & Management*, 6(4): 369–379.

6 Marcopper Mining Corporation (MMC) (1996), 'So the people may know ...' Marcopper flyer reproduced in Bulaong Jnr. (2004), Online resource: http://www.ethicalbusiness.nd.edu/researchScholarship/Consortium%20cases/Marcopper_CaseApril2.pdf Accessed: 4 January 2015.

7 Cooney, J. (1997), 'Placer Dome: "We are responsible".' The Catholic Register. 28 April. p. 17; Coumans, C. (2002), 'Placer Dome case study: Marcopper Mines.' April. Online resource: http://www.miningwatch.ca/sites/www.miningwatch.ca/files/PD_Case_Study_Marcopper_0.pdf Accessed: 4 January 2015; Bulaong (2004), 'A case study on Marcopper'; Dashwood, H.S. (2014), *The Rise of Global Corporate Social Responsibility: Mining and the spread of global norms*, Cambridge University Press, Cambridge. For additional resources on Marinduque see: Placer Dome (2005), 'Fact sheet.' August. Online resource: http://web.archive.org/web/20051125012929/http://www.placerdome.com/__shared/assets/August_2005_Investor_Fact_Sheet2856.pdf Accessed: 4 January 2015; Project Underground and MiningWatch Canada. (2002), 'STD toolkit: Philippines case studies.'

8 USGS (2000), 'An overview of mining-related environmental and human health issues.'

9 Coumans (2002), 'Placer Dome case study'; Macdonald, I. and K. Southall (2005), 'Mining Ombudsman case report: Marinduque Island.' Oxfam Australia. March, Fitzroy.

10 Coumans (2002), 'Placer Dome case study'; Macdonald and Southall (2005), 'Mining Ombudsman case report.'

11 Thomson, I. and R. Boutilier (2011), 'Social license to operate.' In P. Darling, SME *Mining Engineering Handbook* 3rd edn. Chapter 17.2. pp. 1779–1796; Cooney, J. (2014), 'Interview with Rick Cluff,' CBC The Early Edition, British Columbia. 4 December. Online resource: http://www.cbc.ca/player/Radio/Local+Shows/

British+Columbia/The+Early+Edition/Full+Episodes/ID/2625541410/ Accessed: 5 January 2015; Dashwood (2014), *The Rise of Global Corporate Social Responsibility*.

12   Thomson, I. and R. Boutilier (2011), 'Social license to operate'; Cooney (2014), 'Interview with Rick Cluff'; Dashwood (2014), *The Rise of Global Corporate Social Responsibility*.

13   Franks, D.M., Boger, D., Côte, C., and D. Mulligan (2011), 'Sustainable development principles for the disposal of mining and mineral processing wastes.' *Resources Policy*, 36(2): 114–122.

14   Davis Jr., R.A., Welty, A.T., Borrego, J., Morales, J.A., Pendon, J.G. and J.G. Ryan (2000), 'Rio Tinto estuary (Spain): 5000 years of pollution.' *Environmental Geology*, 39(10): 1107–1116.

15   WISE (2014), 'Chronology of major tailings dam failures.'

16   Azam, S. and Li, Q. (2010), 'Tailings dam failures: A review of the last one hundred years.' *Geotechnical News*, December, 50–53.

17   Azam and Li (2010), 'Tailings dam failures.'

18   Azam and Li (2010), 'Tailings dam failures.'

19   Updated data originally published in: Jowitt, S.M., Mudd, G.M. and Z. Weng (2013), 'Hidden mineral feposits in Cu-dominated porphyry-skarn systems: How resource reporting can occlude important mineralization types within mining camps.' *Economic Geology*, 108(5): 1185–1193; and Mudd, G.M. and C.P. Roche (2014), 'Mining in Morobe, Papua New Guinea – Impacts, assurance and self-determination.' Proceedings of Life-of-Mine 2014 Conference, Australasian Institute of Mining and Metallurgy, July 2014, Brisbane, pp. 313–335.

20   United Nations Environment Program (UNEP) (1997), 'Compendium of Summaries of Judicial Decisions in Environment Related Cases: Chile – Environmental Protection, Mining Operations.' Pedro Flores y Otros v. Corporacion del Cobre, CODELCO, Division Salvador. Recurso de Proteccion, Copiapo. Supreme Court of Chile, ROL.12.753.FS.641 (1998), SACEP, UNEP, NORAD Publication Series on Environmental Law and Policy no. 3. Online Resource: http://www.unescap.org/drpad/vc/document/compendium/ch1.htm Accessed: 20 February 2007.

21   International Institute on Environment and Development (IIED) and World Business Council for Sustainable Development (WBCSD; 2002), *Breaking New Ground: Mining minerals and sustainable development. The report of the MMSD project*. London: Earthscan.

22   For more on the potential of paste and thickened tailings technologies see: Boger, D. (2013), 'Rheology of slurries and environmental impacts in the mining industry.' *Annual Review of Chemical and Biomolecular Engineering*, 4: 239–257. For more on the potential to design mining and processing for tailings outcomes see: Edraki, M., Baumgartl, T., Manlapig, E., Bradshaw, D., Franks, D., and C. Moran. (2014), 'Designing mine tailings for better environmental, social and economic outcomes: a review of alternative approaches.' *Journal of Cleaner Production*, DOI: 10.1016/j.jclepro.2014.04.079.

23   Boger, D.V. (2009), 'Rheology and the resource industries.' *Chemical Engineering Science*, 64(22): 4525–4536; Boger (2013), 'Rheology of slurries.'

24   Boger (2013), 'Rheology of slurries.'

25   International Tanker Owners Pollution Federation (ITOPF) (2014), 'Oil tanker spill statistics 2013.' London; ITOPF (2013), 'Oil tanker spill statistics.' London.

26   United Nations Environment Programme (UNEP) and Office for the Co-ordination of Humanitarian Affairs (OCHA) (2000), 'Spill of liquid and suspended waste at the Aurul SA retreatment plant in Baia Mare.' Cyanide Spill at Baia Mare Romania Assessment Mission 23 February–6 March. Geneva; Regional Environmental Centre for Central and Eastern Europe (REC) (2000), 'The cyanide spill at Baia Mare, Romania: Before, during and after.' Szentendre, Hungary. Online resource: http://archive.rec.org/REC/Publications/CyanideSpill/ENGCyanide.pdf Accessed: 22 December 2014.

27   See for example: Moran, R. (2001), 'More cyanide uncertainties: Lessons from the Baia Mare, Romania, spill – water quality and politics.' Mineral Policy Centre Issue Paper

no. 3. Online resource: http://www.earthworksaction.org/files/publications/mcu_final. pdf Accessed: 9 November 2014.

28 Mudder, T., Botz, M. and K. Hagelstein (2006), 'Cyanide science and society.' Unpublished manuscript. Wyoming: TIMES Limited.

29 Mudder, T. and M., Botz (2004), 'Cyanide and society: A critical review.' *The European Journal of Mineral Processing and Environmental Protection*, 4(1): 62–74; Mudder et al. (2006), 'Cyanide science and society.'

30 United Nations Environment Programme (UNEP) and International Council on Metals and the Environment (ICME) (2000), 'A workshop on industry codes of practice: Cyanide management.' Ecole des Mines, 25–26 May, Paris, France. Online resource: http://commdev.org/files/1807_file_cyanide_report.pdf Accessed: 22 December 2014.

31 Bateman, P. (2010), 'Cyanide management: Ten years since Baia Mare.' *Mining Environmental Management*, 13–15 July. Online resource: http://www.euromines.org/sites/default/files/publications/cyanide-management-ten-years-baia-mare---july-2010. pdf Accessed: 22 December 2014.

32 International Cyanide Management Institute (ICMI) (2014), 'Directory of signatory companies.' Online resource: http://www.cyanidecode.org/signatory-companies/directory-of-signatory-companies Accessed: 10 November 2014.

33 The requirement is outlined in the IFC Environmental, Health and Safety Guidelines for mining projects under Performance Standard 3, Resource Efficiency and Pollution Prevention; International Finance Corporation (IFC) (2007), 'Environmental, health and safety guidelines for mining.' December. Online resource: http://www.ifc.org/wps/wcm/connect/1f4dc28048855af4879cd76a6515bb18/Final%2B-%2BMining.pdf?MOD=AJPERES&id=1323153264157 Accessed: 22 December 2014.

34 The critique can be found in: IndustriALL, Construction, Forestry, Mining and Energy Union, United Steelworkers, Earthworks and MiningWatch Canada (2013), 'More shine than substance: How the RJC certification fails to create responsible jewelry.' May; The RJC issued a response to the critique: Responsible Jewellery Council (RJC) (2013), RJC Response to 'More shine than substance.' Report. June. Online resource: http://www.responsiblejewellery.com/files/RJC-Response-to-More-Shine-than-Substance-Report-130613.pdf Accessed: 7 January 2015.

35 Mudd, G. (2009), 'The sustainability of mining in Australia: Key production trends and their environmental implications for the future.' Research report no. RR5, Department of Civil Engineering, Monash University and Mineral Policy Institute, Revised April 2009; Mudd, G. (2010), 'The environmental sustainability of mining in Australia: Key mega-trends and looming constraints.' *Resources Policy*, 35 (2): 98–115; International Council on Mining and Metals (ICMM) (2012), 'Trends in the mining and metals industry. Mining's contribution to sustainable development.' October. London.

36 Mudd (2009), 'The sustainability of mining in Australia'; Mudd (2010), 'The Environmental sustainability of mining in Australia.'

37 Northey, S., Haque, N. and G. Mudd (2013), 'Using sustainability reporting to assess the environmental footprint of copper mining.' *Journal of Cleaner Production*, 40: 118–128.

38 Northey et al. (2013), 'Using sustainability reporting.'

39 Northey et al. (2013), 'Using sustainability reporting.'

40 International Council on Mining and Metals (ICMM) (2012), 'Water management in mining: A selection of case studies.' May. London.

41 Cote, C.M., Cummings, J., Moran, C.J., and K. Ringwood (2012), 'Water accounting in mining and minerals processing.' In J. Godfrey and K. Chalmers (eds), *Water Accounting: International approaches to policy and decision-making*. Cheltenham, UK; Northampton, MA: Edward Elgar, pp. 91–105.

42 Glaister, B.J. and G. Mudd. (2010), 'The environmental costs of platinum–PGM mining and sustainability: Is the glass half-full or half-empty?' *Minerals Engineering*,

23(5): 438–450; Mudd, G. (2012), 'Sustainability reporting and the platinum group metals: A global mining industry leader?' *Platinum Metals Review*, 56(1): 2–19.

43 Hooke, R., Martín-Duque, J. and J., Pedraza. (2012), 'Land transformation by humans: A review.' *GSA Today*, 22(12): 4–10.

44 Sonter, L., Barrett, D., Soares-Filho, B. and C.J. Moran (2014), 'Global demand for steel drives extensive land-use change in Brazil's iron quadrangle.' *Global Environmental Change*, 26: 63–72.

45 Sonter et al. (2014), 'Global demand for steel.'

46 Sonter, L., Moran, C.J. and D. Barrett (2013), 'Modelling the impact of revegetation on regional water quality: A collective approach to manage the cumulative impacts of mining in the Bowen Basin, Australia.' *Resources Policy*, 38(4): 670–677; Erskine, P. (2014), 'Ecological rehabilitation, past, present and future.' Keynote presentation to Best Practice Ecological Rehabilitation of Mined Lands 2014, 25 September, Singleton.

47 Barrett, D., Sonter, L., Almarza, A., Franks, D.M., Moran, C.J., Cohen, T. and C. Hedemann (2010), 'Quantitative approach to improving the business of biodiversity investment.' Final report. Centre for Water in the Minerals Industry, University of Queensland. Australian Coal Association Research Program. Project Number: C17030.

48 Unger, C., Lechner, A., Glennn V., Edraki, M. and D. Mulligan (2012), 'Mapping and prioritising rehabilitation of abandoned mines in Australia.' Proceedings of the Life-of-Mine Conference. Online resource: https://www.cmlr.uq.edu.au/Portals/0/MMLF/LOM%20Paper%20Unger%20et%20al%20July%202012.pdf Accessed: 9 November 2014.

49 Tremblay, G. and C. Hogan (2012), 'Canada's National Orphaned and Abandoned Mines Initiative.' Natural Resources Canada. Presentation to the Managing Mining Legacies Forum, 16–17 July. Online resource: https://www.cmlr.uq.edu.au/Portals/0/MMLF/Canada's%20National%20Orphaned%20and%20Abandoned%20Mines%20Initiative%20(NOAMI).pdf Accessed: 9 November 2014.

50 Tremblay and Hogan (2012), 'Canada's National Orphaned and Abandoned Mines Initiative.'

51 International Council on Mining and Metals (ICMM) (2003), 'Mining and protected areas.' Position statement. September. London.

52 United Nations Environment Programme World Conservation Monitoring Centre (UNEP-WCMC) (2013), 'Identifying potential overlap between extractive industries (mining, oil and gas) and natural World Heritage sites.' December.

53 Natural Value Initiative (NVI) (2011), 'Tread lightly: Biodiversity and ecosystem services risk and opportunity management within the extractive industry.' October. Online resource: http://www.naturalvalueinitiative.org/download/documents/Publications/NVI%20Extractive%20Report_Tread%20lightly_LR.pdf Accessed 13 May 2015.

54 International Council on Mining and Metals (ICMM) and International Union for Conservation of Nature (IUCN) (2014), 'Biodiversity performance review.' Executive summary. November. London.

55 Commonwealth Department of the Environment (DoE) (2014), 'Australia's biodiversity conservation strategy – case studies.' Online resource: http://www.environment.gov.au/biodiversity/conservation/strategy/case-studies Accessed: 8 November 2014.

56 Villegas, C., Weinberg, R., Levin, E. and K. Hund (2012), 'Artisanal and small-scale mining in protected areas and critical ecosystems programme (ASM-PACE)' A Global Solutions Study, September. Online resource: http://www.profor.info/sites/profor.info/files/docs/ASM_PACE-GlobalSolutions.pdf Accessed: 13 May 2015.

57 Buxton, A. (2013), 'Responding to the challenge of artisanal and small-scale mining. How can knowledge networks help?' London: International Institute for Environment and Development.

58 Levin, E. (2012), 'Understanding artisanal & smallscale mining in protected areas and critical ecosystems: A growing global phenomenon.' Presentation for ASM Protected

and Critical Ecosystems London Roundtable. November; ICMM (2012), 'Trends in the mining and metals industry.'

59 Buxton (2013), 'Responding to the challenge of artisanal and small-scale mining.'

60 Hentschel, T., Hruschk, F. and M. Priester (2002), 'Global report on artisanal & small-scale mining.' Report for the Mining, Minerals and Sustainable Development Project no. 70. International Institute for Environment and Development and World Business Council for Sustainable Development. January, London.

61 Buxton (2013), 'Responding to the challenge of artisanal and small-scale mining.'

62 Telmer K. and M. Veiga (2009), 'World emissions of mercury from small scale and artisanal gold mining.' In R. Mason and N. Pirrone (eds), *Mercury Fate and Transport in the Global Atmosphere: Emissions, Measurements and Models*. New York: Springer, pp. 131–172.

63 Hilson, G. (2006), 'Abatement of mercury pollution in the small-scale gold mining industry: Restructuring the policy and research agendas.' *Science of the Total Environment*, 362(1–3): 1–14.

64 Fraser B. (2009), 'Peruvian gold rush threatens health and the environment.' *Environmental Science and Technology*, 43 (19): 7162–7164; Pachas C., VH. (2013), 'A vision for ecological gold mining in Peru.' ASM-PACE blog. 19 July. Online resource: http://www.asm-pace.org/blog/item/9-peru-madre-dios-artisanal-mining-biodiversity.html Accessed: 3 November 2014.

65 Brooks, W.E., Sandoval, E., Yepez, M.A. and H. Howard (2007), Peru Mercury Inventory 2006. Reston, VA: US Geological Survey.

66 Gardner, E. (2012), 'Peru battles the golden curse of Madre de Dios.' *Nature*, 486(7403): 306–307; Pachas (2013), 'A vision for ecological gold mining in Peru.'

67 Elmes, A., Yarlequé Ipanaqué, J.G., Rogan, J., Cuba, N. and A. Bebbington (2014), 'Mapping licit and illicit mining activity in the Madre de Dios region of Peru.' *Remote Sensing Letters*, 5(10): 882–891.

68 Asner, G., Llactayo, W., Tupayachi, R. and E. Ráez Luna (2013), 'Elevated rates of gold mining in the Amazon revealed through high-resolution monitoring.' *Proceedings of the National Academy of Sciences*, 110(46): 18454–18459; Gardner (2012), 'Peru battles the golden curse of Madre de Dios.'

69 Swenson J., Carter C., Domec J.-C. and C. Delgado (2011), 'Gold mining in the Peruvian Amazon: Global prices, deforestation, and mercury imports.' *PLoS ONE* 6(4): e18875.

70 Asner et al. (2013), 'Elevated rates of gold mining in the Amazon.'

71 Swenson et al. (2011), 'Gold mining in the Peruvian Amazon'; Ashe, K. (2012), 'Elevated mercury concentrations in humans of Madre de Dios, Peru.' *PLoS ONE* 7(3): e33305.

72 Gardner (2012), 'Peru battles the golden curse of Madre de Dios.'

73 Joshua Fisher, The Earth Institute, Columbia University, pers. comm.; for a detailed history of attempts to address the challenges presented by ASM see: Hilson, G. and J. McQuilken (2014), 'Four decades of support for artisanal and small-scale mining in sub-Saharan Africa: A critical review,' *The Extractive Industries and Society*, 1(1): 104–118. For an account of strategies from the field see: Collins, N. and L. Lawson (2014), 'Investigating approaches to working with artisanal and small-scale miners: A compendium of strategies and reports from the field.' International Mining for Development Centre. Online resource: http://im4dc.org/wp-content/uploads/2013/09/Collins-ASM-FR-Completed-Report.pdf Accessed: 13 May 2015.

74 United Nations (2012), The Future We Want. Resolution adopted by the General Assembly on 27 July 2012. A/RES/66/288: p. 44.

75 United Nations (2014), 'Open Working Group proposal for Sustainable Development Goals.' Full report of the Open Working Group of the General Assembly on Sustainable Development Goals. A/68/970.

4 Development

Sudbury to Sewell

The human settlements that mirror mines show great geographic diversity. There are towns, like Broken Hill (Australia), Sudbury (Canada), Outokumpu (Finland) and Ouro Preto (Brazil) that were founded by mining. There are places like Cornwall (England) and the Kolar Gold Fields (India) that have followed the boom and the bust. There are towns like Sewell (Chile) and Viivikonna (Estonia) that are now home to ghosts. There are mining towns like Johannesburg (South Africa), Denver (United States) and Kuala Lumpar (Malaysia) that have become metropolitan capitals. And there are cities like Toronto (Canada), Perth (Australia), London (United Kingdom) and Santiago (Chile) that are the capitals of mining finance.

Mining is at the base of the economy, but the fortunes of the industry have inconsistently been fortuitous for the people of the regions and the countries endowed with mineral wealth. Mineral extraction is concentrated in a handful of traditional mining regions. When measured by value, mining is concentrated in Australia (13.3%), China (12.7%), the former Soviet Union (11%), the USA (4.2%), Europe (3.5%) and Canada (2.6%).[1] But mining has continued to expand in the developing world. Twenty-two percent of global mineral extraction now occurs in resource rich developing countries (Chile, Brazil, Peru, South Africa, Zambia, and the Democratic Republic of the Congo).[2] Importantly, from a development perspective, there is a large number of countries where mining plays a significant role in the economy and where the locations of ore bodies correspond with locations of high development need (Table 3).

Development, the opportunity for improvement, owes its popularisation to US President Harry Truman, who in 1949 evoked the application of knowledge and skills for the betterment of people. In the 1960s and 1970s social development emerged as a critique of development as it was then espoused, focused too closely on national economic measures. Social development refers to the institutions, social infrastructure and social relations that enable human progress. In the 1980s sustainable development infused an ecological dimension, and in the 1990s, Indian economist Amartya Sen and Pakistani economist Mahbub ul Haq tasked us with the concept of human development, to emphasise the personal; the human choices and human capabilities that foster a long and healthy life and an adequate standard of living.

Table 3 Mineral rich low, lower-middle, and upper-middle income countries (poverty measured as a function of proportion of people living at less than $2/day)

Country	Resource	Natural resource exports (% total exports; 2006–10)	Natural resource fiscal revenue (% total revenue; 2006–10)	HDI 2011/ Poverty (%)
Low-income country				
Democratic Republic of Congo	cobalt, copper, oil	94	30	0.29/80
Liberia	gold, diamond, iron ore	NA	16	0.33/95
Niger	uranium	NA	NA	0.3/76
Guinea	bauxite, iron ore	93	23	0.34/70
Mali	gold	75	13	0.36/77
Low-income country (prospective natural resource rich country)				
Sierra Leone	diamonds, iron ore	NA	NA	0.34/76
Afghanistan	copper, gas	NA	NA	0.4/NA
Madagascar	oil & gas, nickel	NA	NA	0.48/90
Mozambique	gas, bauxite, coal	NA	NA	0.32/82
Central African Republic	diamonds, gold	NA	NA	0.34/80
Tanzania	gold, gems	NA	NA	0.47/88
Togo	phosphate	NA	NA	0.44/69
Kyrgyz Republic	gold	NA	NA	0.62/29

Lower-middle income country				
Mauritania	iron ore	24	22	0.45/44
Lao PDR	copper, gold	57	19	0.52/66
Zambia	copper	72	4	0.43/82
Papua New Guinea	oil, copper, gold	77	21	0.47/57
Uzbekistan	gold, gas	NA	NA	0.64/77
Mongolia	copper	81	29	0.65/49
Guyana	gold, bauxite	42	27	0.63/17
Ghana	gold, oil	NA	NA	0.54/54
Lower-middle income country (*prospective natural resource rich country*)				
Guatemala	gold, silver	NA	NA	0.57/30
Upper-middle income country				
Peru	copper, gold	8	19	0.73/15
Botswana	diamonds	66	63	0.63/NA
Suriname	bauxite, gold	11	29	0.68/NA
Mexico	oil, silver	15	36	0.77/8
Russia	oil, nickel, bauxite	50	29	0.76/0
Chile	copper	53	23	0.81/2

Source: International Monetary Fund, 2012, 'Macroeconomic policy frameworks for resource-rich developing countries'

In this chapter we explore the mining industry's engagement with development and ask whether resource development has lived up to the expectations and aspirations of the public. The chapter begins with consideration of mining's relationship with development. Mining has traditionally encouraged enclave style economic development. Ambitiously, captains of industry, development economists and the Pontiff himself, have promoted the notion that human and social development should be the defining objective of the industry. The chapter then discusses the forward and backward linkages that bind mineral extraction to their host economies and looks at how governments and companies have tried to maximise these linkages, by profiling The Africa Mining Vision, the Queensland Government's Sustainable Resource Communities policy and corporate policies, such as Anglo American's Socio-Economic Assessment Toolbox. In the final section the chapter interrogates the corporate social investments that have become commonplace in the sector, through the case of the Collahuasi copper mine, and asks if these investments are aligned to human development goals or to business objectives.

An agent of social development?

Cape Town is not the centre of South African mining, but for a week each year in February, it temporarily becomes the mining capital of the world. The *Investing in African Mining Indaba* attracts more than 7,000 financiers, prospectors, executives, investors and government officials to Cape Town – not because Cape Town hosts a mining bourse or a clutch of service companies, which it doesn't; they come because Cape Town is a lovely place to be. Like most such events, going to Indaba is about the side-events and the side-conversations. Cape Town's bustling food scene and the dramatic, cloud-draped Table Mountain, are encouraging scenery for deals about development to be done.

A month after accepting the position as CEO of Anglo American in 2013, Mark Cutifani, still CEO of Anglo Gold Ashanti, addressed the *Indaba* crowd in Cape Town's huge convention hall. While the tradition is for CEOs to deliver an address on the outlook for the company, and the general tenure of the speeches at *Indaba* range between a mere dislike of government regulation, to anaphylaxis, Cutifani focused his talk on what the mining industry could offer governments and their citizens. In 2010, Anglo American was the most profitable company in the developing world.[3] But at the peak of the boom, a subtle shift occurred, governments were now in a stronger negotiating position, and the very large profits accrued by the industry, meant citizens were demanding their share.

Cutifani called on the industry to be comfortable with its role as a 'social development agent', if it is to be recognised as a 'development industry'. He claimed that mining drives more than 45% of world economic activity, and 'we should be the "Development Partner" that supports and catalyses the creation of wealth for all'.[4] The industry was experiencing pressure from governments to increase their social and economic contribution in response to inflated commodity prices. Labelled 'resource nationalism' by parts of the industry, governments were legislating for increased returns, across areas such as local procurement, local employment, infrastructure, community development, royalties and taxation. Some of these were domains where previously the industry's contribution had been voluntary.[5] Cuitifani's positioning, in part, was a response to this trend but it also reflected the expansion of mining into new localities, as high prices and demand brought resource development to locations new to mining, particularly in Africa, Asia and Latin America.

Development economist Sir Paul Collier, speaking at the same convention hall a year later, went further, arguing that the industry needed to embrace a sensible and singular narrative. Corporate Social Responsibility presents the industry as a charity, which is not credible. Profit maximisation presents the industry as indifferent, which when followed by companies, fouls necessary relationships with government and the workforce. Instead the industry is better placed, he argued, to project itself as a fundamental driver of development, responsible for managing a major natural asset; requiring a decent return, but in turn generating revenue, shared infrastructure and business development in the service of the nation and local communities. Collier reasoned, that like banks the mining industry is a custodian of the wealth of others and thus should expect close oversight from government and civil society.

Development agencies, too, have embraced these trends. Erik Solheim was the Minister presiding over Norway's *Oil for Development* programme when he suggested to Australian Prime Minister, Kevin Rudd, that Australia, too, should share it's experience in mining governance with mineral endowed developing countries to improve environmental and social outcomes. The AUD$127 million Mining for Development initiative was announced in 2011. Canada followed suit with the establishment of the Canadian International Resources and Development Institute.[6] UNDP also released a Strategy for Supporting Sustainable and Equitable Management of the Extractive Sector for Human Development in late 2012.[7]

Other prominent institutions have engaged in the debate. His Holiness Pope Francis welcomed senior mining executives to the Vatican for the first time in September 2013. In a written message to those gathered he asked them to 'reflect on the importance of their human and environmental responsibilities' and to examine their conscience 'on what must be done so that their industry may offer a constant positive contribution to integral human development'.[8] The 'Day of Reflection' was hosted by Cardinal Peter Turkson and the Pontifical Council for Justice and Peace. CEOs in attendance included Sam Walsh (Rio Tinto), Mark Cutifani (Anglo American; a key instigator of the dialogue), Gary Goldberg (Newmont) and the President of the ICMM, Anthony Hodge.[9] The Catholic Church has been active in many community campaigns around mining, from the Pascua Lama project in Chile, through to the Mindex project in The Philippines – the later a campaign for which Father Edwin Gariguez was awarded the 2012 Goldman Environmental Prize.

The idea of the mining industry as a development industry does not sit well with some in civil society, who believe the rhetoric cloaks an extractivist mentality, or those in the industry who believe it oversteps the industry's responsibilities and encroaches on the mandate of government. The debate has helped to move beyond the idea that mineral resources are inherently cursed and define the conditions under which the afflictions of resource development can be effectively managed and human development can be enhanced. The idea could hold some potential to provide organisational direction and act as a driver for change. Whether the narrative has the authenticity that local communities and governments are expecting or can encourage the industry to mobilise the relational skills necessary to deliver on development is less clear. The MMSD argued that if well governed the mining industry can positively contribute to development. The rhetoric of mining as a 'development industry' sets a far more ambitious target. One that is harder to live up to.

Backward, forward

During the 50s and 60s it was relatively common in some countries for governments to negotiate state agreements with resource developers that included infrastructure, downstream processing and the establishment of company towns. Long distance commuting has since replaced the company town in many regions, shifting employees away from the mine site, and downstream processing has become increasingly competitive, leading to the export of commodities without value addition, even in countries like Australia and Canada. Automation may further erode the local value proposition of mining, as the remote operation of mines becomes a reality.[10]

For governments and societies wishing to leverage mining development for wider social and economic development there are four key areas of focus. The first is development associated with the core business activity of the mining project. This includes the production, or backward linkages, where domestic companies and employees provide goods, services and infrastructure for the operation; the processing and value addition, or forward linkages, where minerals can be refined and transformed into other products; and the skills and capabilities developed within the sector that can be applied in other sectors (sometimes known as horizontal linkages).

The second is development that has a dual-purpose. This mainly refers to the negotiation of shared infrastructure. An example might be a rail line, port or technical college that can be built to a specification that would assist sectors like agriculture, manufacturing or tourism to also grow. The third is the macroeconomic contribution of mining. This consists of fiscal linkages, where taxation and royalties can be invested in priority areas of the economy, and consumption linkages, where economic demand, wages and the profits of domestic business can stimulate domestic consumption. Finally, the mining industry may make direct social investments in, for example, health and education programmes that can be aligned with development priorities.[11]

'Politicians are always fixated on the downstream value addition, and beneficiation, but that is less important,' says Paul Jourdan, the principal author of the African National Congress's study on State Intervention in the Minerals Sector.[12] Paul believes the benefits of mining are most apparent in the backward, production linkages. 'Of the successful countries we looked at,' he said, 'only those that got into the capital goods for mining had succeeded (mining equipment, machinery *et cetera*). Those industries are knowledge intensive and reinvent themselves in other sectors. It basically forms a nursery for industrial development out of which other things can come.'

Paul was a geologist, oceanographer and African National Congress cadre, before going into exile in Mozambique in 1975. The son of an Anglican priest in a South African township, he grew up witnessing the raw end of South African apartheid. Along with many other exiles he made a conscious decision to switch to policy-making, believing that to contribute to a future post-apartheid state, policy skills would be necessary. When he returned to South Africa he was deployed to the National Union of Mine Workers, looking at what a free South Africa might mean for the mining industry. He took on the role of ANC coordinator for minerals and energy policy and was later asked to lead a major study on State Intervention in the Minerals Sector (SIMS) for the ANC. The SIMS study looked at best practice across a score of countries to find out what makes minerals a blessing rather than a curse. They visited Australia, Botswana, Brazil, Chile, China, Finland, Malaysia, Namibia, Norway, Sweden, Venezuela and Zambia to learn from their experiences. Sections of the ANC were calling for outright nationalisation, but the SIMS report instead found that the pre-requisites for success were investment in technical training, and technology research and development. No country had successfully used mineral wealth to drive development that had not also succeeded in STEM education, that is, science, technology, engineering and mathematics. The report also highlighted the need for more sophisticated fiscal regime, the introduction of a resource rent tax, putting known mineral assets to tender, state investment in the acquisition of geological knowledge, the use of sovereign wealth funds for windfall rents, and a regional development fund for investment in infrastructure, among other proposals.[13]

The Africa Mining Vision

Antonio Pedro is another geologist turned policy maker. He began his career working on rare metals in the pegmatites of the Alto Ligonha District of Mozambique. 'When I started it was a period when there were very few geologists in Mozambique,' said Pedro during our interview 'so immediately after I finished my first degree, I was asked to take on managerial responsibilities.' Pedro worked at the Mozambique Ministry of Mineral Resources, the geological survey and a government owned gem-mining company. He went on to represent Mozambique in the Southern African Development Community helping to develop the first programme of action on mining. From these early experiences of policy reform, Pedro has quietly coordinated a series of major African initiatives aimed at ensuring the continent's mineral resources are used for broad based development.

In 1996, Pedro joined the Eastern and Southern African Minerals Development Centre[14] in Tanzania as Director General and then the United Nations Economic Commission for Africa (ECA) in 2001, where he now holds the position of Director of ECA's Sub-regional Office for Eastern Africa in Rwanda. His early work at ECA focused on how to create better linkages between the extractive industries and other sectors of the economy, promoting concepts like economic clusters and infrastructure corridors. Some of these ideas were captured in initiatives like the African Union's New Partnership for Africa's Development as well as the 'Big Table', a dialogue between African Ministers of Finance and Economic Planning and their counter parts in the OECD to discuss the African development issues. The 2007 Big Table was on "Management of Africa's natural resources for growth and poverty reduction", jointly organised by ECA and the African Development Bank.[15] 'This was well after MMSD,' said Pedro 'so we thought it was important to look at where minerals in Africa were and the extent to which the reforms promoted by The World Bank in the 1990s had reduced poverty and promoted wealth development in Africa.' What they found was that 'all of the enclaves continued to exist and that poverty had essentially not been reduced'. Out of the Big Table, the ECA in 2008 picked up the issue of reform of mineral regimes. Pedro put together the International Study Group on Africa's Mineral Regimes (ISG) and the ISG finalised its report, "Minerals and Africa's Development: The International Study Group Report on Africa's Mineral Regimes" in 2011. The findings were presented to the second African Union Conference of Ministers Responsible for Mineral Responsible Development.[16]

With the support of the United Nations Industrial Development Organization, the United Nations Commission on Trade and Development, AfDB and the African Union Commission, the Study Group drafted a blueprint called the Africa Mining Vision (AMV).[17] The AMV was adopted by the African Union Heads of State at the February 2009 African Union Summit. The AMV provides a framework for integrating mining into development policy across the continent. The implementation of the AMV is now supported by the African Mineral Development Centre (AMDC), a one-stop facility housed at ECA in Addis Ababa, Ethiopia and is being implemented at the country level through country mining visions (CMVs). According to Antonio Pedro:

> This has been a very intensive exercise to understand what it is that would drive change … to create what we call the movement. The movement is nothing revolutionary. If we only leave to government the responsibility for implementing an ambitious programme like the AMV then we might not succeed, because it is not always true that the interests of the government are the interests of the people. We need to unleash pressure groups, strengthen civil society organisations, equip parliamentarians with skills and knowledge and be part of an international process. Promoting sustainable development is a joint responsibility where shareholders, investors, companies and so on, have an equal responsibility in shaping change … If you look at how the world has evolved from the early days of MMSD to now there's been

considerable room to embrace some of these new ideas. If we had proposed the AMV in the 1980s and 1990s, it would not fly, because the context was not appropriate. With the failure of the Washington Consensus there is more policy space and the ideas of the AMV are more welcomed by everyone … we cannot change things overnight but we need to engage in serious conversation and strengthen the business rationale of these ideas.

The AMV is ambitious but coordinated reform of mineral regimes is what is needed to upturn the 'race to the bottom' phenomena. In the next section we look at some of the policies put in place by companies and governments since MMSD to strengthen the socio-economic contribution of mining.

The social way

In the late 1990s Anglo American PLC took a strategic decision to strengthen corporate governance in safety, health, environment and community. The company, which was once a conglomerate, was refocusing back to its core mining business, and with that change came a requirement for stronger corporate governance of environmental and social matters. New policies included a requirement for community engagement plans, but no guidance was provided on what the plans should entail and the quality of the plans that were being produced was varied. 'Most of the people doing community engagement had no background or qualification in community relations,' says Jonathan Samuel, Group Head of Government and Social Affairs at Anglo American, 'because, on the whole, qualifications in the area of community relations didn't exist at the time.' There was a view that social performance or community relations was about people, so the responsibilities for community relations were commonly given to the human resources, or sometimes, the environment function within the business.

It was in this context in 2002 that the company developed the Socio-Economic Assessment Toolbox (SEAT). SEAT was intended to give more structure and clarity about the company's expectations, as well as practical guidance on community engagement and relationship building. The guidance sets out a process for assessing and managing social impacts, with SEAT reports and plans expected to be updated every three years. The guidance ranges from how to enhance local procurement and support alternative livelihoods, to grievance-handling and contractor management.

'We're judged by our worst operation; like footballers who are judged by their last match,' explained Jon. 'There's an awful lot of scope to do things wrong in our sector, so its very important that you have controls in place, to make sure if things do go wrong it is not because you haven't had the right starting point, in terms of systems.' Jonathan Samuel was involved in the development of the first version of SEAT, while based at sustainability consultancy Environmental Resources Management (ERM). Jon project managed Version 2 of SEAT, released in 2007, before joining Anglo American. Version 3 was released in 2012 and the toolbox has been adapted or used by a range of companies, including Shell and a number of junior mining companies.[18] 'In a sense, SEAT created a management system that tried to talk about "social" in the same sorts of terms that we talked about our other operational activities,' said Jon. 'It gave us something to coalesce around … standard operating protocols and systemised processes.'

SEAT played an important role in the growth of community relations as a function within Anglo American. Dedicated and skilled staff members were recruited into the organisation and over time have increased in seniority. Over a period of ten years the company has built community relations teams at all of its sites, with some teams staffed with between ten and 15 people. 'The social staff used to be about as junior as you could get,' said Jon, but now there are 'more people, who are more carefully selected, who are more senior, and better trained within the function, alongside an appreciation that other senior staff in other functions also need to be trained in the management of social issues.' Jon has since led the development of a range of initiatives to complement SEAT, including a corporate policy on social management, called *The Social Way*, to sit above the SEAT guidance, and a training programme, called the Advanced Social Management Program (ASMP).

ASMP is an intensive professional development programme spanning six months and involving two week-long, face-to-face training sessions, as well as regular projects and tutoring. Around 40 senior executives from the company take part each year and the programme has been run annually since 2009. The programme has had a catalytic effect within the business, with the aim to change the way people think about how they do their day jobs across different corporate functions. ASMP is delivered collaboratively by the Cambridge Institute for Sustainability Leadership and The University of Queensland's Centre for Social Responsibility in Mining (CSRM), part of the Sustainable Minerals Institute. Professor David Brereton has been involved in the ASMP since it's beginning. 'What has been most encouraging about the programme is not just its longevity (now entering its seventh year), but the fact that we have seen a steady increase both in the seniority of the participants and the diversity of functions that are represented. This is an encouraging sign that progress is being made in elevating awareness within companies of the importance of the social domain and the need for greater internal alignment,' he said.

Professor Brereton was the foundation Director of CSRM. The centre started in 2001, just as the MMSD process was coming to a head. David led the development of the first University-level professional development qualification for community relations practitioners in the resources industries, which began in 2008. CSRM's graduate programme in community relations now has contemporaries at Queens University, Canada, the *Pontificia Universidad Católica de Chile*, and The University of Witwatersrand, South Africa (developed in partnership with consultancy Synergy Global). I asked David about what has changed in the profession of community relations since the MMSD:

> When I first started at CSRM, most of the people working in community relations roles had come there from different parts of the business, such as

environmental management and geology. There was little, if any, training provided to equip company personnel work, the prevailing view being that anyone who was 'good with people' and had a modicum of common-sense could do the job. Thankfully, the industry has now moved on from this and there has been considerable investment in building specialist knowledge and skills, both by bringing in community relations practitioners from outside the industry (especially civil society) and investing in professional development programmes and upskilling for company personnel. In the case of the CSRM programme, for example, the financial and in-kind support of the Minerals Council of Australia was crucial to getting this initiative off the ground ... While some companies in the industry are currently in a retrograde phase, with a focus on cost reduction and productivity improvement trumping all other concerns, I believe that we are not too far away from seeing the full-scale professionalisation of the community relations function.

As mining companies like Anglo American strengthened their corporate policies and capabilities on community engagement and development, and international financial institutions, like the IFC, were placing performance standards on borrowers, the absence of government regulation of the social aspects of mining became more glaring. In Western Australia, for example, Chevron invoked the IFC Performance Standards, when voluntarily undertaking a social impact assessment as part of the approvals process for the proposed Gorgon gas project, because the Western Australian Government lacked a policy framework for social impact assessment.[19] On the other side of the Australian continent, the Queensland Government was also facing pressure from the mayors of its mining regions, unhappy that development was bypassing their towns.

The Sustainable Resource Communities Policy

In the mid-2000s the Bowen Basin coal region of Central Queensland, Australia, was experiencing severe local social and economic challenges associated with a sharp upturn in coal mining. Pressure on housing supply and accommodation facilities, stretched social services and infrastructure, fatalities on local roads, and difficulty retaining employees in the non-mining industries were some of the challenges mayors of small mining communities were facing all across the basin. The problems were not the fault of any one mine, but the cumulative effects of the more than 50 coal projects operating in the basin.[20]

Lisa Pollard came into contact with these problems while working with the Queensland Department of Communities. The Department had received some funding to station a domestic violence worker in one of the communities of the Bowen Basin but they could not find anywhere for the employee to live. Lisa has a background in social impact assessment so was interested in understanding the source of the problems.

The local mayors from the region began to agitate in the press. The first response of the State Government was to send the Director Generals of the relevant departments up to the region to talk through the issues with the 15 (or so) mayors, but in the absence of a policy response little progress was made. Lisa was tasked with formulating such a response, now working from within the Department of Tourism, Regional Development and Industry. She advocated the formation of a Partnership Group between the Local Government Association of Queensland, the Queensland Resources Council (the peak representative body of mining and energy companies operating in Queensland) and the Queensland Government to guide the policy design and provide a forum for discussion.

In September 2008 the Sustainable Resource Communities Policy was announced.[21] The Partnership Group was complemented by Local Leadership Groups to discuss practical responses to local challenges in each of the State's three resource regions. A Social Impact Assessment Unit was established to encourage greater coordination across government and to oversee the introduction of social impact management plans (SIMPs). SIMPs, a requirement of new mining and petroleum projects, were to outline the forecasted changes to communities and the strategies companies would take to manage the social and economic impacts. SIMPs were the first of their kind in Australia, and one of only a few globally.[22]

I had recently joined the University of Queensland from my position leading the Social and Economic Unit at the Queensland Department of Natural Resources and Water, and was asked provide advice to the Queensland Government on the design of SIMPs. In 2009, we published a review of leading practice strategies for managing the social impacts of resource developments, and developed design principles for SIMPs.[23] In September the following year, under the leadership of Freya Walton, the Social Impact Assessment Unit issued a guideline on the preparation of SIMPs.[24] The guideline was developed after widespread public consultation.

Between 2010 and 2012 at the height of the mining and gas boom in Queensland all new projects were required to prepare and negotiate a SIMP. For some companies, like Anglo American, equivalent corporate policies, and skilled teams, were already in place. For other companies the expectations outlined in the policy were novel. A staff member from one large mining company, for example, was re-assigned from his position in the human relations function to be the company's new community relations manager, on the morning that he was due to begin negotiations with the Queensland Government on the content of the SIMP.

A change of government, in November 2012, ended Queensland's experiment with Social Impact Management Plans. The new Liberal National conservative government in Queensland came to power promising to streamline approvals processes and remove unnecessary 'greentape'. In the lead up to the election, despite their role in the formulation of the Sustainable Resource Communities Policy, the Queensland Resources Council lobbied hard for the repeal of the plans, arguing that the conditions had been excessively prescriptive and overlapped with government responsibilities. The QRC also contended that industry should only be responsible for the 'direct', not the cumulative, impacts of projects.[25] In taking this recidivist position the QRC contradicted the lessons of Pangue and the principles of the ICMM.

Mines with existing social impact management plans were given the option to abandon the plans. Many chose to keep them in place. For at least one company the decision to keep the SIMP in place was motivated by the Equator Principles that were a condition of their project financing. The government instead put in place a 'Royalties for Regions' scheme. Lisa Pollard was again one of the public servants responsible for designing the policy, ensuring that the new priorities of the government were matched with a deep knowledge of the issues and the policy approaches that had come before. It didn't take long for mayors from Queensland's resource regions to again agitate. Gladstone Mayor Gail Sellers submitted a motion at the Local Government Association of Queensland conference in October of 2014 calling on the association to pressure the Queensland Government to bring back Social Impact Management Plans.[26]

In the following section we look at the corporate social investments that have become a common feature of the industry's approach to community development, through the example of the Collahuasi copper mine.

The bird-poo war

Collahuasi is the third largest copper mine by production in Chile, and the fourth largest producing copper mine in the world.[27] It is located in the Atacama Desert, 180km southeast of the city of Iquique in the Tarapacá region of Chile's far north. The mine lies adjacent to the Bolivian border and is around 500km from the border with Peru. In fact, the Tarapacá region of Chile was until 1883 the Tarapacá province of Peru. The province was annexed by Chile following the *Guerra del Guano* ('the bird-poo war'), a conflict more politely known as The War of the Pacific. We can trace the antecedents of many contemporary issues in Tarapacá to this war and the story of how Collahuasi has approached its community development activities is no different.

Northern Chile has a very long history of mining. Copper was mined by pre-Hispanic peoples, and the region was an important source of saltpetre (sodium nitrates) during the 19th century. The rich mounds of seabird droppings that make up the nitrate deposits accumulated over millennia and were mined for use as an agricultural fertiliser and in the production of gunpowder. The principal nitrate deposits were previously within the territory of Peru (Tarapacá, Tacna, Arica) and Bolivia (Antofagasta). Moves by Bolivia and Peru to expropriate nitrate assets and nationalise production angered the Chilean business enterprises that had done most to develop the industry and the sizable Chilean population living in the region, sparking the war and full annexation of the region by Chile. Synthetic nitrate production put an end to the industry in the 1940s leaving ghost towns where once proud communities stood, and copper progressively expanded its footprint in the last decades of the 20th century.

The Collahuasi mine consists of three low-grade porphyry copper deposits: Ujina, Rosario and Huinquintipa. Explored by Shell, Chevron and Falconbridge during the 1980s the ore bodies were geologically defined in 1991 and the mine was commissioned in 1999. The mine is now owned by a joint venture between Glencore Xstrata (44%), Anglo American (44%) and a consortia of Japanese companies including Mitsui (12%). At an altitude of 4,800m the Collahuasi mine sits atop the Andean Altiplano, or high plain. The altitude of the mine is so high that it claimed the life of Falconbridge CEO Franklin Pickard who suffered a heart attack shortly after arriving to the site by plane in 1996 un-acclimatised to the thin air.

I began working with Collahuasi in October of 2009, thankfully arriving on the Altiplano by road.[28] In November of the year before Collahuasi experienced a conflict with one of the coastal fishing villages, or *caletas*, in the vicinity of the mine's port where copper concentrate is shipped to refineries in China, Chile, Japan and India. Collahuasi's new CEO Jon Evans was looking for a changed approach to the company's community relationships and I worked with Luciano Malhue, the Community Relations Manager, to develop such a strategy. One of the first changes Jon Evans introduced was to build a dedicated 'Community Relations' team and shift the existing staff working on such issues from their prior positions within the 'External Affairs' division. The size of the team was expanded and individual staff were made responsible for maintaining relationships with each of the communities across the logistics corridor of the mine (an area spanning 40,000km² and 18 communities). The communities represent diverse backgrounds, values and interests, from Aymara indigenous communities and coastal *caletas*, to urban communities of mine workers, established horticultural towns, such as Pica, and the regional capital of Iquique. The prior lack of a presence within many of the communities across the logistics corridor was one of the reasons for the escalation of the conflict. Collahuasi did not have an ear to the issues that mattered to their neighbours and was left exposed when complaints first began to be raised.

Residents of Chanavayita, a coastal fishing *caleta* near the Port of Patache raised concerns about an odour emitting from Collahuasi's portside processing plant commissioned in 2005. The role of the plant is to remove the molybdenum byproduct from the mineral concentrate prior to export. The odour was not felt as strongly in the *caletas* immediately adjacent to the facility. Instead coastal winds blew the sulphurous odour onto the coastal range, pushing it north around 10kms before it wafted back onto Chanavayita. When the concerns were first raised they were hard to believe. Without an existing relationship to the community the company was not sensitive to their concerns and in the absence of a satisfactory response members of the community rioted on the *Panamericana* highway in November 2008, burning tires, and blocking the arterial road to the north of the country. The conflict and the media it attracted translated the community's whispers into a strong voice that could be heard. Plant operations were suspended by the company, and later operated at reduced capacity until a technical fix was engineered.

As part of the community relations strategy a formal process was introduced to handle community grievances and complaints, a social impact assessment was conducted following Anglo American's Socio-Economic Assessment Toolbox, to better understand and respond to the social context and key performance indicators were developed to define and focus the priorities of the Community Relations team.

The strategy was also an opportunity to reorientate the company's community development programme. Like many contemporary mining companies Collahuasi makes large contributions to the community through a series of foundations and direct corporate social investments. Consistent with Xstrata's policy to contribute 1% of pre-tax group profit to community development initiatives.[29] The investments amounted to many million dollars per year. We looked at the focus of the programmes and the extent to which they involved the intended recipients in programme design and delivery. Most of the investments were focused on activities without a clear link to the business or its objectives, and some didn't make strong sense from a development perspective. One of the largest investments was the building of a replica ship and museum dedicated to the *Esmeralda*, a famous casualty of the *Guerra del Guano*.

La Tirana and the Esmeralda

In May of 1879, a wooden hulled Chilean naval ship, the *Esmeralda*, ran afoul of the superior armour of a Peruvian vessel, the *Huáscar*, as the vessel raided the Chilean naval blockade of Iquique. Before the *Esmeralda* met its fate, sinking under the repeated ramming of the Peruvian ship, Captain Arturo Prat led a daring boarding party and perished on the deck of the *Huáscar*. The bravery of Arturo Pratt is still remembered fondly by Chileans and the Battle of Iquique is one of the most memorable events of the War.

One hundred and thirty-one years later, as part of the Chilean Bicentenary, Collahuasi embarked on a project to commemorate the event. The proposal was to build a full-scale replica of the ship off the coast of Iquique to serve as a museum and cultural attraction. The *Museo Corbeta Esmeralda* is a large social investment. The investment made sense from a number of perspectives. The museum celebrated the history of the region and the Chilean national identity, it promoted tourism in Iquique, and was a very visible investment. These are the kind of investments that public relations officers love, they are easy to sell and they build a reputation across the wider populace.

When I reflected on the investment in this project I wondered what type of reputation the company was building. Would, in the retrospect of history, the company be able to point to unequivocal economic and social development outcomes as the legacy of such vast copper wealth? To be sure, Collahuasi was also investing significantly in health and education, and tourism is an already important industry in Tarapacá, that is a wise industry to build upon. Many Chileans would also view the *Museo Corbeta Esmeralda* as an obviously important project. But I, as an outsider without the cultural connection to the event, wondered if other investments might have been better placed to simultaneously meet the business and the human development objectives that large corporate social investments have the potential to achieve. Could it be that in the search for the big and the visible, that the small fissures of opportunity, with perhaps even greater ramifications, are obscured from view?

We began by looking at the business risks faced by Collahuasi. The Community Relations team mapped the environmental and social issues that where translating into the biggest challenges to the business. Not surprisingly, given the conflict in Chanavayita, environmental issues (odour, dust, water, energy, and the transport of dangerous goods) came out on top. This was closely followed by relationships with Aymara communities, as at the time Chile was engaging in a national conversation about the implementation of the International Labour Organization Convention 169 on indigenous and tribal peoples. Lower down the list were business participation (employment, local business development, etc.) and the provision of skills and education, which are crucial to ensure an educated workforce and the success of the business.

When mapped against social investment spending the results were startling. The majority of social investment spending was in areas that were not defined as priorities from a business risk perspective. Investments in sports, arts, culture and community health dominated the programme. Areas defined as medium risk (enterprise development, education and social development) and high risk (environment and indigenous) captured a minority of the corporate social investment spend. The medium and high-risk areas were ripe for greater investment in innovative programmes such as participatory environmental monitoring and entrepreneurship programmes but for whatever reason these investments were not as high on the priority list when spending decisions were being made.

The analysis made me wonder why it is that companies that otherwise would adhere to the bottom line in all of their other dealings would set aside such a mission when it comes to social investments? Is there a lesser imperative when undertaking activities that are seen to be 'doing good' to apply business rigour?

In the extractives sector, as we have seen, many companies have stepped into areas where development actors have long been working, and have yet to differentiate themselves as unique actors. In many cases social development is considered a supplementary exercise in corporate philanthropy, rather than a long-term obligation to leave a legacy from resource extraction.

I was also interested in the geographic distribution of the spending. Northern Chile is a region where inequality follows geography. Many small towns in the region still record poverty rates of around 30–40%. Criteria were developed by the Community Relations team to determine strategic locations for investment. Examples included the proximity to the operation and logistics corridor, employee residence, presence of key stakeholder groups and poverty levels. The analysis revealed a spending bias toward larger population centres, such as Iquique, while strategic, yet smaller locations were under-represented even when normalised for population.

One example was the city of Alto Hospicio, tucked behind the coastal range near Iquique and home to a large proportion of the mine's contract workforce.

Here infrastructure and social services are particularly stretched. The city has exploded in size during recent decades, expanding from 5,588 people in 1992, to 50,214 in 2002 and 94,254 in 2012.[30] Alto Hospicio is home to a restive workforce, looking to improve their lot. The living conditions of the city are thought by many of these workers to be disproportionate to the hours that they toil. This seemed to me to be a good location to increase investment in social infrastructure and for the company to reap the additional benefits of improved labour relations.

Identifying the small fissures of opportunity that simultaneously advance human development and business objectives can be difficult. One opportunity that I thought might have been worthwhile exploring was in the small town of La Tirana, located 70km inland of Iquique and home to a little over 500 people. La Tirana is a town with high development needs. The rate of poverty among its small number of inhabitants is high and the infrastructure in the town is scant. The most notable feature of the town is its Catholic Church, built in 1886.

In mid-July each year, La Tirana welcomes more than 200,000 pilgrims, drawn to the town to feast and dance in honour of Our Lady of Mount Carmel, the Virgin Mary, Chile's patron Saint. The *Fiesta de La Tirana* is Chile's largest religious festival. In 2009 the Chilean Ministry of Health cancelled the festival due to health issues related to outbreaks of swine flu. In 2013 the same virus threatened again to halt the festival. Health officials were worried that the poor sanitation infrastructure in the town would exacerbate the health risks in the event of an outbreak.

When guided by the synergies between business and human development, sometimes unique opportunities present. A quiet investment in sanitation could have simultaneously improved the health outcomes of some of the poorest people in the region, and boosted regional tourism. La Tirana is not a town that provides employees for the mining industry or an important political centre. The town is not crucial to the production of copper. But if mining companies are motivated to invest in alternative livelihoods within the regions they are working and to leave a post-mining legacy, then La Tirana presented no worse an opportunity then the *Museo Esmeralda*, with the added human development dividend. Toilets may not make for good public relations but there is no doubt that the pilgrims to the region would have noticed.

Development-relevant

The scale of corporate social investment in the mining industry is staggering. The top 15 mining companies contribute a combined total of US$1.7 billion dollars a year in social investment (Figure 5). If we were to compare this combined investment from the mining industry to global overseas development assistance, these 15 mining companies would register as the 16th highest development donor (Figure 6) – an investment larger than Finland.

It is true that social investments are undertaken because of development demands of local communities and governments, and due to the lack of

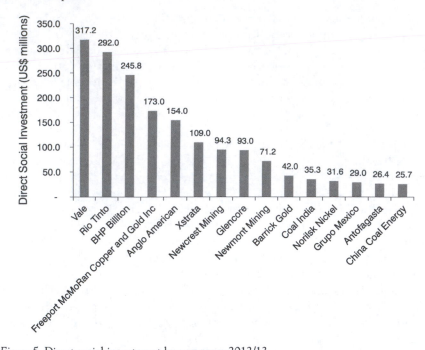

Figure 5 Direct social investment by company, 2012/13

Source: Compiled from respective corporate sustainability reports

government investment in services and infrastructure in many of the regions where many companies operate. But when we dig into the specific activities that are supported by corporate social investment in the mining industry, we see that much of the spending is uncoordinated and is not strategic, even from a business perspective. Companies have been encouraged to invest in corporate philanthropy but without a strong background in development practice they may be wasting the potential that could come from better alignment between business objectives and development priorities and better coordination across development actors. The focus on corporate social investments may also mask the much larger development that can come from leveraging the core business activities of mining, such as procurement, infrastructure and business development.

In recent years, a handful of business schools have trained their sights on the challenge of mining and social development. Michael Porter, from the Harvard Business School, and Mark Kramer, from the Harvard Kennedy School, coined the phrase 'Creating Shared Value' to describe a management strategy whereby companies create value by leveraging their business activities to address social problems. The Shared Value Initiative and FSG published a White Paper in late 2014, applying the concept to the extractives sector.[31] The Kellogg Innovation Network at the Kellogg School of Management has also been leading a multi-

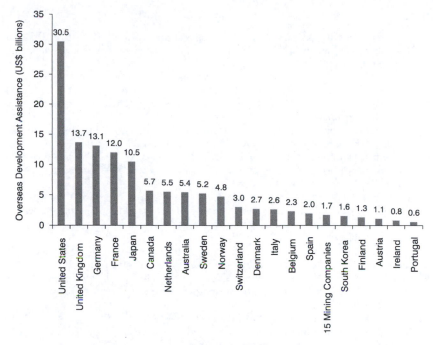

Figure 6 Overseas development assistance by country, 2012

Source: OECD, 2013, 'Net official development assistance from DAC and other donors in 2012'

stakeholder dialogue on the Mining Company of the Future. They too released a White Paper in late 2014 outlining a framework for how mining companies might become 'development partners.'[32]

The description of the mining industry as a 'development industry' is at present an overstatement. In this chapter we have seen that some of the major companies are engaged in development debates, have expanded their capabilities, and committed resources. More effort has been put into localising procurement and employment, and investments have been made in social development, but many projects still represent enclaves within the economies and societies in which they work and it is difficult to see the collective outcomes from such large amounts of corporate spending in social investment.

Instead of a 'development industry', what might be more accurate is to talk about the degree to which the industry is development-relevant. Miners are not the main social development actor (that remains the responsibility of governments, development organisations, and communities themselves) and they should not be expected to loose sight of their core business, which remains mining, but the core business activities of the industry can be designed in such a way that they are relevant to broad-based development. In the next chapter we look at the confluence of mining and conflict, and the recent initiatives designed to resolve conflict more constructively.

Notes

1 2011 data; International Council on Mining and Metals (ICMM) (2012), 'Trends in the mining and metals industry. Mining's contribution to sustainable development.' October. London.

2 ICMM (2012), 'Trends in the mining and metals industry.'

3 United Nations Conference on Trade and Development (UNCTAD) (2011), 'World Investment Report 2011: Non-equity modes of international production and development.' Geneva.

4 International Council on Mining and Metals (ICMM) (2013), 'Mining's contribution to sustainable development.' Address by Mark Cutifani, CEO, Anglo Gold Ashanti. 7 February, Mining Indaba, Cape Town. Online resource: https://www.youtube.com/watch?v=n__qA79cjtI & https://www.icmm.com/document/5043 Accessed: 9 January 2015.

5 McNab, K., Keenan, J., Brereton, D., Kim, J., Kunanayagam, R. and T. Blathwayt (2012), 'Beyond voluntarism: The changing role of corporate social investment in the extractives sector.' Brisbane: Centre for Social Responsibility in Mining and The University of Queensland.

6 The social democratic government of Prime Minister Kevin Rudd was replaced with the conservative government of Prime Minister Tony Abbott in late 2013. Extractive sector development assistance was reshaped at this time to follow a more explicit aid-for-trade approach in line with the approach taken by Canadian Prime Minister Stephen Harper.

7 United Nations Development Programme (UNDP) (2012), 'Strategy note. UNDP's strategy for supporting sustainable and equitable management of the extractive sector for human development.' December. New York.

8 Bertone, T. (2013), 'Pope Francis' greeting to mining industry representatives for Day of Reflection.' 7 September. Online resource: http://www.zenit.org/en/articles/pope-francis-greeting-to-mining-industry-representatives-for-day-of-reflection Accessed: 9 January 2015.

9 Reguly, E. (2013), 'Industry's reckoning: Why are world's top miners at the Vatican?' *The Globe and Mail*, 9 September.

10 For a detailed study on the potential social ramifications of automation in the Australian mining industry see: McNab, K., Onate, B., Brereton, D., Horberry, T., Lynas, D., and D.M. Franks (2013), 'Exploring the social dimensions of autonomous and remote operation mining: Applying social licence in design.' Prepared for CSIRO Minerals Down Under Flagship, Mineral Futures Collaboration Cluster, by the Centre for Social Responsibility in Mining and the Minerals Industry Safety and Health Centre, Sustainable Minerals Institute, The University of Queensland, Brisbane.

11 International Council on Mining and Metals (ICMM) (2013), 'Approaches to understanding development outcomes from mining.' July. London; Hailu, D., Gankhuyag, U. and C. Kipgen. (2014), 'How does the extractive industry promote growth, industrialization and employment generation?' Paper presented to the United Nations Development Programme and Government of Brazil, Dialogue on the Extractive Sector and Sustainable Development – Enhancing Public–Private–Community Cooperation in the context of the Post-2015 Agenda, Brasilia, Brazil, 3–5 December.

12 African National Congress (ANC), (2012), 'Maximising the developmental impact of the People's mineral assets: State intervention in the minerals sector.' March.

13 ANC (2012), 'Maximising the developmental impact of the People's mineral assets.'

14 Now known as the Southern and Eastern African Mineral Centre.

15 United Nations Economic Commission for Africa (UNECA) and African Development Bank (AfDB) (2007), 'The 2007 Big Table. Managing Africa's natural resources for growth and poverty reduction.' Summary report. 1 February.

16 United Nations Economic Commission for Africa (UNECA) and African Union (2011), 'Minerals and Africa's development.' The International Study Group Report on Africa's Mineral Regimes. Addis Ababa, Ethiopia.

17 African Union (2009), 'Africa mining vision.' February. Online resource: http:/pages. au.int/sites/default/files/Africa%20Mining%20Vision%20english_0.pdf Accessed: 7 February 2015.

18 Anglo American (2003), 'SEAT: Socio–Economic Assessment Toolbox.' London; Anglo American (2007), 'SEAT: Socio–Economic Assessment Toolbox.' Version 2. London; Anglo American (2012), 'SEAT Toolbox: Socio–Economic Assessment Toolbox.' Version 3. London. Online resource: http://www.angloamerican.com/~/media/Files/A/Anglo-American-PLC-V2/documents/communities/seat-toolbox-v3. pdf Accessed: 7 February 2015.

19 Chevron Australia (2005), 'Draft Environmental Impact Statement/Environmental Review and Management Programme for the Gorgon Development.' Chapter 14. *Social and Cultural Environment – Effects and Management.* September. Online resource: https://www.chevronaustralia.com/docs/default-source/default-document-library/ chapter_14_social_and_cultural_environment_risks_and_management.pdf?sfvrsn=0 Accessed 13 May 2015.

20 For more on the topic of cumulative impacts in resource regions see: Franks, D.M., Brereton, D. and C.J. Moran (2010), 'Managing the cumulative impacts of coal mining on regional communities and environments in Australia.' *Impact Assessment and Project Appraisal,* 28(4): 299–312; Franks, D.M., Brereton, D. and C.J. Moran (2013), 'The cumulative dimensions of impact in resource regions.' *Resources Policy,* 38(4): 640–647.

21 Queensland Department of Tourism Regional Development and Industry (QDTRDI) (2008), 'Sustainable Resource Communities Policy. Social impact assessment in the mining and petroleum industries.' September. Brisbane.

22 Franks, D.M. and F. Vanclay (2013) 'Social Impact Management Plans: Innovation in corporate and public policy.' *Environmental Impact Assessment Review,* 43: 40–48.

23 Franks, D.M., Fidler, C., Brereton, D., Vanclay, F. and P. Clark. (2009), 'Leading practice strategies for addressing the social impacts of resource developments.' Centre for Social Responsibility in Mining, Sustainable Minerals Institute, The University of Queensland. Briefing paper for the Department of Employment, Economic Development and Innovation, Queensland Government. November. Brisbane. Online resource: https://www.csrm.uq.edu.au/publications?task=download&file=pub_ link&id=287 Accessed: 7 February 2015.

24 Queensland Department of Infrastructure and Planning (QDIP) (2010), 'Social impact assessment. Guideline to preparing a social impact management plan.' September.

25 Roche, M. (2012), 'Queensland's resources outlook.' CEDA Resources Outlook, Queensland Resources Council. 30 October.

26 McBryde, E. (2014), 'Gladstone mayor wary of mining exploitation.' *The Gladstone Observer,* 3 October. Online resource: http://www.gladstoneobserver.com.au/news/ mayor-is-wary-of-mining-exploitation/2407590/ Accessed: 14 January 2015.

27 International Copper Study Group (2013), 'The World Copper Fact Book 2013.' Portugal.

28 Section based, in part, on a conference presentation and written paper given by the author and colleagues from Collahuasi to the First International Symposium on Social Responsibility in Mining, Santiago, 2011; Franks, D.M., Malhue, L., Acuña, M, Canelo, K and Freiburghaus, C. (2011), 'Social performance indicators at the Collahuasi copper mine, Northern Chile.' Proceedings of the First International Seminar on Social Responsibility in Mining, Santiago, 19-21 October.

29 Davis, M.L. (2007), Sustainable Development Policy. December. Xstrata plc.

30 Instituto Nacional de Estadísticas (2007) División Político-Administrativa Y Censal. Santiago de Chile. Online resource: http://www.ine.cl/canales/chile_estadistico/territorio/ division_politico_administrativa/pdf/DPA_COMPLETA.pdf Accessed: 4 June 2014;

Instituto Nacional de Estadísticas (2012) División Político-Administrativa Y Censal. Santiago de Chile; it should be noted that the 2012 census was withdrawn due to data inconsistencies.

31   Hidalgo, C., Peterson, K., Smith, D., and H. Foley. (2014), 'Extracting with purpose creating shared value in the oil and gas and mining sectors' companies and communities.' Shared Value Initiative and FSG. October.

32   Kellogg Innovation Network (KIN) (2014), 'Reinventing mining: Creating sustainable value introducing the Development Partner Framework.'

5 Conflict

Near and far

Conflict, ranging from low-level tensions to escalated violence, is a central character in the story of mining. Minerals have fuelled wars and inspired revolutions. They have shaped the course of world events and their influence has stretched far beyond the locales where the ore is actually unearthed. At more humble scales, nearer to the sites of extraction, mining has also sparked conflict with local communities.

In this chapter we will survey the association of mining and minerals with conflict, both near to, and far from, the sites of extraction, and look at the efforts by different actors to prevent conflict, or mediate it in more constructive ways. The first half of the chapter will focus on mining and civil conflict. We will examine the Fatal Transactions campaign, the establishment of the Kimberley Process Certification Scheme, and the subsequent proliferation of certification schemes across the sector that aim to break the association of mineral resources with conflict and unsustainable practices. In the second half of the chapter we narrow the focus to company–community conflict, exploring the incidence, costs, and issues motivating conflicts between mines and local communities and the dialogue and grievance-handling processes that have been employed to avoid and resolve them. We begin in Sierra Leone, a small West African nation on the Atlantic coast, known for its religious tolerance, its history as a refuge for thousands of freed African slaves, and for its beautiful, gem-quality diamonds.

The belligerent's best friend

According to the United Nations Environment Programme (UNEP) natural resources have played a role in at least 40% of all intrastate conflicts.[1] In describing conflict trends in the post-Cold War period the Report of the International Commission on Intervention and State Sovereignty noted that 'conflict has been directed towards the capture of resources and towards plunder' and that the 'weakness of state structures and institutions in many countries has heightened the challenges and risks of nation building, and sometimes tempted armed groups to try to seize and themselves exploit valuable assets such as diamonds, timber and other natural resources'.[2]

There are, of course, many societies where mineral endowments have been, and continue to be, a source of economic and social development and many actors and institutions have highlighted the central role that good governance plays in determining which of the vastly different pathways resource endowed countries may take.[3] Natural resources can also play an important role in supporting peace-making, and rebuilding after conflict, which is the impetus behind the UNEP Post-conflict Peacebuilding and Natural Resources Programme.[4]

In his important article 'The political ecology of war: Natural resources and armed conflicts', Philippe Le Billon identified four key variables that may influence the character of conflict over natural resources:

- the distribution of resources ('point' resources may be more easily controlled than 'diffuse' resources);
- the proximity of resources to sites of political power ('point' resources close to sources of power are prone to state violence or *coup d'état*, while 'point' resources located on the margins of controlled territory are prone to capture by rebels);
- the transferability of the resource (diffuse resources may be more easily sold and thus are prone to warlordism, if their location is distant from centres of power, or rioting/rebellion if their location is proximate); and
- the lootability of the resource (resources that require minimal processing – lootable resources – lend themselves to capture by rebels while non-lootable resources – where sophisticated capital is necessary for processing – may encourage the capture or extortion of the state).[5]

In Sierra Leone, a 'lootable', easily concealable, high value, 'point' resource lay in alluvial fields on the periphery of the country. Between 1991 and 2002 civil conflict in Sierra Leone claimed 70,000 lives and displaced 2.6 million people (more than half the population).[6] Diamonds fuelled the conflict, providing cash for belligerents to purchase arms and incentives to capture and clear land. This bloody civil war (along with the contemporaneous conflict in Angola) firmly established in the global public consciousness the association of minerals with conflict, and spurred international efforts, such as the Kimberley Process Certification Scheme, to break such links. It is worth, then, looking further into the history of this conflict and how a coordinated international response emerged.

In 1991, Revolutionary United Front (RUF) rebels invaded Sierra Leone from the neighbouring country Liberia, under the leadership of Foday Sankoh, and backed by Liberian warlord Charles Taylor. The disaffected youth that filled the ranks of the RUF made easy gains against the corrupt and inept Momoh regime and earned a terrible reputation for brutal amputations of civilians. In 1992, a group of junior military officers led by Captain Valentine Strasser overthrew the Momoh regime and installed a National Provisional Ruling Council (NPRC) in Sierra Leone. The new regime showed early signs of success against the RUF but by 1995 the rebels regained the momentum and control of large swaths of territory, and marched on the capital Freetown. The NPRC turned to the South African mercenary group Executive Outcomes (EO) to repel the RUF back into the interior of the country and retake the diamond mining regions in the east. The war and control of key territory ebbed and flowed with significant fatalities, atrocities and changes in government. In October of 1999, the UN sent peacekeepers to Sierra Leone and in 2000 British forces intervened. The war came to an end in 2002.

Inequality in the diamond fields has been a source of destabilisation in eastern Sierra Leone for decades. The first contract for diamond mining was awarded to De Beers' Sierra Leone Selection Trust (SLST) in 1934. The SLST was granted a 99-year monopoly but by the mid-1950s, 75,000 diamond miners were active in Sierra Leone, undermining the De Beers monopoly and establishing a new smuggling route into neighbouring Liberia.[7] Popular dissatisfaction in the Kono diamond fields led to rioting, which was initially quelled by mercenaries in the employ of De Beers SLST, but nevertheless forced the government to terminate the SLST monopoly in 1955.[8]

During the civil war in the 1990s combatants on all sides exploited the diamond resource. NPRC troops mined diamonds in Kono, using them to procure weapons[9] and in the late 1990s the RUF re-established the smuggling route into Liberia yielding an estimated US$25–125 million per year.[10] It wasn't just belligerents that benefited from the trade; international terrorist networks were allegedly also involved in the trafficking of Sierra Leone's diamonds.[11]

Diamonds, once symbols of purity, wealth and celebrity, were, in the late 1990s, starting to take on a crimson hue. In 1997 Charles Taylor, by then President of Liberia, attended a dinner in honour of Nelson Mandela in the Presidential Lodge in Pretoria, South Africa. Taylor was seated with super model Naomi Campbell and Mandela himself. Campbell was an ambassador for the Nelson Mandela Children's Fund. Carole White, Campbell's former agent, told the United Nations Special Court for Sierra Leone in 2010 that Campbell was flirting with Charles Taylor at the dinner and that Taylor offered to have his men bring her a pouch of rough diamonds. The stones were alleged by prosecutors to have been smuggled by Taylor from the fields of Sierra Leone.[12]

White recalls that two of Charles Taylor's men drove to Johannesburg that evening to fetch the stones for Campbell, returning to the guesthouse of the Presidential Lodge in the early hours.[13] Campbell told the court: 'When I was sleeping, I had a knock at my door and I opened my door. Two men were there and they gave me a pouch and said: "A gift for you."'[14] White recalls that the gift arrived wrapped in paper and when unwrapped six small greyish pebbles were revealed to the disappointment of Campbell who was expecting cut and polished stones.[15] 'I saw a few stones, they were very small, dirty looking stones,' Campbell told the court; 'I'm used to seeing diamonds shiny and in a box.' The next morning after receiving advice from close friends Campbell chose not to keep the stones.[16] This proved a wise decision because the issue of blood diamonds was about to receive a lot more attention.

Fatal Transactions

In 1999, five European aid and advocacy organisations launched the Fatal Transactions campaign (Global Witness; Medico International; International Peace Information Service; Netherlands Organisation for International Assistance; and the Netherlands Institute for Southern Africa). In just a few short years the terms 'conflict diamonds' and 'blood diamonds' went from inglorious terms with almost no public recognition to lines on the script of a Leonardo DiCaprio Hollywood blockbuster, as more than 100 non-government organisations joined the campaign.

Like other consumer awareness campaigns Fatal Transactions aimed to generate media coverage, but the key to its success was that it combined investigative reporting with savvy marketing and subversive branding, turning the carefully curated image of diamonds as symbols of luxury and purity in on itself. The campaigners sent mock diamond rings in jewellery boxes to select fashion editors and jewellery retailers, accompanied with labels that detailed negative statistics about the diamond trade and conflict in Angola.

Anne Jung, one of the founders of Fatal Transactions, cites two key investigative reports as providing the evidence base and catalysts for the campaign: the December 1998, Global Witness report, 'A rough trade: The role of companies and governments in the Angolan conflict'; and the January 2000 Partnership Africa Canada report, 'The heart of the matter: Sierra Leone, diamonds and human security.'[17]

Fatal Transactions did not call for a wide consumer boycott of diamonds out of fear that significant harm would result from denying development in localities without conflict and devastating the livelihoods of thousands of diamond cutters. The first press release of the campaign explicitly stated that, 'This campaign is not anti-diamond but it is anti-war' and cited Botswana, Namibia and South Africa as countries where diamond revenue was argued to have brought economic benefit.[18] From the very beginning the goal of the campaign was to mobilise consumer awareness to push for an effective system of controls and to use the threat of a wider boycott to push governments and industry into action.[19] Diamonds, unlike many other mineral commodities, are purchased directly by the general public and are thus exposed to public sentiment. 'As we approach the millennium,' said Global Witness conflict diamonds campaigner Alex Yearsley in the press release, 'it is incredible that there are no meaningful controls in place to ensure that diamonds do not fund conflict.'[20]

Within days of the first press release, De Beers, the largest player in the diamond market, announced that it would no longer source diamonds from Angola.[21] Diamond mining is a highly concentrated industry. Just four large-scale mining companies accounted for 76% of the global supply of rough diamonds in 2002 (De Beers Consolidated Mines, Alrosa, Rio Tinto and BHP Billiton).[22] The remainder, however, was (and continues to be) sourced by thousands of artisanal and small-scale miners from alluvial fields dispersed throughout the world. Estimates of the trade of conflict stones ranged between 3 and 15% of global rough diamond trade.[23] Earlier attempts by Belgian MPs to ban imports from The National Union for the Total Independence of Angola (UNITA) in 1993 were unsuccessful due to the difficulty in identifying the origin of stones once mixed with stones from other locations and the potential for the unilateral response by Belgium to drive trade to competitor countries.[24] For these reasons, Fatal Transactions called for a global approach to diamond certification.

In March 2002, Global Witness was jointly nominated with Partnership Africa Canada for the 2003 Nobel Peace Prize by US law-makers in recognition of their efforts to bring the issue of conflict resources to global attention. Their campaigns ran in parallel with efforts by other NGOs, such as Amnesty International and the Network Movement for Justice and Development (from Sierra Leone), and the United Nations, to resolve the conflicts in Sierra Leone and Angola. All of these initiatives dovetailed to support the creation of the Kimberley Process Certification Scheme in 2003. Before we look at the establishment of the scheme we revisit some of the history of diamond production in Africa and the mine from which the scheme draws its name.

'Big Hole' and the de Beer brothers

The city of Kimberley is in South Africa's Northern Cape. In 1869 an 83.5-carat diamond was found on a property called *Vooruitzigt* owned by two brothers, Johannes Nicolaas and Diederik Arnoldus de Beer. A handful of diamonds emerged from nearby alluvial diggings in previous years, but it was this discovery that started the 'New Rush' and the beginnings of the Kimberley mine. As thousands of people rushed to the fields to unearth new wealth, the digs caught the attention of competing colonial interests. When the British emerged with the prize in hand, the Secretary of State for the Colonies, Lord Kimberley, insisted that the 'vulger' Dutch name *Vooruitzigt* be replaced with 'decent and intelligible names'. One of his diplomats duly obliged, and named the new territory Kimberley, after his Lordship.[25]

The Kimberley mine is how industrialisation found Africa, and how the colonial 'Scramble for Africa' began. From 1871 to 1914, 50,000 miners hand dug the *Colesberg Kopje* hill into a 'Big Hole' reaping thousands of kilograms of diamonds in the process.[26] One of the new migrants was a young Englishman by the name of Cecil Rhodes. In 1870, Cecil was sent to Africa as a teenager to assist his brother who ran a cotton farm. The family hoped that the dry warm climate might improve his asthma. Within a year the cotton farm failed and the Rhodes brothers found themselves in Kimberley trying their luck with diamonds.[27] They started by renting water pumps to the miners. Interspersed with studies at Oxford, Cecil progressively consolidated his business interests in the diamond fields.

For the first few years the digging was easy at Kimberley but soon the soft, yellow, weathered regolith gave way to the hard, blue primary ore and technical challenges such as water management required increasing sophistication and industrialisation. Rhodes partnered with Charles Rudd to purchase claims and they accepted the contract to pump water out of three of the principal mines.[28] As industrialism transformed mining, so too it transformed the town, and in 1882 Kimberley became the first town in the southern hemisphere to install electric street lighting.[29]

In March of 1888, backed by South African diamond magnate Alfred Beit and the Rothschild family, Rhodes and his business partner Charles Rudd merged their business interests with their main rival Barney Barnato to establish De Beers Consolidated Mines, the name was a nod to the claim where it all began. The new company held a monopoly of diamond mining in the country and partnered with a London-based cartel, the Diamond Syndicate, to control supply and set high prices. This practice of restricting supply to inflate value continued long after Cecil Rhodes' death in 1902.[30]

De Beers is still today the world's leading diamond company. The firm was taken over by Ernest Oppenheimer in 1927. Oppenheimer was once a rival agent to the De Beers cartel and before taking over De Beers he established mining firm Anglo American with American businessman J.P. Morgan. Oppenheimer consolidated De Beers global monopoly of the diamond trade, which largely held until the year 2000.[31] The Oppenheimer family relinquished their remaining ownership of the company in 2011 by selling their interest to Anglo American.

In 1896 South Africa's first School of Mines was established in Kimberley, part funded by De Beers. The School was relocated to nearby Johannesburg in 1904 and later formed the core of the University of Witwatersrand in 1922. Johannesburg, like Kimberley, owes its origins to a mining rush in the gold bearing reefs of the Witwatersrand plateau in 1886. 'Wits' is one of South Africa's top-ranked universities and still retains a strong mining programme. The university hosts the Centre for Sustainability in Mining and Industry, directed by former MMSD Research Manager, Professor Caroline Digby.

Rhodes continued to expand his mining interests following the founding of De Beers, using the proceeds to extend the territorial interests of the English colonies. With Rudd he established Gold Fields of South Africa in 1887 (which is still an active mining company with eight contemporary mines in South Africa, Ghana, Peru and Australia), and his British South Africa Company consolidated mineral rich territories in southern and central Africa to collectively form 'Zambesia'. The territories were renamed 'Rhodesia' by settlers in 1895 with Southern Rhodesia later becoming Zimbabwe and Northern Rhodesia, Zambia.

Lord Kimberley also continued to lend his name to significant things and events. The geologist Professor Ernst Cohen recognised in 1872 that the Kimberley deposits were cylindrical volcanic pipes and, in 1887, at a meeting of the British Association for the Advancement of Science, the term kimberlite was coined by Henry Carvill Lewis. Kimberlite pipes are the geological formations of once-molten volcanic rock that carry diamonds from the earths mantle to its surface.[32] Kimberlite pipes are the most important source of mined diamonds today. They are the target for industrial mining and are also the source of alluvial diamond fields as the eroded pipes disperse diamonds across the surrounding river plains.

Lord Kimberley would unwittingly also lend his name to a diamond certification scheme brokered by the UN to stem the trade of conflict diamonds following the conflicts in Sierra Leone and Angola.

The Kimberley Process Certification Scheme

In May 2000, representatives of Southern African diamond producing states met in Kimberley to discuss the issue of conflict diamonds. Follow up meetings were held in Namibia and Pretoria in September and were attended by representatives of most of the main diamond producing and importing countries in the world. It is from this series of meetings that the Kimberley Process Certification Scheme (KP) emerged.

Around the same time the diamond industry started to organise, and the World Federation of Diamond Bourses and the International Diamond Manufacturers Association created the World Diamond Council to develop and implement a tracking system for diamonds; however, the notion of an industry-run self-regulatory scheme was overtaken by the pace of events.

The UN General Assembly passed Resolution 55/56 in December 2000 that supported the creation of an international certification scheme for rough diamonds, and by November of 2001 a proposal for the KP was submitted to the UN General Assembly. The working document was finalised in March of 2002,[33] and a full working scheme was in place by January 2003 and endorsed by UN Security Council Resolution 1459.

The KP requires participant countries to certify shipments of rough diamonds as conflict free; to trade only with other participant countries; and to provide statistical information on production and trade. The scheme is underpinned by national legislation, export and import controls, and supported by national-level institutions. The scheme fosters knowledge exchange between participant countries to improve implementation of the scheme and responsible mining more generally. KP countries (now numbering 81) cover 99.8% of the global production of diamonds. The trade in diamonds is also backed by a voluntary system of warranties created by the World Diamond Council and endorsed by participant countries.[34]

Civil society can take a good deal of the credit for fomenting the conditions that led to quick implementation of the KP; however, a number of other parallel UN initiatives also played an important role. The inaugural meeting of the KP followed the release of the report of the UN Panel of Experts on Angola Sanctions in March of 2000 under the leadership of Ambassador Robert Fowler of Canada, that detailed how diamonds were fuelling the conflict in Angola, and named and shamed the companies, governments and other actors involved in the trade. A similar UN Panel of Experts on Sierra Leone Diamonds and Arms, chaired by Ambassador Martin Chungong Ayafor of Cameroon, reported its findings in December of 2000.

Estimating the success of the Kimberley Process is difficult. The KP is widely credited with stemming the trade in conflict diamonds;[35] however, the scheme did come into effect *after* the hostilities in Angola and Sierra Leone ceased. Earlier attempts to control the illicit diamond trade in the late 1990s through both UN and US sanctions proved unsuccessful because they did not require certification from the country of extraction – just from the country of last export.[36] The KP on the other hand is a comprehensive scheme and was established through a multi-stakeholder process with the involvement of governments (as participant countries), and industry and civil society (as observers). The diamond industry, while preferring a self-regulatory approach, did come to view the KP as inextricably linked to their business success, as well as a form of insurance, a way to distance the large-scale mining industry and large traders from the atrocities occurring in some producing countries.[37] The NGOs behind Fatal Transactions claimed the KP as a campaign achievement but continued to harbour reservations about the scope and definition of 'conflict diamonds', the auditing system (which did not conform to the gold standard of 'independent third party monitoring') and the voluntary nature of the controls on trade.

Some of these concerns were raised even before the scheme started. The United States General Accounting Office found in 2002 that the proposed structure of the Kimberley Process 'does not contain the necessary accountability to provide reasonable assurance that the scheme will be effective in deterring the flow of conflict diamonds'.[38] This was based on their assessment that some high-risk activities were only subject to 'recommended' controls, and that only voluntary controls and self-regulated monitoring and enforcement are required after the entry of the stone in the first foreign port until the final point of sale. The GAO predicted that 'these and other shortcomings provide significant challenges in creating an effective scheme to deter trade in conflict diamonds'.[39]

In June 2009, Ian Smillie, of Partnership Africa Canada, one of the founders of the Kimberley Process, resigned his position as civil society representative. In his resignation letter he said, 'I feel that I can no longer in good faith contribute to a pretence that failure is success,' citing the inability of the scheme to respond efficiently and effectively to multiple challenges.[40] Global Witness followed suit in December 2011, withdrawing from the KP as an official observer. Two of their main concerns were the lack of independent verification of supply chain control and the endorsement by the KP of diamonds originating from the Marange region of Zimbabwe, where human rights violations by the national army were not considered by the KP to be within the definition of conflict diamonds. 'Despite intensive efforts over many years by a coalition of NGOs,' stated the Global Witness press release that announced the withdrawal, 'the scheme's main flaws and loopholes have not been fixed and most of the governments that run the scheme continue to show no interest in reform.'[41]

When I spoke to Annie Dunnebacke, Deputy Campaigns Director of Global Witness, in its London offices, she explained to me the rationale for withdrawing from the process:

It's not doing what it said on the tin. It is not addressing the conflict diamond issue as most reasonable people would understand conflict diamonds. If you go to somebody in the street – somebody who cares about what they buy – and you say does it matter what uniform the guy was wearing when he raped and killed? Obviously it doesn't ... [Because of] the administrative way that the Kimberley Process is organised, the fact that it is consensus-based decision-making just consistently led to either no decision, sort of paralysis because nobody could agree, or constantly [choosing] the lowest common denominator. So it was the very weakest option, rather than continuously trying to improve and do better and really meet the objectives of the scheme, and a real lack of political will on the part of the governments to hold each other to account.

Despite the flaws, 'the Kimberley Process has chalked up some notable achievements in the past ten years,' according to Global Witness, 'including pioneering a tripartite approach to solving international problems, and helping some of the countries that were worst-hit by diamond-fuelled wars to increase their official diamond revenues.'[42] Medico International described the KP as the biggest success of the Fatal Transactions campaign, while simultaneously noting that the contradictions in the scheme presented the campaign with its greatest challenge.[43]

A key measure of the success, or otherwise, of the KP must include the broader effect of the scheme on the landscape of mining 'soft' regulation. On this measure the performance of the KP is less equivocal. The KP, like The Cyanide Code (discussed in Chapter 3), was at the forefront of a wave of minerals certification schemes (see Table 4). While some are focused specifically on conflict, others attempt to set standards across the broad array of sustainable development issues. Unlike the KP, the vast majority of schemes do not involve government. Instead, they are voluntary standards developed by industry and/or civil society.

Each scheme has its own story to tell. For instance, Cristina Echavarría, one of the South American Regional Coordinators of the MMSD (who we met in Chapter 1), worked closely with artisanal and small-scale miners as part of the Alliance for Responsible Mining to help produce the Fairmined gold standard. Gold certified under this scheme was crafted into the 2014 Palme d'Or, the highest prize awarded at the Cannes Film Festival. The Responsible Jewellery Council is one of the more established certification schemes (introduced in Chapter 3). It first took shape after an Australian research project, the Mining Certification Evaluation Project (MCEP), which was led by WWF-Australia and the CSIRO (the Australian federal government agency for scientific research). Another scheme, the Initiative for Responsible Mining Assurance, released a draft standard in 2014 after years of debate between industry, civil society, labour union and affected community representatives. Each of these schemes may go on to leave their own legacies, but the legacy of the KP is that it provoked genuine enthusiasm for multi-stakeholder approaches to certification and mineral governance.

Table 4 Selected sustainability standards relevant to the mining and minerals sector

Year	Standard	Commodity/scope	Focus
1996	International Standards Organization 14000	All	Environmental management
2000	International Cyanide Management Code	Gold	Safety and environment
2000	Kimberley Process Certification Scheme	Diamonds	Conflict
2004	Alliance for Responsible Mining/ Fairmined	Artisanal gold, silver, platinum	Environment, social, labour
2005	Responsible Jewellery Council Code of Practices	Precious metals and stones	Environment, social, labour
2005	Green Lead Project	Lead	Environmental management
2006	Initiative for Responsible Mining Assurance	Large scale mining	Environment and social
2006	Diamond Development Initiative	Artisanal diamond miners	Livelihoods and development
2007	Responsible Steel	Australian steel (full lifecycle)	Environment and social
2008	ITRI Tin Supply Chain Initiative	Tin (mine to smelter)	Conflict
2009	OECD Due Diligence Guidance for Responsible Supply Chains of Minerals from Conflict-Affected and High-Risk Areas	Tin, tantalum, tungsten and gold	Conflict
2010	International Standards Organization 26000	All	Social responsibility
2010	EICC-GESI Conflict Free Smelter program	Smelters and refiners	Conflict
2011	International Conference on the Great Lakes Region Regional Certification Mechanism	Tin, tantalum, tungsten and gold	Conflict
2011	World Gold Council Conflict-Free Gold Standard	Gold	Conflict
2012	Bettercoal	Coal mining	Environment, social, labour
2012	Aluminium Stewardship Initiative	Aluminium (full lifecycle)	Environmental and social

The legacy of blood diamonds

The restaurant was otherwise empty. We sat opposite the wide timber bar watching as two heavily built Nigerian ex-servicemen entered and demanded protection money from the Lebanese proprietor. Such was our introduction to Koidu, the dusty frontier town, in the Kono District of eastern Sierra Leone.

As we have seen, the alluvial diamond fields on the outskirts of the town played an important role in the Sierra Leone civil war. Alluvial diamonds are no longer the lifeblood of the economy in Kono or elsewhere in Sierra Leone, but artisanal mining for diamonds, gold and other commodities does provide a supplementary source of income for many of the country's poorest people.[44]

Large-scale mining, on the other hand, is experiencing somewhat of a renaissance in Sierra Leone with the development of the African Minerals Tonkolili magnetite project near Makeni (which is reported to have lifted GDP growth in Sierra Leone to 20% in 2013)[45] and the expansion of the large-scale diamond mine, Koidu Holdings. Koidu Holdings exploits a primary kimberlite deposit in the Kono District that is currently under expansion. The mine reportedly employs nearly 3,000 people and supplies 60% of the 500,000 carats of diamonds it mines each year to jeweller Tiffany & Co.[46]

The history of Koidu Holdings mine is entangled with the history of the conflict. The mine resumed operations in 2003 after the war. It is alleged that former NPRC junta leader, Valentine Strasser, awarded the Koidu diamond concession to the business arm of the South African mercenary group EO in 1995, in part-payment for its role in repelling the rebels. The transaction was allegedly brokered by Tony Bukingham of the Branch-Heritage Group. Bukingham is reported to have introduced EO to the NPRC. The CEO of Koidu, Jan Joubert, is a former EO mercenary himself, as are others in his employ.[47] The Beny Steinmetz Group Resources progressively increased its investment from part owner in 2002 to full control of the mine in 2007.[48] We meet Beny again in the next chapter where his alleged role in a corruption scandal related to the Simandou iron project in Guinea is under investigation by the US Justice Department.

Our arrival to Koidu was a decade after peace finally returned to the country. Our mandate was to assist the Sierra Leone Environmental Protection Agency (SL-EPA) to prioritise their mining rehabilitation efforts. With the support of the United Nations Environment Programme (UNEP) and the International Mining for Development Centre, an initiative of the Australian aid programme, we visited large-scale and artisanal mining sites across the country to identify rehabilitation risks and provide advice to the SL-EPA on how to address them (see Figure 7).[49] UNEP has a dedicated programme on Post-Conflict Peacebuilding and Natural Resources that provides direct assistance to governments. David Jensen and Oli Brown from UNEP were important supporters of our time in Sierra Leone, but were also key supporters of the strengthening of the SL-EPA along with other donors such as the European Union.

Jatou Jallow is Executive Chairperson of the SL-EPA. She has taken the organisation from a staff of four, without a computer or a vehicle in 2009, to an

Figure 7 Mural on wall, Koidu, Sierra Leone (top); streetscape panorama, Koidu (middle); disturbed land, alluvial diamond diggings, Tongo Fields, Sierra Leone (bottom)

Credits: D.M. Franks and P. Erskine, 2012

organisation of more than 60 employees. Eight decades of alluvial mining have left scars across vast tracts of once fertile and arable land in the eastern and southern provinces of Sierra Leone, while governance systems during and immediately following the conflict ground to a halt.[50] The war also severed the responsibilities of the large-scale mining industry for the legacies of mining. After the large-scale mines were ransacked and companies went bankrupt, the new owners of the ore bodies after the war did not accept all of the historical rehabilitation liabilities. The SL-EPA has been part of addressing this by methodically renegotiating mining contracts for better environmental outcomes.

'We have been very tenacious in ensuring that we raise public awareness and people now understand the consequences of environmental degradation and not making provisions for rehabilitation,' said Jatou Jallow when I asked her how the SL-EPA has so quickly won the respect of a wide spectrum of actors in the country. Jallow credits the support of the Office of the President, civil society and international donors and agencies for the SL-EPA's achievements in driving change in the performance of the large-scale mining sector. 'When we had Oli Brown [from UNEP] here and we were going up and down with the UN vehicle [the companies] knew their secrets could no longer remain in Sierra Leone [and] they had to start changing,' said Jallow. Now, almost all of the mining projects operating in Sierra Leone have environmental officers on site, a key change and a performance metric of the new agency. The sophistication of the companies with regard to community relations, however, is still nascent and local conflicts at two sites have resulted in civilian fatalities in recent years. In the following sections we look at the other side of the conflict story – the conflicts between mines and local communities and the dialogue and grievance-handling processes that have been employed to avoid and resolve them.

Community rising

When the MMSD concluded in 2002 global commodity prices started to pitch steeply upward and they remained high throughout the rest of the decade. This was a new heady era for mining, a boom that contrasted the bust of the nineties. Copper (482%), thermal coal (668%), iron ore (1276%) and gold (405%) all posted very dramatic price rises as demand from China and to a lessor extent India outstripped the capacity of the industry to meet supply.[51] Market capitalisation was up, the appetite for investment returned and new projects were mooted in familiar and unfamiliar territory.

The major mining companies exited the Global Mining Initiative with renewed confidence. They had engaged with the critiques of global civil society, they felt that they had listened and had formulated an appropriate response. Professionals with new capabilities and ideas were drafted into the ranks of the industry and a series of new 'soft' regulatory initiatives were providing a new governance framework.

The scale of mining investment in the second half of the decade was unprecedented. Industry scrambled to take advantage of the new price environment and megaprojects were the configuration of choice, at least for the

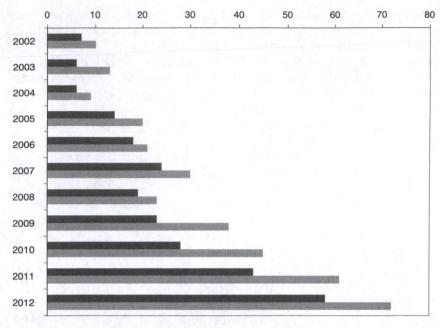

Figure 8 Number of mine-community conflicts by year; dark grey data represents cases compiled from the Business and Human Rights Resource Centre; light grey data represents cases compiled by the ICMM

Source: ICMM, personal communication

majors but also for the companies aspiring to join the major's club. Traditional mining economies, such as Australia, Brazil, Canada, Chile, Russia, South Africa and the USA, dominated the investment, however mining also expanded in Mongolia, Mozambique, Madagascar, Guinea, and Peru, among others. Many of the new mining investments did not find ready acceptance and a series of the global mining industry's marquee projects faltered at the hands of local community opposition. It proved far more difficult than companies had expected to negotiate their way into unfamiliar territory or even into the locations where they had operated for decades.

The ICMM has charted a dramatic rise in mining community conflict over the course of the past decade, finding that conflicts have dramatically increased year on year (Figure 8). Similar trends are evident from data collected by the IFC Compliance Advisor Ombudsman and the Fraser Institute. The extractive industries (mining, oil and gas, and chemicals) accounted for 50% of the 120 cases brought to the CAO between 1999 and mid-2013. Mining projects represented 18 of the cases, with 37 complaints related to oil and gas.[52] The 2013 annual survey of mining companies published by the Fraser Institute for the first time asked about the effect of community opposition on mining. Thirty-six percent of the 489 respondents reported that public opposition had affected the permitting or approval process of their operations over the prior year.[53]

These local-scale conflicts represent a subtle but significant shift when compared to the deep controversies in which mining was embroiled in the nineties. The MMSD process was launched after sustained pressure on the industry largely from Western-based NGOs. These groups, however, were no longer the primary source of industry pressure in the post-MMSD period, and the global headquarters of mining firms were no longer the primary target. Instead local communities affected by mining found their own voice and made their own connections (including with each other). Their implements of change were different. Lobbying, campaigning and international diplomacy, were replaced with direct action, legal proceedings, and dialogue tables. Conflict itself became a regulator of reform, rather than appeals to corporate social responsibility or industry wide reputation. To be sure the local campaigns were amplified through international networks, in part facilitated by the very same NGO's that had led the global activism the previous decade. But the local campaigns primarily had a local audience, and the change that was being sought was about the shape of the mining project itself, not the performance of the industry as a whole. In essence, the many local scale conflicts that greeted the sector in the post-MMSD period represent a democratisation of activism around mining.

Looking back then over the past two decades what becomes apparent is that the mining industry has been subject to two distinct, though related crises. The nexus between mining and community (situated in the context of the environment and livelihoods) has been central to both, but in quite different ways. The first crisis occurred at the bottom of the commodity cycle. It consisted of international civil society challenging the environmental legacy of an entire industry. The second, and most recent crisis has occurred during a sustained commodity boom where local communities were challenging the legitimacy of individual proposed mining projects before a bar of gold was even poured, or a cathode of copper was plated.

The costs of company-community conflict

In 2002 the final report of the MMSD, *Breaking New Ground*, reported that 'Most companies [we]re struggling to establish a clear business case for pursuing [sustainable development].'[54] With conflict manifesting at more local scales in the decade since, an undeniable business case has now emerged for companies that are attuned to the shifting trends. Delays, project modifications, increased demands on senior-staff time and the abandonment of projects, all have the potential to substantially drive up the costs of doing business.

Early in his mandate, Professor John Ruggie, UN Secretary-General's Special Representative on Business and Human Rights, was shown the findings of an internal company analysis of non-technical risks from one of the international oil majors. The company had examined the costs of non-technical (social and political) risks across 12 of their projects, and scaled the results to the remainder. The company found a staggering loss of >US$6 billion over a two-year period – a double-digit percentage of operating profits. Rachel Davis, at the time one of Professor Ruggie's legal advisors, and now Managing Director of business and

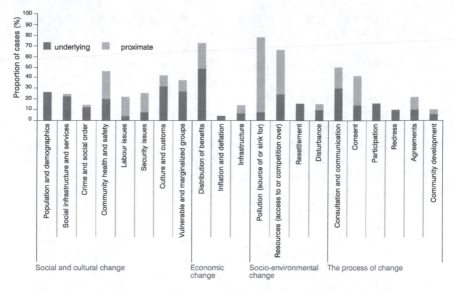

Figure 9 Cases of mine-community conflict: Issues in dispute (*n*=50)

Source: Davis and Franks, 2014, 'Costs of company–community conflict in the extractive sector'

human rights organisation, Shift, heard about separate research that Warwick Browne and I were undertaking at the Centre for Social Responsibility in Mining, looking to quantify the costs of mining conflict with local communities. In our subsequent joint research, Rachel and I interviewed 45 corporate finance, legal and sustainability professionals in the mining and oil and gas industries to understand the costs of conflict with local communities and the ways that companies are approaching this problem.[55] We also analysed 50 cases of mine-community conflict, across different commodities, geographies and types of company, to understand the issues in dispute, how conflicts manifest and the stage in the conflict cycle where conflict was most prevalent.

What we found was that environmental issues are the most common issues precipitating conflict, but behind these, socio-economic issues, and unmet expectations about consultation and consent, play an important role in shaping the broader mine–community relationship (see Figure 9). Pollution and access to/competition over environmental resources commonly trigger conflict (with water and land looming large in the case pool analysed). The distribution of project benefits, changes to local culture and customs, and the quality of ongoing processes for consultation and communication where important underlying issues that affected the nature of the relationship between the parties, but did not necessarily precipitate the conflict.

When we looked at the stage in which mine–community conflicts were arising we observed that mining projects are particularly vulnerable in the feasibility and construction stages (see Figure 10). We found an over-representation of conflicts during these early stages that were leading to the suspension or abandonment

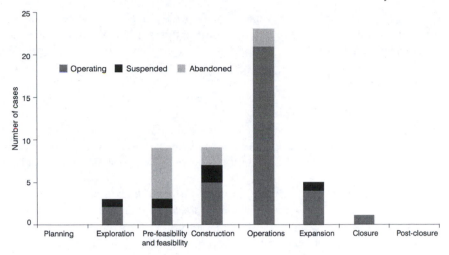

Figure 10 Cases of mine-community conflict: Operating stage (*n*=50)

Source: Davis and Franks, 2014, 'Costs of company–community conflict in the extractive sector

of projects due to conflict. One explanation is that these periods can represent dramatic transitions for local communities with major project impacts being experienced for the first time and large influxes of, often temporary, workers from other geographic locations.

The feasibility and construction phases, however, also represent time periods when local community and civil society organisations, if mobilised, have the greatest opportunity to influence whether, and if so how, projects proceed. This is in part because the project is smaller and easier to contest but also because at later stages of the project cycle capital has been sunk into an area, changes become costly to retrofit, revenues begin to be generated, and there are increased incentives for companies and governments to 'defend' their projects. Civil society organisations were found to mobilise and build campaigns around major government and corporate decision points, such as final investment decisions or impact assessment processes. The feasibility and construction stages are simultaneously a mobilisation point for project opponents and a period of vulnerability for project proponents.

Our interviews revealed that the most frequent costs experienced by companies are due to delay. Delays of world-class mining investments (worth between 3–5 billion dollars) will cost a company roughly US$20 million per week as a result of conflict (in Net Present Value terms). The greatest costs of conflict were identified as the opportunity costs arising from the inability to pursue projects and/or opportunities for expansion or for sale. There are two broad types of costs here. The first is the cost of the lost capital already spent on a project. The second, and by far the most significant, is the lost future value of developing the resource.

For example, in the highlands of Northern Peru, plans by US based Newmont Mining Corporation and Peruvian company Buenaventura to open the Minas

Conga copper and gold project spurred region-wide protests over water security, which ultimately led in 2011 to the suspension of the project during construction. The suspension put at risk US$2 billion of capital that investors had already sunk into the project in the 2 years before suspension. The estimated life production of the deposit was 15–20 million ounces of gold and 4–6 billion pounds of copper. At 2014 prices this translates to roughly US$45 billion of forgone value, with cash costs of production commonly around a third to half of this value. Other suspended or abandoned projects include: Vedanta's Lanjigarh bauxite project in Orissa, India; Barrick's US$8.5 billion Pascua Lama project in central Chile; the Esquel gold project in Argentina and the Tambogrande copper and gold project in Peru.

The most overlooked costs relate to staff time. Few companies factor in such costs, but the drain on senior management time when confronted with conflict can be substantial. We heard reports from companies that senior managers were spending up to 50% of their time managing conflict at some sites. The issue of staff time was viewed by interviewees as an opportunity cost, where instead of putting out fires, senior managers could have been spending their time on productive activities and relationships that generate genuine value.

While we were surprised by the very significant scale of the costs revealed by our research, other recent studies are reporting similar findings. An empirical study of 19 publicly traded junior gold mining companies, undertaken by Witold Henisz and colleagues at The Wharton School, at The University of Pennsylvania, found that two thirds of the market capitalisation of these firms is a function of the individual firm's stakeholder engagement practices, whereas only one third of the market capitalisation is a function of the value of the gold in the ground.[56] A 2012 study by Credit Suisse calculated ESG (Environmental, Social & Governance) impacts on share price for the Australian Stock Exchange and found AUS$21.4 billion in negative valuation impact (hydrocarbon and mining represented AUS$8.4 billion; an average of 2.2% impact on the target price).[57]

What this emerging body of research is demonstrating is that contrary to popular belief some of the seemingly most vulnerable and marginalised people in society, including indigenous peoples, can have huge economic clout. The companies that fail to grasp this reality and run roughshod over communities are pursuing a high-risk business strategy. Financial markets are beginning to discount the value of projects based on these risks and if companies are motivated by the bottom line then they should aim for high environmental and social standards. It is no longer a moral imperative but a business imperative as well.

Of course, there are also costs experienced by communities as a result of conflict and situations where communities are not in a position to translate the risks that they may be experiencing into business risks for a company. Social actors commonly mobilise at immense personal risks to themselves. In the 50 cases of conflict we analysed a full 21 cases involved a fatality. The vast majority of these deaths were community members who typically died at the hands of state security forces called in to defend mining and mineral processing operations from riots and blockades. We decided to explore this issue further, in part prompted by the very severe labour conflicts occurring at Marikana and other mines in the platinum belt in of South Africa in mid-2012. We tracked publicly reported fatalities resulting from mine-community conflict over a 12-month period (1 October 2011 to 30 September 2012) and we were startled to find 84 reported fatalities. More research is needed to track conflict related fatalities over time, however, to emphasise the significance of this figure, the figure of 84 reported fatalities is comparable to the total number of workforce fatalities at ICMM member company mine sites in a given year (90 in 2012, and 91 in 2013).[58]

Getting to the table

There are many contextual reasons as to why the mining industry was, and continues to be, subject to major local level resistance. Communities are now far more connected than they have ever been before. Communication technologies are driving advances in global democracy. Campaigns on one side of the world are now easily visible to people on the other and the pulse of mining investment has dramatically increased the number of projects in the early, more vulnerable stages of the project development cycle. However, the performance and the response of the industry is also a major factor. When grievances are raised by individuals and communities, but ignored or dismissed by companies and governments, there is often no other avenue to seek remedy than to escalate conflict.

In the 50 cases of mine–community conflict that Rachel Davis and I analysed there were commonly opportunities for companies to respond to issues before they had escalated into costly conflict. Conflict is not necessarily a measure of outright opposition. Sometimes communities would just like to assert a more equal platform for development to occur on their own terms, consistent with their own values.

Where MMSD advocated an industry-wide dialogue in response to an industry-wide crisis, many companies have not chosen the path of greater dialogue with their critics when they have run into conflict at more local scales. Instead engagement has too often been too superficial. Far too many companies have employed an approach sometimes known as 'decide, announce and defend', choosing to prioritise public relations and communications in an effort to convince communities of the benefits of a mining project. Many have also increased the level of direct social investment in local communities mistakenly thinking that this will win public support. As a means to build one-on-one relationships in a relatively neutral environment or to leverage shared value, corporate social investments have their place, but as a strategy to reduce conflict they have proved remarkably ineffective and have fuelled public cynicism.[59]

Bruce Harvey, speaking at the time as Global Practice Leader for Communities and Social Performance at Rio Tinto, argued that the practice of community relations has in the past been 'patchy' and 'ad hoc', but 'there is actually a way of doing this work properly'. Bruce says that, 'Project directors who understand the "social project" will by and large succeed, those who don't, will not.'[60] Even in the face of significant costs many in the industry have been slow to recognise that the extraction of resources is as much a 'social project' as it is a technical one. The industry has demonstrated highly varied capabilities and maturity in conflict resolution, the practice of community relations and indeed in environmental performance. Employing capable sustainability professionals into organisations is one thing, placing these professionals in positions of influence is another.

Management often turn to community relations staff for advice during the heat of conflicts. Associate Professor Deanna Kemp and Dr John Owen, colleagues of mine from the Centre for Social Responsibility in Mining, have coined the term 'post-crises recognition regression' to explain a common situation where the effectiveness of sustainability and community relations professionals is temporary, and occurs only for the duration of a crisis.[61] Community relations staff often find it difficult to translate their understandings of conflicts and their insight more generally to decision-makers in higher levels of management outside a crisis context. Sustainability and community relations professionals need to become more effective at using business case arguments to make their case, even while at the same time responding to community in vastly different terms.

Company–community relationships can in some important respects be viewed just like any other human relationship. I sometimes use the analogy of a marriage. When a marriage ends in bitter divorce, just how often do you hear about the same couple getting remarried? Once a marriage ends there is so much baggage and broken trust that the prospect of amicable relations can be remote. Unlike technology, one can't assume that a relationship can be fixed once it is broken. Issues must be addressed before they escalate. Avenues for dialogue and public influence over projects need to be open across the lifecycle of a project, and especially during the early phases of project design.

Breaking New Ground advocated the use of project-level, non-judicial grievance-handling mechanisms to receive, track and respond to complaints from the public. The report was one of the first, if not the first, study to propose the use of grievance-handling mechanisms by private sector companies, with the recommendation stemming from Luke Danielson's experience with the Pangue Independent Review and the subsequent formation of the IFC's Compliance Advisor Ombudsman. Few companies adopted the recommendation until the 2006 revision of the IFC Performance Standards required high risk projects to implement them[62] and the aforementioned UN Secretary-General's Special Representative on Business and Human Rights, Professor John Ruggie, emphasised the importance of 'remedy' in his 'Protect, Respect, Remedy' framework. Carolyn Rees was responsible for implementing this pillar of the Ruggie mandate and when combined with the example set by Meg Taylor, the IFC's Compliance Advisor Ombudsman, the uptake of grievance-handling in the mining sector has started to improve.

Rio Tinto, Newmont, Anglo American, Glencore Xstrata and Barrick Gold all now require their sites to have a project-level grievance mechanism; however, the majority of mining companies do not. A 2013 report by CAER and Oxfam Australia found that only five (9%) of the 53 mining and energy extraction companies listed on the ASX200 (the 200 largest companies on the Australian

Stock Exchange) reported having a grievance-handling mechanism.[63] Even for the companies with established mechanisms, they may not be living up to the their potential. Associate Professor Deanna Kemp and colleagues reviewed the practical application of grievance-handling processes at six mine sites and found that in their current form, and on their own, they may be insufficient as a means to advance justice.[64] MiningWatch Canada has also raised concerns about the 'rights compatibility' of some mechanisms.[65]

New innovations in digital technology are assisting to improve the accessibility of grievance-handling mechanisms. Ulula, for example, is implementing a real-time SMS-based information platform to anonymously handle complaints and from local community members. Antoine Huety, the founder of Ulula was the former Deputy Director of the Revenue Watch Institute and the platform is currently under trial at a mining project in Peru.

Grievance-handling is not the only process that companies, civil society and governments are employing to bridge difference and resolve conflict. In Latin America, a new generation of organisations are experimenting with participatory processes to foster dialogue and resolve conflict at project, regional and national levels. Dialogue tables are a platform for relationship building and a forum for exploring disparate perspectives outside of the pressures of individual project negotiation processes. Dialogue tables allow participants an opportunity to move beyond the stereotypes they may have about different stakeholders.[66] Peru's long-standing *Grupo de Dialogo Mineria y Desarrollo Sostenible* (Dialogue Group on Mining and Sustainable Development), established 13 years ago, has grown to a network of over 500 people. More recently similar groups have emerged in Argentina, Chile, Ecuador, Brazil and Colombia, and there is interest in establishing dialogue processes in Guatemala, Dominican Republic and Panama. A network also now exists across Latin America to provide technical support and promote the exchange of knowledge between dialogue initiatives.[67] Participatory processes for water monitoring, where local community groups are involved in data collection and analysis and thus have the opportunity to build greater trust in the integrity of data, have also been trialed as methods to avoid and reduce conflict.[68]

While the industry is coming to fully realise the power of local communities, we are at an important juncture in the global mining sector. The recent plunge in commodity prices has led some companies to shed jobs, especially in the environmental and social performance areas. Companies are signalling to the market that they are serious about getting costs under control. But they are also signalling that the role of community relations professionals has yet to be fully understood or embedded within the corporate consciousness. The mining industry seems to be missing the potential opportunities for cost savings that can come from investing in improved relationships with communities. In the following chapter we look at the issue of transparency and the impact of the Publish What You Pay campaign, The Extractive Industries Transparency Initiative, and The Natural Resource Charter on natural resource governance.

Notes

1 United Nations Environment Programme (2009), 'From conflict to peacebuilding: The role of natural resources and the environment.' Expert Advisory Group on Environment Conflict and Peacebuilding. Nairobi.

2 International Commission on Intervention and State Sovereignty (2001), 'The responsibility to protect.' November, International Development Research Centre, Ottawa, p. 4.

3 International Council on Mining and Metals (2006), 'The challenge of mineral wealth: Using resource endowments to foster sustainable development.' August. London; United Nations Sustainable Development Solutions Network (2013), 'Harnessing natural resources for sustainable development: Challenges and solutions.' Good Governance of Extractive and Land Resources Thematic Group, United Nations Sustainable Development Solutions Network. Technical report for the post-2015 development agenda. September. Online resource: http://unsdsn.org/wp-content/uploads/2014/02/TG10-Final-Report.pdf Accessed: 11 July 2014.

4 For more on the issues of mineral development in post-conflict settings see: Boege, V. and D.M. Franks (2012), 'Reopening and developing mines in post-conflict settings: The challenge of company–community relations.' In P. Lujala and S.A. Rustad (eds) *High-Value Natural Resources and Post-Conflict Peacebuilding*. Milton Park and New York: Earthscan, pp. 87–120; for accounts of the potential role of mineral resources in peace-building see: UNEP (2009), 'From conflict to peacebuilding'; and, Lujala, P. and S.A. Rustad (eds) (2012), *High-Value Natural Resources and Post-Conflict Peacebuilding*.

5 Billon, P. (2001), 'The political ecology of war: Natural resources and armed conflicts.' *Political Geography*, 20(5): 561–584.

6 United Nations Development Programme (2006), 'Evaluation of UNDP assistance to conflict-affected countries: Case study – Sierra Leone.' Evaluation Office. New York.

7 Sierra Leone Truth and Reconciliation Commission (SLTRC) (2004), *Witness to Truth: Report of the Sierra Leone Truth and Reconciliation Commission*. Accra, Ghana; Kawamoto, K. (2012), 'Diamonds in war, diamonds for peace: Diamond sector management and kimberlite mining in Sierra Leone.' In P. Lujala and S.A. Rustad (eds) *High-Value Natural Resources and Post-Conflict Peacebuilding*, pp. 121–145.

8 SLTRC (2004), 'Witness to truth.'

9 Kawamoto (2012), 'Diamonds in war.'

10 United Nations Security Council (UNSC) (2000), 'Report of the Panel of Experts appointed pursuant to Security Council resolution 1306 (2000), paragraph 19, in relation to Sierra Leone.' S/2000/1195. December; SLTRC (2004), 'Witness to truth.'

11 Farah, D. (2004), *Blood From Stones: The secret financial network of terror*. New York: Broadway Books.

12 Special Court for Sierra Leone (SCSL) (2010), 'Transcript.' The Prosecutor of the special court v. Charles Ghankay Taylor. SCSL-2003-01-T. 10 August 2010.

13 SCSL (2010), 'Transcript.'

14 Campbell (2010), Testimony to the Special Court for Sierra Leone. Online resource: https://www.youtube.com/watch?v=bItA7VstArE Accessed: 1 July 2014.

15 SCSL (2010), 'Transcript.'

16 Campbell (2010), Testimony to the Special Court for Sierra Leone.

17 Global Witness (1998), 'A rough trade: The role of companies and governments in the Angolan conflict.' December. London, United Kingdom. Online resource: http://www.globalwitness.org/sites/default/files/pdfs/A_Rough_Trade.pdf Accessed: 11 July 2014; Smillie, I., Gberie, L., and R. Hazleton (2000), 'The heart of the matter: Sierra Leone, diamonds and human security.' Partnership Africa Canada. January. Ottawa, Canada; Jung, A. (2008), '10 years of Fatal Transactions.' Online resource: http://www.medico.de/media/input-referat-10-years-of-fatal-transactions.pdf Accessed: 1 July 2014.

18 Global Witness (1999), 'Campaign launched to stop billion dollar diamond trade from funding conflict in Africa.' Press release: 3 October. Online resource: http://www.africa.upenn.edu/Hornet/irin_10499.html Accessed: 1 July 2014.

19 Billon, P. (2006), 'Fatal Transactions: Conflict diamonds and the (anti)terrorist consumer.' *Antipode*, 38(4): 778–801.

20 Global Witness (1999), 'Campaign launched.'

21 Jung (2008), '10 years of Fatal Transactions.'

22 General Accounting Office (2002), 'Significant challenges remain in deterring trade in conflict diamonds.' Statement of Loren Yager, Director, International Affairs and Trade, Testimony Before the Subcommittee on Oversight of Government Management, Restructuring and the District of Columbia, Committee on Governmental Affairs, US Senate. 13 February. GAO-02-425T.

23 GAO (2002), 'Significant challenges remain.'

24 Billon (2006), 'Fatal Transactions.'

25 Roberts, B. (1976), *Kimberley, Turbulent City*. Cape Town: David Philip & Kimberley Historical Society; Mitchell, R. (1986), 'Historical aspects of kimberlite petrology.' In R. Mitchell, *Kimberlites: Mineralogy, geochemistry and petrology*, New York: Springer, pp. 1–6.

26 Williams, G.F. (1905), *The Diamond Mines of South Africa*. New York: B. F. Buck & company. Online resource: https://openlibrary.org/books/OL7219289M/The_diamond_mines_of_South_Africa Accessed: 27 June 2014; Roberts (1976), *Kimberley, Turbulent City*.

27 Thomas, A. (1997), *Rhodes: The race for Africa*. London: London Bridge.

28 Rotberg, R.I. (1988), *The Founder: Cecil Rhodes and the pursuit of power*. New York: Oxford University Press.

29 Morris, M. and J. Linnegar (2004), *Every Step of the Way: The journey to freedom in South Africa*. Cape Town, South Africa: Human Sciences Research Council Press.

30 Epstein, E.J. (1982), *The Rise and Fall of Diamonds: The shattering of a brilliant illusion*. New York: Simon and Schuster; Kretschmer, T. (1998), 'De Beers and beyond: The history of the international diamond cartel.' London Business School Case. Online resource: http://pages.stern.nyu.edu/~lcabral/teaching/debeers3.pdf Accessed: 27 June 2014.

31 Kretschmer (1998), 'De Beers and beyond.'

32 Mitchell (1986), 'Historical aspects of kimberlite petrology.'

33 Kimberley Process Certification Scheme (KPSC) (2002), 'Essential elements of an international scheme of certification for rough diamonds, with a view to breaking the link between armed conflict and the trade in rough diamonds.' 20 March. Kimberley Process Working Document nr 1/2002; the following year Global Witness also published a discussion paper on the design of the scheme: Global Witness (2003), 'Conflict diamonds: Possibilities for the identification, certification and control of diamonds.' June.

34 Kimberley Process Certification Scheme (2014), 'About: Kimberley process basics.' Online resource: http://www.kimberleyprocess.com/en/about Accessed: 21 July 2014.

35 See for example: Grant, J. (2012), 'The Kimberly process at ten: Reflections on a decade of efforts to end the trade in conflict diamonds.' In P. Lujala and S.A. Rustad (eds), *High-Value Natural Resources and Peacebuilding*, London: Earthscan; Wright, C. (2012), 'The Kimberly Process Certification Scheme: A model negotiation.' In P. Lujala and S.A. Rustad (eds), *High-Value Natural Resources and Post-Conflict Peacebuilding*. London: Earthscan; Bieri, F. (2010), *From blood diamonds to the Kimberley Process: How NGOs cleaned up the global diamond industry*. Surrey: Ashgate.

36 GAO (2002), 'Significant challenges remain.'

37 Bone, A. (2012), 'The Kimberly Process Certification Scheme: The primary safeguard for the diamond industry.' In P. Lujala and S.A. Rustad (eds), *High-Value Natural Resources and Peacebuilding*. London: Earthscan.

38 GAO (2002), 'Significant challenges remain,' p. 11.
39 GAO (2002), 'Significant challenges remain,' *Highlights*.
40 IRIN (2009), 'Credibility of Kimberley Process on the line, say NGOs.' Online resource: http://m.irinnews.org/Report/84949/GLOBAL-Credibility-of-Kimberley-Process-on-the-line-say-NGOs#.U_PR4dkazCQ Accessed: 15 August 2014.
41 Gooch, C. (2011), 'Why we are leaving the Kimberley Process – A message from Global Witness Founding Director Chairman Gooch.' 5 December. Online Resource: http://www.globalwitness.org/library/why-we-are-leaving-kimberley-process-message-global-witness-founding-director-charmian-gooch Accessed: 1 July 2014; Global Witness (2011), 'Global Witness leaves Kimberley Process, calls for diamond trade to be held accountable.' Press release: 5 December. Online resource: http://www.globalwitness.org/library/global-witness-leaves-kimberley-process-calls-diamond-trade-be-held-accountable Accessed: 1 July 2014.
42 Global Witness (2014), 'The Kimberley Process.' Online Resource: http://www.globalwitness.org/campaigns/conflict/conflict-diamonds/kimberley-process Accessed: 22 July 2014.
43 Jung (2008), '10 years of Fatal Transactions.'
44 Maconachie, R. and T. Binns (2007), '"Farming miners" or "mining farmers"?: Diamond mining and rural development in post-conflict Sierra Leone.' *Journal of Rural Studies*, 23(3): 367–380; Maconachie, R. and G. Hilson (2011), 'Artisanal gold mining: A new frontier in post-conflict Sierra Leone?' *The Journal of Development Studies*, 47(4): 595–616.
45 World Bank (2014), 'Sierra Leone.' Online resource: http://www.worldbank.org/en/country/sierraleone Accessed: 22 July 2014.
46 Akam, S. (2012), 'Sierra Leone diamond firm: From war booty to IPO.' Reuters. 4 April. Online resource: http://www.reuters.com/article/2012/04/04/us-sierraleone-diamonds-idUSBRE83311520120404 Accessed: 4 July 2014; Manson, K. (2013), 'Battlefields, diamonds and the "hell" of the MBA.' *Financial Times*, 7 October. Online resource: http://www.ft.com/intl/cms/s/2/95a65f74-08b7-11e3-8b32-00144feabdc0.html#axzz36TQvDNpe Accessed: 4 July 2014.
47 Coll, S. (2000), 'The other war.' *Washington Post Magazine*, 9 January. Online resource: http://www.washingtonpost.com/wp-dyn/content/article/2006/11/28/AR2006112800682.html Accessed: 4 July 2014; SLTRC (2004), 'Witness to truth'; Keen, D. (2005), *Conflict and Collusion in Sierra Leone*. US and UK: Palgrave Macmillan; Akam (2012), 'Sierra Leone diamond firm'; Manson (2013), 'Battlefields, diamonds and the "hell" of the MBA.'
48 Koidu Holdings (2012), 'Company history timeline.' Online resource: http://www.koiduholdings.com/company-history.php Accessed: 4 July 2014.
49 Franks, D.M. and P. Erskine (2012), 'Mine site rehabilitation in Sierra Leone – A rapid appraisal of selected sites.' Centre for Mined Land Rehabilitation, The University of Queensland, Brisbane.
50 United Nations Environment Programme (UNEP) (2010), 'Sierra Leone: Environment, conflict and peacebuilding assessment.' Technical Report, February, Geneva.
51 Thermal coal rose from US$25/t in 2003 to a peak of US$192/t in 2008, before dropping to US$65/t in 2014. Iron ore rose from US$13/t in 2003 to a peak of 179/t in 2011, before dropping to US$80/t in 2014. Copper rose from US$1700/t in 2003 to a peak of US$9,900/t in 2011, before settling to US$6,700/t in 2014. Gold rose from US$350/ounce to US$1770/ounce in 2011, before settling to US$1200/ounce in 2014; World Bank (2014), 'Global Economic Monitor (GEM) Commodities.' Online resource: http://data.worldbank.org/data-catalog/commodity-price-data Accessed: 30 October 2014.
52 Taylor, M. (2013), 'Indigenous people and the resource extraction industry: Towards public, transparent and human rights compliance standards.' Compliance Advisor Ombudsman (CAO), Presentation to the ATNS Symposium, University of Melbourne,

25 June 2013. Online resource: http://atns.net.au/symposium/Day%20One/Dame%20 Meg%20Taylor%20ATNS%20Symposium%2025%20June%202013.pdf Accessed: 28 July 2014.

53 Wilson, A. and M. Cervantes. (2014), 'Fraser Institute Annual Survey of Mining Companies 2013.' The Fraser Institute, Vancouver, Canada. Online resource: http:// www.fraserinstitute.org/uploadedFiles/fraser-ca/Content/research-news/research/ publications/mining-survey-2013.pdf Accessed: 28 July 2014.

54 IIED and WBCSD (2002), *Breaking New Ground*, p. xviii.

55 Davis, R. and D.M. Franks (2014), 'Costs of company–community conflict in the extractive sector.' Corporate Social Responsibility Initiative Report no. 66. Cambridge, MA: Harvard Kennedy School. Online resource: http://www.hks.harvard.edu/m-rcbg/CSRI/research/Costs%20of%20Conflict_Davis%20%20Franks.pdf Accessed: 7 February 2015; Franks, D.M., Davis, R., Bebbington, A.J., Ali, S.H., Kemp, D., and M. Scurrah (2014), 'Conflict translates environmental and social risk into business costs.' *Proceedings of the National Academy of Sciences*, 111(21): 7576–7581.

56 Henisz, W., Dorobantu, S. and L. Nartey (2013), 'Spinning gold: The financial returns to stakeholder engagement.' *Strategic Management Journal*, 35(12): 1727–1748.

57 Credit Suisse (2012), 'Australian ESG/SRI. $21.4bn in ESG concerns on Australian stocks.' July.

58 International Council on Mining and Metals (2014), 'Benchmarking safety data: Progress of ICMM members.' Online resource: http://www.icmm.com/publications/ safety-data Accessed: 21 August 2014.

59 Martinez, C. and D.M. Franks (2014), 'Does mining company-sponsored community development influence social licence to operate? Evidence from private and state-owned companies in Chile.' *Impact Assessment and Project Appraisal*, 32(4): 294–303.

60 Harvey, B. (2013), ComRel conversations. Interview with Bruce Harvey by Dr Deanna Kemp. Centre for Social Responsibility in Mining, University of Queensland. Online resource: https://www.csrm.uq.edu.au/docs/ComRel_Conversations_2_Bruce_Harvey_ Transcript.pdf Accessed: 28 July 2014.

61 Kemp, D. and J.R. Owen (2013), 'Community relations in mining: Core to business but not "core business".' *Resources Policy*, 38(4): 523–531.

62 Wilson, E., and E. Blackmore (2013), 'Dispute or dialogue: Community perspectives on company-led grievance mechanisms.' London: International Institute for Environment and Development.

63 Hill, C., Leske J. and S. Lillywhite (2013), 'The right to decide: Company commitments and community consent.' CAER and Oxfam Australia, Belconnen, Australia.

64 Kemp, D., Owen, J.R., Gotzman, N., and C.J. Bond (2011), 'Just relations and company–community conflict in mining.' *Journal of Business Ethics*, 101(1): 93–109.

65 MiningWatch Canada (2013), 'Barrick ignores UN High Commissioner for human rights recommendation regarding Papua New Guinea rapes.' Press release: 28 October. Online resource: http://www.miningwatch.ca/news/barrick-ignores-un-high-commissioner-human-rights-recommendation-regarding-papua-new-guinea-rap Accessed: 30 July 2014.

66 Arbeláez-Ruiz, D. and D.M. Franks. (2014), 'Getting to the table: How a new generation of organisations is improving dialogue and recording conflict over mining in Latin America.' *Americas Quarterly*, 8(2): 111–113.

67 Arbeláez-Ruiz and Franks (2014), 'Getting to the table.'

68 Atkins, D., and S. Wildau (2008), *Participatory Water Monitoring: A guide for preventing and managing conflict*. Advisory note. Compliance Advisor Ombudsman. Washington, USA.

6 Transparency

Dirty deals, done dirt-cheap

The grilled chicken sandwich and fries arrived just after 3pm on a warm Sunday afternoon, in Florida, in April of 2013. Fifty-one year-old French businessmen Frédéric Cilins was lunching at Tampa International Airport. His guest was Mamadie Touré, the widow – and the youngest of the four wives – of Guinea's long-serving authoritarian President Lansana Conté. Cilins conveyed an offer of US$11 million for Touré's part in an allegedly corrupt deal to acquire the northern half of the Simandou iron ore deposit. Touré was wearing a wire.

Cilins was convicted by a New York Federal Court in 2014 after pleading guilty to obstructing a criminal investigation. While lunching in Florida he asked Touré to leave the United States to avoid questioning by a US federal grand jury. He also pleaded for her to destroy the paper trail that linked her to the deal.

Cilins is an associate of billionaire diamond dealer, Beny Steinmetz, and an intermediary for Beny's company, BSGR. Cilins assisted BSGR to acquire the mining rights to Blocks 1 and 2 of Guinea's Simandou iron ore deposit – one of the world's largest known untapped deposits of iron ore. These rich iron-ore concessions underlie the forested Simandou ranges. The concessions were held by Rio Tinto, which is building a US$20 billion mine–rail–port project on neighbouring Blocks 3 and 4 with the Aluminium Corporation of China, the International Finance Corporation, and the Government of Guinea.

In mid 2008 President Conté stripped Rio Tinto of the rights. In December, just days before Conté's death, the rights were awarded free to BSGR. Touré fled across the border to Sierra Leone and later to Florida. BSGR sold 51% of the allegedly ill-gotten deposit to Rio's rival, Brazilian miner Vale for US$2.5 billion – a figure twice the annual budget of Guinea.

Alpha Condé, the newly elected President of Guinea ordered a review of Guinea's mining concessions. The review committee found in April of 2014 that the concessions had been granted corruptly and the rights were subsequently striped from Vale and BSGR. The committee did not find that Vale participated in the scandal, but graft investigations are ongoing, across three continents.[1]

This chapter details global efforts to shine a light on the dirty deals that rob citizens of their mineral wealth. The growth of the transparency agenda is charted by initiatives, such as the Publish What You Pay coalition, The Extractive Industries Transparency Initiative, and The Natural Resource Charter, and reforms led by the G8, the US Congress and the European Commission. We start by looking at how yet another Global Witness report catalysed global action, this time on the topic of transparency. The report, *A Crude Awakening*, would be to the Extractive Industries Transparency Initiative, what *A Rough Trade* was to the Kimberley Process. Two hard hitting investigative reports about one country in Africa, set off two of the most important governance initiatives in the extractive industries.

A crude awakening

Angola is a former Portuguese colony on the Atlantic coast of southern Africa. For most of the second half of the 20th century Angola found itself rapt in conflict. First, a battle for independence (1961–1974). Then a civil war (1975–2002). Angola was a stage to battles of its own and others making. Rival independence movements were backed by rival economic systems. The Popular Movement for the Liberation of Angola (MPLA) was backed by the Soviet Union and Cuba. The National Union for the Total Independence of Angola (UNITA) was backed by the United States and South Africa.

Oil and diamonds financed the civil war. Revenues from the international oil majors, like BP and Chevron, propped up the MPLA government, while diamonds, purchased by De Beers, funded UNITA. On the diamond side, the solution lay in controlling the flow of illicit diamonds, but on the oil side, the prospect of the international oil majors divesting from Angola appeared remote. *Global Witness*, a London-based NGO that had already exposed the role of diamonds in the Angolan conflict, decided to focus on the flow of oil revenues. The strategy was to pressure the international oil companies to disclose their payments to the Angolan government and to support efforts by the International Monetary Fund and The World Bank to encourage fiscal transparency in Angola.

In December of 1999 Global Witness published *A Crude Awakening: The role of the oil and banking industries in Angola's civil war and the plunder of state assets*. The report detailed the links between conflict and oil in Angola, arguing that, 'It is simply not good enough to continue in the same vein, so we are challenging the oil industry to adopt a policy of "full transparency".'[2] In particular, the report used BP's increasingly progressive stance on accountability to recommend that the 'BP–Amoco alliance sets a "benchmark for corporate transparency and accountability" by publishing their full set of Angolan accounts, both in Angola and internationally – not just the consolidated, audited, year-end accounts available in the annual reports.'[3] The report also recommended companies 'make available copies of all contracts signed with Sonangol [the Angolan State petroleum company] and the Angolan government'.[4]

Simon Taylor is the co-founder of Global Witness. He spent the months following the release of the report talking to representatives from companies such as BP, Shell and Stat Oil about the potential for a mechanism for the disclosure of payments made to the Angolan government. Simon aimed to convince the few company representatives willing to take his call that a collective industry response to transparency was needed. There was in principal agreement from some companies for transparency around payments. Taylor argued, though, that there were obvious risks for companies if they disclosed alone, and instead he pushed for a mechanism to force companies to disclose. This would both protect the willing companies and bring on board all of the companies who did not want to disclose. It was clear that, even at these early stages, a mandatory mechanism would not be supported by even the most progressive companies in the oil or mining industries, but there was some interest in a voluntary approach.

After months of bilateral conversations the UK Foreign & Commonwealth Office hosted a meeting in September of 2000 to discuss the disclosure of company payments in Angola. The meeting was chaired by Peter Hain, then UK Minister for Africa, and included representatives from Shell, BP, Norsk Hydro and Stat Oil, as well as David Murray, from Transparency International UK. The meeting was the first formal multi-stakeholder gathering to discuss revenue transparency. Chevron, Marathon, Exxon, Total and Elf were noticeably absent. Simon Taylor recounted to me the achievements of the meeting:

> Within ten minutes [the BP representative] destroyed the meeting ... I was furious, it took me six months to get this thing going and so at the end of the meeting I sort of had a go at him. I said, 'Look, I'm really quite frankly disgusted at what you did in the meeting there; of all of the companies, you should have been at the forefront. Instead you killed the conversation and we ended up having a vacuous conversation about nothing for the next hour, which didn't achieve anything. What the hell were you trying to do?' His response was, 'Oh well, we'll show the laggards how it's done, we have a plan, I'll come back to you.'

BP Chief Executive, John Browne, whom we met in Chapter 2, decided to take a lead on the issue. Browne reflected on the decision in his memoir: 'Global Witness was right in suggesting it was time for a radical rethink of international best practice. And we would make a start. We would break the mould because we had nothing to hide.'[5] On 6 February 2001, BP Group Managing Director Richard Olver wrote to Global Witness and committed BP to publish its payments to Angola, including taxes, levies, signature bonus payments and payments to the state oil company, Sonangol. After a week of follow-up conversations with BP, Global Witness released a press release on 12 February that reported the contents of the letter and the story was front-page news in the *Financial Times*.[6]

BP was hoping that disclosure would put it at the vanguard of corporate social responsibility. The Angolan government did not share this view. Sonangol, which was a partner in BP's Angolan blocks, wrote to BP threatening to invoke article 40 of the production sharing agreement – cancellation of the contract – should BP breach the confidentiality provisions. A copy of the letter was sent by Sonangol to all of the other oil companies operating in Angola.[7] Intriguingly the letter to BP was dated 6 February – the same day as BP's letter to Global Witness and prior to the Global Witness press release. Just how the Angolan government became aware of BP's intentions is unknown. The decision by BP to voluntarily disclose the payments risked billions of dollars of investment – and ended any illusions that the solution to revenue transparency lay in disclosure by individual companies. John Browne was summoned to a meeting with President dos Santos in Luanda, Angola's capital, and BP backed down from the commitment in light of the risks.[8]

Global Witness, returned to its investigative work, releasing the report *All the Presidents' Men* in March of 2002. The cover of the report parodied the poster of the Robert Redford film of the same name. The mock credits read:

> The devastating story of oil and banking in Angola's privatised war. 'ALL THE PRESIDENTS' MEN': DIRECTORS' CUT • A Global Witness Report • Starring [French President] JACQUES CHIRAC and [Angolan President] JOSE EDUARDO DOS SANTOS • Co-starring [Russian President] BORIS YELTSIN as himself • Special guest appearances by [US President] GEORGE W BUSH and [Vice-President] DICK CHENEY • Based on an original idea by [French Foreign Minister] CHARLES PASQUA and [French intelligence officer] JEAN-CHARLES MARCHIANI • Lack of transparency by most of the INTERNATIONAL OIL AND BANKING INDUSTRIES • Introducing the notion of 'PUBLISH WHAT YOU PAY' • No rating: uncensured by the INTERNATIONAL COMMUNITY.[9]

This was the first use of the campaign slogan 'Publish What You Pay'. The report called on companies to '[e]mbrace a unified stand on full transparency of payments to national governments amongst all companies in the oil sector for all countries of operation'.[10]

Shortly after the release of the report Taylor attended a meeting of the Open Society Institute in Johannesburg, South Africa. Founded by billionaire investor and philanthropist George Soros, the Open Society Institute aimed to help societies transition from communism, and to promote democratic accountability. Soros attended the Johannesburg meeting. Taylor shared the idea of a global campaign around the notion of Publish What You Pay (PWYP) and Soros liked the idea. A network of London-based individuals worked with Taylor and Soros to build the formal PWYP coalition, including Katherine Astill (Catholic Agency For Overseas Development), Gavin Hayman (Global Witness), David Murray (Transparency International UK), Fiona Napier (Save the Children UK), Mabel van Oranje (Open Society Institute), and Sophia Tickell (Oxfam Great Britain). George Soros launched the campaign in June of 2002, bringing on board thirty civil society organisations. Henry Parham joined as the International Coordinator of PWYP in 2002, holding the position until 2007. PWYP is now a network of over eight hundred member organisations in more than forty countries.[11]

Meanwhile, academic literature on the 'resource curse' was mounting. The 'resource curse' refers to the apparent paradox that countries with greater abundance or dependence on natural resources tend to demonstrate a greater risk of conflict, poor economic growth and repression. Coined by Richard Auty in his 1993 classic, *Sustaining Development in Mineral Economies*,[12] the concept helped to frame a series of studies in the later 1990s, and supported calls for greater transparency in the management of mineral and oil wealth. Influential academic pieces during this period include, the 1998 working paper by Paul Collier and Anke Hoeffler on the confluence of civil war and natural resource abundance, the 1997 working paper by Jeffrey Sachs and Andrew Warner showing a negative correlation between economic growth and natural resource dependence, and the 2001 Oxfam America report, *Extractive sectors and the poor*, by The University of California academic, Michael Ross.[13]

Michael is now Professor of Political Science and Director of the Centre for Southeast Asian Studies at The University of California, Los Angeles. I asked Michael about the impact of the Oxfam America report and how it came to be written:

> In 1999 I published my first piece on [the resource curse], which was a review article in an academic journal … Around that same time I met Paul Collier, when he was by chance visiting the University of Michigan where I was working. He invited me to spend my sabbatical year, which was coming up, at The World Bank where he was about to take over as research director. That was a key move for me, I had a chance to be around a lot of very smart people who were working on all kinds of development issues, I had a chance to look at the bank and learn something about the bank and how it was working, and I had a chance to be around Collier, who is very stimulating and generous with his time and very supportive. All of those things led to a whole new research agenda for me, which at the time was kind of fairly obscure in political science looking at the consequences for developing countries for having significant resource abundance … I remember one day coming out of the bank and there was a big protest across the street, NGOs were protesting [World Bank] lending support for extractive industry projects … The demonstration was interesting because it helped clue me into the fact that NGOs were mobilising on this issue and I was interested in it [from an academic perspective].

Michael got in touch with Keith Slack from Oxfam America through old networks that Michael had developed while active in Greenpeace. Keith was looking for help with a report on poverty and the extractive industries. The resulting report was due to be launched in Washington on 12 September 2001. The launch was thrown into chaos when planes struck the World Trade Centre and the Pentagon. Despite the false start, the report was widely disseminated. The study used econometric analysis to examine the relationship between mineral and oil dependence and outcomes for the poor. It found a strong negative correlation between a country's level of mineral dependence and its ranking on the UN's Human Development Index. The report called for 'full disclosure of all financial transactions between extractive firms and host governments' and for 'international funders to only support projects in which the host government specifies in advance how the resource revenues are to be used to alleviate poverty'.[14] Oxfam used this report, and others, to push for reforms to lending practices, including through The World Bank's Extractive Industries Review. According to Michael:

> Today, everybody associated with the intergovernmental organisations that have any sort of stake in this are more or less on board with the transparency agenda and many of the other tenets of extractive industry reform. At the time ... there was nothing like that and it was met with a lot of hostility initially. The old view of this as simply being a pure issue of economic development ... those views really still were quite prevalent. Now, the change to me is quite astounding. I keep stumbling across new initiatives both in the NGO world and among inter-governmental organisations and at the time there wasn't anything like that.

One of the most important initiatives was the Extractive Industries Transparency Initiative (EITI). The EITI was one of the first successes of the PWYP coalition and the growing transparency movement.

The Extractive Industries Transparency Initiative

The debate on the resource curse, conflict and extractive resources was live among academics, civil society and multi-lateral institutions, but conversations were also beginning to happen in the halls of government. The UK Department for International Development (DfID) started to engage more deeply in the issue of revenue transparency in the lead up to the Rio +10 summit, held in Johannesburg, South Africa, in late August of 2002. George Soros wrote a letter to UK Prime Minister Tony Blair in May of that same year alerting Blair to the issue of revenue transparency and the letter reportedly convinced the UK government that the issue was worth acting on. BP CEO John Browne, too, met with the Prime Minister to urge action.[15]

DfID staff put together an initiative about transparency for Blair to announce in Johannesburg. The Extractive Industries Transparency Initiative was written into Blair's speech, but the speech was not delivered as planned. His speaking slot was moved due to a diplomatic stoush with Zimbabwean President Robert Mugabe. The 'announcement' only appeared in the written remarks released after the summit. The UK would support the establishment of a voluntary compact on transparency to encourage better accountability of resource revenues. Sir Robert Wilson, Chairman of Rio Tinto, Brian Gilbertson, Chief Executive of BHP Billiton, and Tony Trahar, Chief Executive of Anglo American, welcomed Blair's 'announcement' and pledged to work with other companies, governments and civil society to develop the framework.[16]

The PWYP coalition, too, cautiously welcomed the EITI, though continued to question whether a voluntary initiative would work. PWYP was building a movement for mandatory disclosure. The EITI, like PWYP, was premised on citizen accountability but it also looked to engage citizens in a process of disclosure – and bring all the players, including governments and companies, willingly into that process.

In June of 2003 the first EITI conference was held at Lancaster House in London. One hundred and forty participants representing seventy governments attended the conference. Prime Minister Blair opened the event:

> I welcome the efforts of non-governmental organisations and international agencies to improve understanding, to put this issue on the international agenda and to stimulate public debate … Of course, we can't solve the problem overnight. Nor do we believe that this initiative is the only thing to be done. By setting a framework for concrete action, I firmly believe that the initiative can make a significant contribution to ensuring that the proceeds from mining and energy industries are used for development … Well, to succeed we need joint action by governments and companies, working in tandem. We need to link 'Publish What You Pay' with 'Publish What You Earn'.[17]

After offering up the idea, DfID was now tasked with making it work. Ben Mellor led the International Secretariat of EITI from within DfID between 2004–2007. I caught up with Ben over a scratchy phone line from Khartoum where at the time he was the Head of DfID in Sudan. He now Heads the DfID office in Nigeria. 'The key issues early on were about building support, working out what EITI actually meant, establishing the EITI sourcebook [the implementation guide] and setting up the processes to spin off the EITI into an independent secretariat,' said Ben.

Momentum was important in the early stages. Signing up to the EITI was as easy as a letter of support at the beginning because it was important to demonstrate reach, and it would have been incredibly difficult to differentiate countries prior to development of any detailed standards. Maximising the reach of the initiative would create the necessary constituency for future success when the requirements of involvement were progressively tightened. 'Then after we got that we said, "Okay, now we've got broad enough credibility, people understand what the brand is, people understand what we're trying to do here, then you have to say the brand is now worth something to people, so now if you want to stay in, you have to do a little bit more," and that's when we started kicking people out who hadn't done anything.'

Ben highlights the importance of networking, and 'just talking all the time'. People were interested but cautious. The EITI was viewed by companies as a better alternative than the go-it-alone approach BP tried in Angola or mandatory disclosure. 'I don't think without a bit of external pressure the [companies] would have necessarily shifted, [though] some of the more progressive companies might have done,' said Ben. An industry-wide rule levelled the playing field.

Decision-making was consensus driven and great effort was put into corralling ideas into collective positions. 'I found the phrase "collaborative thuggery" in some book that I read at the time,' said Ben, 'and I remember thinking that was quite a good description because we made sure that everybody collaborated, but if they stepped out of line, my job was to beat them up and get them back into line.' Face-to-face meetings were important, whether it was meetings with George Soros in New York or with government representatives in Indonesia, it meant a lot of travel. One year Ben made the top ten list of travel mile offenders within DfID, a remarkable feat given his employ in a diplomatic agency full of frequent flyers. Informal meetings gradually became more formal and an International Advisory Group was set up to advise on the process.

The EITI approach began to take shape. EITI was not a voluntary standard for companies. It was more akin to a disclosure standard implemented by governments. The EITI sought country-by country commitments to establish multi-stakeholder groups to publish annual reports on the payments received by government and the corresponding payments made by companies.[18] In 2006 the EITI Board was constituted and Peter Eigen, founder of Transparency International, was appointed as its Chair. The following year the International Secretariat opened in Oslo, marking the end to DfID's role as the secretariat during the establishment phase. As of 2008, not a single EITI candidate country had been deemed compliant. At the time of writing, however, EITI boasts 31 compliant countries, 17 candidate countries, and 90 supporting companies. Ninety-two institutional investors have signed a statement supporting EITI, collectively managing over US$16 trillion in investment.[19] International Financial Institutions have even made EITI implementation a condition of lending to governments, for example, in Gabon and the Central African Republic.

EITI has exposed corruption and made it easier for citizens to access data. In the Democratic Republic of Congo, EITI reports exposed a discrepancy in payments reported by one of the tax collecting agencies. The agency could not account for US$26 million of royalty payments. Judicial action is likely. In Nigeria US$8.3 billion in tax payments were found missing by EITI reports, of which US$443 million has since been recovered. The Liberia EITI discovered discrepancies in the procedure for awarding contracts and a subsequent audit found 62 of the 68 concessions had not complied with the laws and regulations.[20]

One of the EITI's biggest successes is that it has made transparency ordinary. Rt. Hon. Clare Short was Secretary of State for International Development in the Government of Prime Minister Tony Blair from 1997 to 2003. She was the Minister who oversaw the early establishment of EITI and since 2011 she has held the position of EITI Chair. Clare has overseen major reforms of the EITI rules during her term as Chair. A new EITI Standard was released at the March 2013 EITI Conference in Sydney. The conference was attended by 1,200 people from 96 countries, and was billed as 'Beyond Transparency'. Clare revealed to me during our conversation the risks of complacency and why renewal of the standards was so important:

> I think the achievement in this first period was the entrenchment of an
> expectation of transparency and that was a complete shift in culture, but,

now, we have got to make the accountability work and make sure the information informs debate in countries … and then countries can make much more informed decisions about fair contracts, how fast to take it out of the ground, how to use it and what will they do when it is exhausted … I think honestly, if the rules hadn't been changed [in Sydney], I probably wouldn't have done a second term [as chair]. It was becoming a bit of a box-ticking thing. You know, jump through the hoops and you are EITI compliant. I wasn't sure it was really driving the change that was needed. My motivation is that these are massive resources … and if they are used well they can improve the lives of hundreds of millions of people. If they are not they can spread corruption and misgovernment. It's a chance that's time bound to get an enormous advance in development. I mean, if you can improve the lives of lots of people that are having a tough life now, and make sure countries are in a position to manage their resources for the benefit of their own people, then I believe in that. That is why I am in it … Now, we are trying to broaden it to encourage transparency on licensing and contracts … to contextualise reports so they are not just columns of figures.

Professor Michael Ross reflected on the future of the EITI in a keynote speech to the International Mining for Development Conference in May of 2013.[21] The event was held in Sydney and coincided with the EITI global conference. Ross shared with me his appraisal of the EITI and his vision for the next ten years:

Looking back at what EITI has accomplished I really am quite surprised at how far it has gone. I would never have guessed it would bring so many countries aboard. That it would gradually be able to raise transparency standards, regularise them in a meaningful way, all kinds of benefits large and small are associated with EITI that are really quite impressive. In my view it is the very success of EITI during this last phase that should raise the question for people who work on this issue of where this issue should go next.

Ross believes that it is now time for the standard to extract some meaningful commitments from companies. Companies who support the EITI are not asked to live up to explicit standards, nor is the transparency performance of companies monitored. According to Ross this has led to an anomalous position where some companies that nominally support EITI are at the same time fighting against mandatory disclosure in jurisdictions like the United States. 'If companies want to use it as a brand lets make it meaningful. To do so we need to set up some standards and make sure that they are truly followed by companies that have signed on.'

The EITI has indeed made impressive gains for the transparency agenda and wields huge convening power, but the challenge will be to turn, what is essentially a reporting process, into better decisions about the management of natural resources. One effort to use transparency for wider policy change is the Natural Resource Charter.

The Natural Resource Charter

Sir Paul Collier, CBE grew up the son of a butcher in the industrial city of Sheffield in Northern England. His parents left school before they were teenagers. Paul, on the other hand, was given the opportunity to attend Oxford and he made the most of it to rise to the position of Professor of Economics and Public Policy at his alma mater. For more than four decades he has put economics in the service of development in Africa, a dedication that he was awarded a knighthood for in 2014.

Collier was a student at Oxford in 1968. Like many people of the times he was concerned about issues of global poverty. 'Really all you had to be was to be a human being, at the time, to worry about that,' admitted Paul when we spoke along Cape Town's Victoria and Alfred Waterfront. Interested in development economics, Paul learnt about the challenges of Nyasaland, a British Protectorate in Central Africa. The father of a friend Paul met at Oxford was the governor general of Nyasaland. The country was renamed Malawi after independence, but it remained the poorest country in Africa. 'I recognised that Africa is full of millions of people like my parents – opportunity denied,' said Paul. 'That's what got me energised.'

Paul was recruited by Joseph Stiglitz to head the research department of the World Bank in 1998, and he held the position until 2003. The role was a unique opportunity to combine research and policy at a time when there was an increased appetite for reform. After his stint at the World Bank he rejoined the academy and in the summer of 2008, Paul collaborated with Karen Lissakers, then Director of Revenue Watch Institute, to convene a small group of academics and development practitioners. The group included Joseph Bell, Thomas Heller, Michael Ross, Tony Venables, Robert Conrad and Michael Spence, and they were invited to spend a week at Collier's home to map out the resource extraction decision chain – from discovery to use – and to come up with suggestions for the choices that resource endowed governments face. The group felt that an independent perspective, free from institutional baggage and based on deep experience working on the challenges, would be helpful in the search for solutions. The result was 12 'precepts' or principles, framed as a Natural Resource Charter.

The Charter was launched in 2010 at the Annual Meetings of the International Monetary Fund and The World Bank Group. The Charter, has since been adopted as a flagship programme by The New Partnership for Africa's Development (NEPAD) and it is now working to accommodate the Africa Mining Vision into its methodology. Gradually the Charter has also became an organisation. A Technical Advisory Group was formed and Chaired by Nobel Laureate in Economics, Michael Spence. An Oversight Board was constituted and Chaired by Ernesto Zedillo, former President of Mexico. Mo Ibrahim, a prominent Sudanese-British entrepreneur and philanthropist, was counted among the board's members.

Countries like Tanzania have taken up the challenge of implementing the Charter. They have used the Charter to define their own reform agenda. In

December 2013, the Chief Secretary of the Tanzanian civil service, Ambassador Ombeni Sefue, appointed a 14-member Tanzanian team to work through the decision chain of the Charter and to benchmark Tanzania's current performance and develop a plan of action. 'The truth is,' stressed Sefue, 'that this is our own initiative, and it is driven by the government.'[22]

The Natural Resource Charter is not strictly a transparency initiative, but it is steeped in the heritage of the transparency movement and has transparency at its core. Precept 2 reads, 'Resource governance requires decision-makers to be accountable to an informed public.'[23] The charter positions transparency as a tool to promote accountability, and in this subtle shift the Charter hopes to move the focus of reform from the issue of resource revenues to the issues of resource governance. Emphasising this trend, the Natural Resource Charter merged with the Revenue Watch Institute in 2014 to form the Natural Resource Governance Institute. Revenue Watch began in 2002 as a programme of the Open Society Institute. It was spun off into an independent organisation in 2006. The merger gave the Natural Resource Charter greater implementation capacity and helped Revenue Watch to rebrand following its expansion beyond issues of transparency.

Paul has continued to have an important influence on the transparency and resource governance agendas. A copy of his book *The Plundered Planet: Why we must – and how we can – manage nature for global prosperity*,[24] made it into the hands of UK Prime Minister David Cameron. Collier was then invited by Cameron to lead the development agenda of the 39th G8 summit. The summit was hosted in 2013 by the United Kingdom and the official theme was tax evasion and transparency. Collier worked to develop a platform among the members. His message to Cameron was that the G8 should put its own house in order in ways that are helpful to the poorest developing countries. Five of the eight members of the G8 – the US, UK, Italy, Germany and France – committed to join the EITI. Britain announced a legally required public register of true ownership of all companies to expose the practice of using shell companies to hide shady natural resource deals. Europe and Canada agreed to follow the lead of the United States and issue mandatory requirements for resource revenue disclosure. The G8 committed to act on OECD research on the best ways to address profit shifting to low-tax jurisdictions.[25]

'Resources are not a curse, they are an asset,' said Paul. 'They're an asset, which if you screw it up, becomes a curse. But the real story is that there is huge potential for harnessing development.' The reforms by the G8 were underpinned by more than a decade of collective work on increasing transparency for better management of natural resources. In the next section we follow attempts by the United States, Europe and Canada to go beyond voluntary standards and require project-by-project corporate disclosure of resource revenues.

A mandatory standard after all

Years of lobbying and preparatory work by the members of the Publish What You Pay coalition paid off in July 2010, when the Cardin-Lugar Amendment (Section

1504) to the United States Dodd-Frank Wall Street Reform and Consumer Protection Act was signed into law. The financial reforms outlined within the Act were in response to the calamity of the Global Financial Crisis. In the crisis PWYP saw opportunity. And the long-debated and perennially unsuccessful draft bills on revenue transparency in the extractive sector found their vessel into law. The amendment, co-sponsored by Democratic Senator Ben Cardin and Republican Senator Richard Lugar, requires extractive resource companies (oil, gas and mining) who are listed on a US stock exchange to annually disclose their payments to host country governments by country and by project.

The United States Securities and Exchange Commission (SEC) released the rules guiding the revenue disclosures in August of 2012. But in October the American Petroleum Institute, the US Chamber of Commerce, the National Foreign Trade Council, and the Independent Petroleum Association of America sued the SEC claiming the regulations imposed excessive compliance costs, compelled speech in violation of their First Amendment right, and were anti-competitive because they privileged state-owned oil companies not listed on stock exchanges.[26] The District Court for the District of Columbia ruled in July 2013 against the SEC on procedural grounds and vacated the SEC rules applying to Section 1504. The court ruled that the SEC failed to justify the decision to require public disclosure of government payments by extractive companies and to not allow exemptions for countries that prohibit disclosure.[27] The SEC must now redraft the implementing regulations.

In contrast to the oil industry, the mining industry chose not to challenge the SEC. There may be a number of reasons for this. State-owned companies represent a minority of the companies that make up the mining industry, so mining multinationals might be less disadvantaged by transparency rules that would only apply to them. The mining industry participates in fewer joint ventures, so it may be less technically challenging to disaggregate payments by project. The mining sector may even have calculated that transparency reduces investment risks and puts pressure on governments to spend resource revenues wisely. Clare Short believes that the difference in approach may represent 'a general change in the ethos of mining', where the industry has come to understand that you have got to be respectful of people or you are going to get yourselves into trouble. A lesson learnt from having communities directly surrounding mining operations.

An even further reason might be that mandatory transparency regulation is now catching on internationally. Legislation mirroring the Cardin-Lugar Amendment is now in place in Europe and is in preparation in Canada. The 2013 revisions to the EU Accounting and Transparency Directives require listed and large non-listed companies in the extractive sector to report payments to governments. In Canada civil society groups, PWYP Canada and the Revenue Watch Institute, even worked together with the Mining Association of Canada and the Prospectors and Developers Association of Canada to collaboratively recommend an approach for disclosure after Canada signalled its intentions to enact mandatory requirements. The Canadian Association of Petroleum Producers declined to join the group.[28]

Of the world's 100 largest mining companies, 40 are listed on a US stock exchange, and thus captured by Section 1504 of the Dodd-Frank Act; 28 are listed on an EU-regulated exchange, and thus captured by the EU Transparency and Accounting Directives; one is listed on the Oslo Stock exchange and subject to Norwegian transparency rules enacted in January 2014; and 16 are listed on the Toronto stock exchange, and stand to be captured by transparency initiatives in preparation in Canada. Together these jurisdictions account for 58 of the world's largest mining companies.[29]

The issue of transparency has come a long way since *Breaking New Ground*, the final report of the MMSD, suggested that:

> Concerted effort is needed to combat corruption – governments should adopt national legislation to put the anti-corruption convention of the Organisation for Economic Co-operation and Development into effect. Companies could work with organizations such as Transparency International at the national level to establish industry-wide guidance. Industry organizations should consider taking the initiative, possibly in partnership with an international organization such as The World Bank, to establish an international and public register of all payments by mining companies to governments at all levels.[30]

More than a decade later the global achievements in transparency have exceeded the vision of the MMSD. An international standard, supported by a critical mass of governments and companies has been established. More than half of the world's largest mining companies will soon fall under mandatory rules for disclosure of payments by project, and the concept of transparency itself is now being subsumed under the rubric of natural resource governance in new initiatives aimed at improving decision-making in the management of mineral resources for sustainable development. Challenges remain. Countries like Australia and Hong Kong, which are home to major mining companies, have yet to commit to the EITI or develop mandatory disclosure standards.[31] Transfer pricing, tax evasion, tax holidays, corruption and the application of first-in-first-assessed exploration regimes for known mineral deposits are all too common in the sector, as we saw with the travails of Mamadie Touré, the widow Guinea's former President. In the final chapter of the book we look at the issue of agency, and we ask whether, and if so how, the mines are a-changin'.

Notes

1   The above account of the Simandou case drew on the following sources: Radden Keefe, P. (2013), 'Buried secrets: How an Israeli billionaire wrested control of one of Africa's biggest prizes.' *The New Yorker*. 8 July; Ax, J. (2014), 'Frenchman gets two years in U.S. prison for role in Guinea mine scandal.' *Reuters*. 25 July. Online resource: http://www.reuters.com/article/2014/07/25/us-usa-guinea-mining-idUSKBN0FU23S20140725 Accessed: 20 January 2015; Flynn A. (2014), 'Rio Tinto, Guinea seal deal on $US20 billion Simandou mine.' *The Australian*. 27 May. Online resource: http://www.

theaustralian.com.au/business/mining-energy/rio-tinto-guinea-seal-deal-on-us20-billion-simandou-mine/story-e6frg9df-1226932660235 Accessed: 20 January 2015; Comité Technique de Revue des Titres et Conventions Miniers (CTRTCM) (2014), 'Publication of the Report and Recommendation of the CTRTCM on the Licenses and Mining Convention Obtained by VBG.' 9 April. Conakry. Online resource: http://www.contratsminiersguinee.org/blog/publication-report-recommendation-VBG. html Accessed: 20 January 2015; Global Witness (2014), 'FBI surveillance implicates diamond billionaire in plan to subvert US fraud probe.' 9 April. Online resource: http://www.globalwitness.org/sites/default/files/library/GW%20BSGR%20report%20 -%2009.04.14.pdf Accessed: 20 January 2015; Huissier de Justice (2014), Transcription de l'enregistrement audio des conversations entre M. Cilins et Mme Touré.' Online resource: https://s3.amazonaws.com/s3.documentcloud.org/documents/1105519/ transcription-enregistrement-audio-frederic.pdf Accessed: 20 January 2015.

2   Global Witness. (1999), 'A crude awakening: The role of the oil and banking industries in Angola's civil war and the plunder of state assets.' December. London, p. 21.

3   Global Witness (1999), 'A crude awakening,' p. 9.

4   Global Witness (1999), 'A crude awakening,' p. 9.

5   Browne, J. (2010), *Beyond Business*, p. 115.

6   Global Witness (2001), 'Campaign success: BP makes move for transparency in Angola.' Press release: 12 February. Online resource: http://www.globalwitness.org/ library/campaign-success-bp-makes-move-transparency-angola Accessed: 19 January 2015.

7   Global Witness (2002), 'All the Presidents' men.' March. London; Browne (2010), *Beyond Business*.

8   Global Witness (2001), 'Campaign success'; Global Witness (2002), 'All the Presidents' men'; van Oranje, M. and H. Parham (2009), 'Publishing what we learned: An assessment of the Publish What You Pay Coalition.' Browne (2010), *Beyond Business*.

9   Global Witness (2002), 'All the Presidents' men,' cover page.

10   Global Witness (2002), 'All the Presidents' men,' p. 1.

11   Global Witness. (2002), 'Publish what you pay.' Press release: 13 June. Online resource: http://www.globalwitness.org/library/publish-what-you-pay Accessed: 19 January 2015; van Oranje and Parham (2009), 'Publishing what we learned'; Publish What You Pay (PWYP) (2011), 'About us.' Online resource: http://www.publishwhatyoupay. org/about Accessed; 20 January 2015.

12   Auty, R. (1993), *Sustaining Development in Mineral Economies: The resource curse thesis.* London and New York: Routledge.

13   Sachs, J. and A. Warner. (1997), 'Natural resource abundance and economic growth.' Centre for International Development and Harvard Institute for International Development. Harvard University, Cambridge, MA. November; Collier, P. and A. Hoeffler. (1999), 'Justice-seeking and loot-seeking in civil war.' The World Bank, 17 February, Washington, DC; Ross (1999), 'The political economy of the resource curse'; Ross, M. (2001), 'Extractive sectors and the poor: An Oxfam America report.' October. Boston: Oxfam America; The empirical basis for the resource curse has also been challenged by a number of authors, for example: Brunnschweiler, C.N. and E.H. Bulte (2008), 'Linking natural resources to slow growth and more conflict.' *Science*, 320(5876): 616–617.

14   Ross (2001), 'Extractive sectors and the poor,' p. 4.

15   van Oranje and Parham (2009), 'Publishing what we learned'; Browne (2010), *Beyond Business*.

16   Mining Journal (2002), 'UK calls for transparency.' 6 September, 339(8701). Online resource: http://www.infomine.com/news/mining.journal/Sep06-02.pdf   Accessed: 15 January 2015; van Oranje and Parham (2009), 'Publishing what we learned'; Moburg, J. and E. Rich. (2013), 'Beyond governments: lessons on multi-stakeholder

governance from the Extractive Industries Transparency Initiative (EITI).' Online resource: https://eiti.org/files/08_Moberg_Rich.pdf Accessed: 19 January 2015.

17 Blair, T. (2003), Speech by Tony Blair, UK Prime Minister. Extractive Industries Transparency Initiative, London Conference, 17 June. Online resource: http://collections.europarchive.org/tna/20070701080507/http://www.dfid.gov.uk/pubs/files/eitidraftreportspeech.pdf Accessed: 19 January 2015.

18 Moburg and Rich (2013), 'Beyond governments.'

19 Extractive Industries Transparency Initiative (EITI) (2014), 'Investors' statement on transparency in the extractives sector.' November. Online resource: https://eiti.org/files/Investors-November-2014.pdf Accessed: 20 January 2015.

20 Extractive Industries Transparency Initiative (EITI) (2014), 'Progress Report 2014: Making transparency matter.' Online resource: https://eiti.org/files/EITI_ProgressReport_2014_En_Web_Interactif_r.pdf Accessed: 20 January 2014.

21 Ross, M. (2013), 'EITI 2.0.' Keynote address. International Mining for Development Conference, 20 May Sydney. Transcript. Online resource: http://www.resourcegovernance.org/news/blog/eiti-20 Accessed: 17 January 2015.

22 Uongozi Institute (2013), 'Tanzania Natural Resource Charter expert panel launched.' Online resource: http://www.uongozi.or.tz/news_detail.php?news=1873 Accessed: 21 January 2015.

23 Natural Resource Governance Institute (NRGI) (2014), 'Natural Resource Charter.' 2nd edn.

24 Collier, P. (2010), *The Plundered Planet: Why we must – and how we can – manage nature for global prosperity*. New York: Oxford University Press.

25 United Kingdom Prime Minister's Office (2013), '2013 Lough Erne G8 Leaders' Communiqué.' Online resource: https://www.gov.uk/government/uploads/system/uploads/attachment_data/file/207771/Lough_Erne_2013_G8_Leaders_Communique.pdf Accessed: 21 January 2015.

26 Lynch, S. (2012), 'Business groups sue SEC over Dodd-Frank anti-bribery rule.' *Reuters*. October. Online resource: http://www.reuters.com/article/2012/10/11/us-sec-lawsuit-idUSBRE8991NL20121011 Accessed: 21 January 2015; American Petroleum Institute (API) (2012), 'API files court challenge against costly, anti-competitive SEC rule.' October. Online resource: http://www.api.org/news-and-media/news/newsitems/2012/oct-2012/api-files-court-challenge-against-costly-sec-rule Accessed: 21 January 2015; American Petroleum Institute (API) (2013), 'API lauds court win ending SEC's anti-competitive disclosure rule.' July. Online resource: http://www.api.org/news-and-media/news/newsitems/2013/july-2013/api-lauds-court-win-ending-sec-anti-competitive-disclosure-rule Accessed: 21 January 2015; United States District Court for the District of Columbia (US DCDC) (2013), 'American Petroleum Institute et al., v. Securities and Exchange Commission and Oxfam America.' Civil Action no. 12-1668.

27 US DCDC (2013), 'American Petroleum Institute et al.'

28 Balleny, L. (2013), 'Miners less resistant to transparency than big oil.' *Thomson Reuters Foundation*. 1 August. Online resource: http://www.trust.org/item/20130801110131-vilez/ Accessed: 21 January 2015.

29 Publish What You Pay United States (PWYP US) (2014), 'Transparency on the move: Payment disclosure by the world's largest oil, gas & mining companies.' March. Online resource: http://pwypusa.org/sites/default/files/Company%20Coverage%20Fact%20Sheet_Final.pdf Accessed: 21 January 2015.

30 IIED and WBCSD (2002), *Breaking New Ground*, p. xxx.

31 Australia has been on of the largest financial contributors of the EITI is not compliant or a candidate country. In October 2011 the Australian government made a commitment to 'pilot' the EITI. At the time of writing the government has not yet announced whether they will apply to become an EITI candidate.

7 Mountain movers

The bald mountain

Geology is the study of pressure and time. Under pressure all mountains yield, wasting their mass into the sea. Mostly this takes a very long time, but on occasion big things happen fast. In 1979, on a property in the state of Pará, Brazil, a child found a six-gram gold nugget. By the end of the week 1,000 peasant miners rushed the property. Within five weeks there were 10,000. At its peak 100,000 miners worked the deposit. Industrial mining projects can move a mountain in around 10–20 years. The *garimpeiros* of Brazil managed to move Serra Pelada, the 'bald mountain' within about five.[1] Even the powerless can move mountains when they are powered by hope.

In this chapter we look at the dynamics behind change for sustainable development in the mining industry and we return to the questions posed in the preface of this book: How far has the industry come? Has the process of change been authentic? Where has change occurred? And what were the key drivers? Have the people demanding or delivering on change found success? How did they do it?

The chapter begins by looking at the regulatory instruments that have shaped reform. We then turn our analysis to the agents of change and the interactions between them, before finally, we look back on the MMSD to see how far the industry has come, and what the future might hold for the sustainable development agenda.

A governance 'ecosystem'

Each of the change-agents I interviewed during the writing of this book shared with me a unique perspective on whether, and if so how, the mining industry could simultaneously address its environmental impacts and advance human and social development. There was, however, strong convergence on the importance of appropriate governance and oversight in shaping the outcomes of mineral development. Yes, corporate professionals showed a preference toward voluntary approaches, but even within this group there was an acknowledgement that national and global sustainability standards were crucial to the success of mining.[2]

Table 5 Common types of regulation applied to sustainability issues in mining

Types of regulation	How they work?	Featured examples
International standards, legal instruments/norms and frameworks	*Standards*: An international standard setting organization develops a standard that is voluntarily or enforced through certification. Certification may influence consumer behavior, be required by law, or be a condition of membership of an association. *Legal instruments/norms*: International legal instruments compel behavior through international law. International norms are non-legally binding and are adopted as a result of social pressure or peer expectation. *Frameworks*: International frameworks provide advice on effective or desirable policy and practice.	*Standards*: Extractive Industries Transparency Initiative; Kimberley Process Certification Scheme; Guiding Principles on Business and Human Rights; Voluntary Principles on Security and Human Rights; International Standards Organization guidance on social responsibility; International Cyanide Management Code for the Manufacture, Transport, and Use of Cyanide in the Production of Gold; Responsible Jewellery Council Code of Practices; and Initiative for Responsible Mining Assurance. *Legal instruments/norms*: International Labour Organization; Indigenous and Tribal Peoples Convention; and United Nations Declaration on the Rights of Indigenous Peoples. *Frameworks*: Africa Mining Vision; Natural Resource Charter; United Nations Millennium Development Goals; United Nations Sustainable Development Goals; New Partnership for Africa's Development; Protect, Respect and Remedy; International Study Group on Africa's Mineral Regimes; and Global Compact.
Industry standards	An industry develops a standard (commonly led by a peak industry association) that is observed due to peer expectations or to maintain membership of an industry association. Industry associations develop guidance in support of the standards.	International Council on Mining and Metals Sustainable Development Framework; International Council on Mining and Metals; Position Statement on Indigenous Peoples and Mining; The International Union for Conservation of Nature – International Council on Mining and Metals Memorandum of Understanding.

Corporate standards and policies	Corporations adopt policies and standards to guide and direct the practice of the company, its employees or the supply chain.	Anglo American Social Way and Socio-Economic Toolbox; and Rio Tinto Biodiversity Strategy.
Government regulation	Government (national, provincial, local) uses law and policy to proscribe conduct (command and control), persuade (suasive instruments), or incentivize behavior (market based instruments).	Queensland Sustainable Resource Communities Policy (Australia); Northern Contaminated Sites Program (Canada); African National Congress State Intervention in the Minerals Sector (South Africa); and Cardin-Lugar Amendment to the United States Dodd-Frank Wall Street Reform and Consumer Protection Act (United States).
Conditions on finance and share market activism	*Conditions on finance:* Investors impose standards to be followed by loan recipients to reduce the risk associated with investment and to achieve desired performance outcomes. *Share market activism:* Investors use their equity stake to influence management decisions through corporate governance processes.	*Conditions on finance:* International Finance Corporation's Environmental and Social Performance Standards; International Finance Corporation's Compliance Advisor Ombudsman; and The Equator Principles.
Social regulation	Social groups persuade, encourage or force change in the behavior of individuals, institutions, government or corporations. Levers include reputation, conflict and blockades, strikes, elections, agreements, and partnerships. Civil society groups may seek to mobilise public opinion through campaigns and networks.	Publish What You Pay; Fatal Transactions; The Birdlife International – Rio Tinto Partnership; and Western Cape Communities Co-Existence Agreement.
Litigation	A court of law imposes actions on a party in the resolution of a dispute.	Milirrpum v. Nabalco Pty Ltd (1971); and Mabo v. Queensland (1992).

Mining projects become part of the settings in which they are built and they must therefore navigate the contextual and relational dynamics of what Julia Sagebien and Nicole Marie Lindsay have called 'governance ecosystems'. According to Sagebien and Lindsay:

> The relationships forming these interlocking acts of governance can be conceptualised as an ecosystem – a community of interacting organisms and their physical environment – where each organism and specific interaction between components shapes not only the organisms primarily involved in the interaction but also the entire system itself.[3]

The governance ecosystem that now shapes mining consists of an array of regulatory instruments, industry standards, international frameworks, social expectations and norms (see Table 5). Every instrument of reform influences, and is influenced by, all of the others and together they shape the performance of the industry.

We have seen that the past decade has been notable for the creation of international and industry standards for sustainable development in the mining industry. These standards have done a lot to promote and disseminate norms on what the industry should look like. Many of the standards were developed through a multi-stakeholder approach and the industry is awash with 'toolkits' and 'good practice guides' explaining how to implement them. While most of the standards are not binding, their strength is that they have brought constituents to the table willingly. From transparency to conflict, international consensus now exists on the standard of performance that should be expected. Of course consensus is not unanimity, but on the whole the standards are now mostly uncontested. The big challenge that remains is that the influence of these norms has not penetrated as deeply, into the body of mining organisations, or as widely, across the diversity of companies that make up the sector, as would be needed for truly transformative change.

There are a number of companies that have adopted corporate policy that come close to matching the ambitions voiced by civil society. These policies, sometimes developed in consultation with industry critics, or developed as part of a partnership or dialogue process, are a leading indicator of reform. But a gulf exists between the standards committed to on paper and industry performance on the ground. Between the industry's aspirations and its practice. It is not enough for companies to commit to new standards. Practising sustainability is hard. It will require deep changes to the core business of mining. Shifts in technology, shifts in the way projects are designed, and shifts in the way decisions are made. Even the most committed of companies will require outside assistance to translate policy into action, whether by harnessing innovations dreamed up in academic institutions, or by partnering with international agencies, civil society, or the broader public to learn from their unique knowledge and perspectives (see Table 6).

A second gulf that exists is between the policies adopted by the 'ICMM club', and the rest of the pack. This is not to say that bigger companies are necessarily always more responsible. Some small, but incredibly nimble, companies have

Table 6 Additional external influences on corporate sustainability performance

External influence	How it works?	Featured examples
Institutional capacity building	Programmes build the capacity of individuals and institutions to regulate and manage industry.	Mining for Development Initiative and International Mining for Development Centre (Australia); Canadian International Resources and Development Institute; United Nations Environment Programme Post-conflict Peacebuilding and Natural Resources Programme; and United Nations Development Programme Strategy for Supporting Sustainable and Equitable Management of the Extractive Sector for Human Development.
Research programmes, institutes and networks	Research generates new knowledge and innovation, or applies existing knowledge to conceptual and practical problems.	Mining Certification Evaluation Project; United Nations Sustainable Development Solutions Network; International Institute for Environment and Development; Sustainable Minerals Institute, The University of Queensland; Centre for Sustainability in Mining and Industry, University of the Witwatersrand; Mining and the Environment Research Network; Cambridge Institute for Sustainability Leadership. *Other centres of excellence in mining research and teaching*: Centre for Energy, Petroleum and Mineral Law and Policy, University of Dundee; Mining Business School, Universidad Católica del Norte, Chile; Columbia Centre on Sustainable Investment; Colorado School of Mines; Norman B. Keevil Institute of Mining Engineering, University of British Columbia.
Public dialogues and reviews	*Dialogue processes*: Creation of a public space to share experiences and perspectives, reflect, and alter behaviour. *Reviews*: Analysis of a problem and recommendations for changes in policy and practice.	*Dialogue processes*: Mining, Minerals and Sustainable Development Project; Dialogue Group on Mining and Sustainable Development (Peru); and Intergovernmental Forum on Mining, Minerals, Metals and Sustainable Development. *Reviews*: World Bank Extractive Industries Review; and International Finance Corporation Pangue Independent Review.

significant capacity in sustainable development issues. But the companies that belong to the International Council on Mining and Metals have tended to be the ones that have been the object of the most scrutiny and have been the most active in the sustainable development debates. ICMM members account for 40–50% of mining production. This is significant, but more than half of mining production is undertaken by mid-sized, junior, small-scale, artisanal and state-owned miners that have not been as closely engaged in the sustainability agenda. For these miners other forms of regulation are especially important.

Governments have faced dilemmas when regulating the mining industry. A common argument is that 'over regulating' the mining industry creates a disincentive for investment as miners seek out jurisdictions where the obligations are more lax. Maintaining an 'attractive investment climate' has for some countries meant reducing environmental and social obligations on project developers.[4] There is, however, evidence to suggest that such an approach may run counter to the interests of mining companies and their investors, let alone host countries and their communities. Once sunk, mining capital is anchored to the ore bodies that they mine. Academic literature on the factors that influence investment decision-making, suggest a number of unique features that differentiate the mining sector from other forms of foreign direct investment, including: high capital intensity, long lead times, finite life and the fixed geographic locality of mineral ores. James Otto's work on the influences on foreign investment in the mining industry found that the presence of practical legislation and policy to address environmental and social issues were reported to *attract* mineral investment.[5]

One possible explanation is that weak governance ecosystems may increase business risks and jeopardise the prospects for long-term success of developments. We saw in Chapter 5 that conflict between local communities and mining companies can translate the environmental and social risks generated by the industry into business costs for companies. This is one reason that investors place conditions on finance. The IFC Performance Standards and the Equator Principles, in particular, are as much about protecting capital from avoidable risk as they are about promoting responsibility.

There is no doubt that the mining industry has traditionally resisted stronger government regulation. In Chapter 2 we saw that the strong industry response to the issue of Native Title in Australia delayed, but did not stop, the eventual recognition of indigenous rights within the law. More recently the mining industry campaign against the introduction of the Resource Super Profits Tax and emissions trading in Australia not only led to the withdrawal of both proposals but also played an important role in the unseating of Australian Prime Minister Kevin Rudd. When governments do regulate greater environmental and social obligations on the industry these proposals sometimes do not survive the next change in government, lacking a constituency of voters affected by mining to defend the reforms. Governments are also sometimes guilty of imposing inflexible processes that may not actually improve on-the-ground outcomes.

Coordinated action by governments can help to overcome the dilemmas that individual governments face. Frameworks like the Africa Mining Vision and The Natural Resource Charter, and gatherings like the Intergovernmental Forum on Mining, Minerals, Metals and Sustainable Development, promote alignment across jurisdictions to simultaneously lift standards and to minimise any jurisdiction-shopping that does occur.[6]

'Social regulation' also plays a very important regulatory role. In addition to conflict, social groups can influence the conduct of mining companies by denting a company's reputation, encouraging strikes by employees, or extracting concessions within agreements and partnerships. Civil society campaigns such as Fatal Transactions and Publish What You Pay have galvanised international action and been incredibly effective by appealing to public sentiment but also by influencing other types of regulation. Anne Jung, one of the founders of the Fatal Transactions campaign, has written that the central task of campaigning should be to 'create critical publics and simultaneously to bring back politics to the centre stage of claims'. She wrote that campaigners must find 'new forms of action and communication' to 'keep the public interest awake and awaken it in new circles.'[7]

For the commodities that are consumer facing, like gold and precious stones, the threat of a backlash can be very powerful. As we saw in Chapter 5, certification schemes like the Responsible Jewellery Council Code of Practices and the Kimberley Process have provided choice for consumers wanting to purchase responsible jewellery. In the case of thermal coal, for example, consumer awareness about the effects of climate change have led to schemes offering the purchase of green power. For commodities like copper, iron ore or manganese, whose consumers are not the general public, effective action relies on the responsibility of refiners and other entities down the supply chain, government regulation, or direct action against mining companies by social movements.

The governance ecosystem of mining is diverse. Depending on the commodity, the issue, the geography, the company or the government, an extraordinary array of sustainable development outcomes are possible. There are some 'habitats' where oversight of mining is weak and others where the industry is more tightly regulated. Some companies are attracted to weak governance ecosystems; their niche is in high-risk spaces, where the rewards may be larger, and where short cuts are incentivised. Other companies prefer to play it safe where higher environmental and social standards are welcome to the extent that they contribute to more successful, and thus more profitable projects.

The diffusion of sustainability ideas – horizontally between localities, and vertically from the grassroots up and from executives down – requires people.[8] In the following section we look at the agents of change and the art, and science, of their practice.

Inside-out

The whole room looked like it was made of copper and I was standing in the one place on the planet where there was a good possibility that it was. At the far wall, above what looked like an altar, was what looked like a cross. It was the company logo of CODELCO, Chile's state-owned copper company, and we were meeting in the boardroom in Santiago. The host of our meeting directed one of his staff to give the 'safety share', a common ritual in the mining industry where employees tell a story about safety to keep it front of mind. 'I want to share with you my hope that CODELCO is a company that produces happy copper cathodes,' he said. 'Cathodes that are created with environmental integrity across the whole value chain. Cathodes that are pure.'

Half-way across the globe on London's River Thames I spoke to Tom Burke, Environmental Policy Advisor for Rio Tinto and the Former Executive Director Friends of the Earth. We met Tom in Chapter 1 when he played an important role in the design of the Global Mining Initiative (GMI), the parent programme of the MMSD. 'It's not hard to be proud of the GMI because it was quite a big thing,' said Tom, but 'what I am most proud of is birds.' Burke was recruited into Rio Tinto to provoke new ideas. On his first tour of Rio Tinto's mines he met a fellow birder, Pete Outhwaite, at Richards Bay, South Africa. Tom had the idea to engage Rio Tinto's employees in bird watching and conservation programmes. He set up a partnership with Birdlife International. The programme has lasted more than 14 years. 'Things you do for birds are bound to be good for the environment as a whole,' said Tom; 'Birds are universal.'

These two stories, and many others like them, point to an industry that is more comfortable with the sustainable development agenda. Employees are now recruited from a wider range of backgrounds and with a wider range of perspectives. Christine Bader calls these internal change-agents 'Corporate idealists'. In her book, *The Evolution of a Corporate Idealist*, Bader recounts her experience working inside BP. 'I realized that I am part of a global army of people fighting for better environmental and social practices inside multi-national companies – with mixed success,' writes Bader. 'We believe business can be a force for good, even as we struggle with our own contradictions … We defend our companies to investors and campaigners, but insist to our colleagues that we're not doing enough.'[9]

The change-agents working inside companies must navigate a complex corporate landscape. Their role often requires them to understand the mining business and the environmental and social context; to network across the company and outside of it; to mount persuasive arguments to incrementally win improvements in corporate policy and to institutionalise corporate policy into management decisions that improve corporate practice. Their work is necessarily reformist. Most often when they count wins, they are in increments, but they are buoyed by the fact that small changes to big organisations can have huge consequences.[10] Tom Burke shared with me some of the traits that he acquired working inside Rio Tinto:

I've learnt to speak corporate, I've accomplished what I set out to do, which was to learn and understand how big companies work, how business works, how it thinks, and that spreads into all the other things I do. That's been tremendous. You're getting a grounding in a way that you can't get from outside in: what are the conversations that really matter?

Understanding organisational dynamics and constraints and speaking in the language that decisions are made are crucial aspects to being an internal change-agent. Corporate idealists are sometimes viewed with suspicion. Those on the outside are suspicious of their association with the company and those on the inside are suspicious of their association with social movements and affected communities; and of the fact that they come from non-traditional disciplinary backgrounds. This creative friction, however, is from where they draw their success. The ability to operate in multiple worlds helps corporate idealists to propose novel solutions for mutual betterment.

There are people working within companies who play an important role in sustainable development, however, who don't see themselves as idealists. These change-agents draw less from moral or value-based motivations and more from a philosophy of corporate pragmatism. 'I see myself as a manager,' admitted Jon Samuel when I asked him about his motivations working within Anglo American. Jon is Group Head Government and Social Affairs, as we learnt in Chapter Four. 'Some of the people who I've seen who've been most effective actually tend to see themselves as managers, rather than as specialists,' argues Jon. 'I genuinely believe that for mining companies to get this right it's a source of competitive advantage. That's what we talk about, we talk about managing risk; so stopping bad things from happening to us, and trying to create positive space for us as a business.' The precise mix of idealism and pragmatism that motivates corporate change-agents is unique to each person but as the business case for sustainable development has strengthened there becomes less of a reliance on idealists. Sustainability just becomes part of doing business.

The extent of sustainability thinking has grown in some companies, but it is also true that a very substantial proportion companies in the mining industry do not possess the organisational culture or capacity necessary for improvements in performance. Organisations need the right people, with the right competencies, in the right positions. Individuals must be nurtured and supported, and aware of the corporate culture that is necessary to drive change. 'Every case of good practice that we see seems to have common elements,' said Ed O'Keefe, Director of sustainability consultancy, Synergy Global. 'There's always a champion, usually an individual at the heart of it that is driving change,' and frequently cases of good practice come from 'companies that have screwed up, and they've learnt their lessons and they've kind of been shocked into it.' Ed believes that the industry must do more to support practitioners working in sustainability roles, and part of that is by promoting awareness of change management. 'What's really needed is for people to work through that change management process and work out precisely what they need.'

Strengthening professional practice is the focus of the Community Relations Research Unit, ComRel, established at the Centre for Social Responsibility in Mining at the University of Queensland. Associate Professor Deanna Kemp is the Director of the ComRel Unit. She believes that professionals working in Community Relations roles benefit from exchanging experiences and knowledge about their practice. 'I worked in Community Relations in mining for many years myself, and there wasn't anything like this,' said Deanna. 'There was nothing to tap. There was very little knowledge to draw on. There was very little recognition of this as a very important professional area, so I'm building something that I once had a need for.'

Action on sustainability in a corporate setting also requires leadership. Whether it was Tom Burke speaking of Sir Robert Wilson (Chairman of Rio Tinto), Jon Samuel speaking of Cynthia Carroll and Mark Cutifani (CEOs of Anglo American), Bruce Harvey, speaking of Leon Davis, (CEO of Conzinc Rio Tinto of Australia), George Littlewood, speaking of Hugh Morgan (CEO of WMC Resources) or David Rice speaking of John Browne (CEO of British Petroleum), all of these corporate change-agents believed the culture necessary for transitions to sustainable development started at the top.

The change in Rio Tinto's corporate culture to address Indigenous rights, discussed in Chapter 2, is a case in point. Leon Davis took a risk and broke ranks with the industry. He also gave 'permission' to those working within the corporate hierarchy to experiment with a new way of doing business. According to Paul Wand and Bruce Harvey this permission was crucial. 'For the individuals concerned,' they wrote 'this knowledge that possible initial dissent will not result in severance empowered their conviction, and over time it disempowered those with other motivations.'[11] 'Constructive dissent and debate' was an important part of the reform process inside the company that would not have been possible without a licence from the top.

Outside-in

If reform from the inside of companies is enabled from the top, it should be of no surprise that pressure from the outside is powered by the bottom. Social movements and civil society organisations are fundamental to institutional reform. There is not a single case of mining industry reform that was profiled in this book that did not rely on external demands for change. The power of social movements comes from the scale and size of the movement, the tenacity of small groups of committed activists, and the authority of the voices calling for change. In mining the most authoritative voices tend to be from the communities affected by mines.

Paul Jourdan, whom we met in Chapter 4, believes that, 'It's only outside pressure and laws that have caused [the mining industry] to change.' Paul is a veteran of the anti-apartheid movement and spent time in exile in Mozambique. The Mozambique Liberation Front, FRELIMO, won independence to the rallying cry of *a luta continua*, 'the struggle continues'. 'I've never seen any change in the mining industry,' said Paul, 'I've only seen them adapting to new environments.'

Like the inside change-agents, profiled above, those on the outside are guided by various models of change. There are campaigners, there are brokers, and there are those that engage with the industry (Table 7). Campaigners raise awareness and pressure through outreach, media, protests, research and direct action. They organise and they build movements for change. In reality there is an incredible

Table 7 Types of change-agents working inside and outside of the mining industry

	Inside		Outside		
	Managers	Corporate idealists	Engagers	Brokers	Campaigners
	Orientation: The world as it presently is	*Orientation:* The world as it presently is	*Orientation:* The world as it presently is	*Orientation:* The world as it is or as it ought to be	*Orientation:* The world as it ought to be
	Role: Manage sustainability as a necessary business issue	*Role:* Find novel solutions for mutual benefit; bridge inside and outside organisation	*Role:* Form partnerships; engage; understand inside constraints; propose and trial alternatives	*Role:* Assist people with knowledge or moral authority to find an audience; build networks	*Role:* Use outreach, media, protests, research and direct action to raise awareness; build pressure
	Philosophy: Pragmatism	*Philosophy:* Practical idealism and reformism	*Philosophy:* Practical idealism and reformism	*Philosophy:* Progressivism	*Philosophy:* Idealism and radicalism
	Political approach: Respond to the political climate; willing to roll back reforms if necessary	*Political approach:* Respond to the political climate; create internal moments; resist roll back of reforms; preserve assets	*Political approach:* Respond to the political climate; assist insiders to create internal moments	*Political approach:* Create the political climate; help inform people to make better decisions	*Political approach:* Create the political climate; maintain pressure when climate turns
	Who: Corporate managers; traditional backgrounds	*Who:* Specialist corporate professionals; non-traditional backgrounds	*Who:* Professional civil society organisations; and applied academics	*Who:* Specialist civil society organisations; activists; critical and applied academics; international institutions	*Who:* Civil society organisations; activists; citizens; critical academics; affected communities

variety of approaches to campaigning even within a single organisation. What campaigners have in common is a mixture of idealism and radicalism. The Wassa Association of Communities Affected by Mining (WACAM) works with Ghanaian mining communities to build their capacity to advocate about environmental and human rights issues. The *Wahana Lingkungan Hidup Indonesia* (WAHLI), or Indonesian Forum for the Environment, has exposed the environmental and human rights abuses of mining companies operating in Indonesia. The *Observatorio de Conflictos Mineros de América Latina* collates and shares information about community campaigns against mining projects in Latin America. Global Witness is an organisation known for cutting investigative research and deft behind the scenes networking. 'Sometimes it's been like fighting in a trench with a baseball bat,' said Simon Taylor co-founder and Director of Global Witness; 'Other times it's been incredibly subtle and delicate and balanced.'

Vidalina Morales de Gámez is a small-scale farmer and mother of five. She has been organising against large-scale metallic mining in El Salvador since 2006, when she became aware of the El Dorado mining project and its potential impact on her community in the northern department of Cabañas. After first hearing about the project, and the benefits, as described by the project proponents, Vidalina sought out the perspectives of other impacted communities. It started as a personal interest, but Vidalina then 'got organised', joining with others to be part of wider coalitions of resistance. Vidalina explained to me her motivations:

> One of the first reasons in which I became involved in this struggle is because I, and my ancestors, have lived close to the land. Our survival is based on harmony with nature. With the water. With the earth. With everything in our environment. That has been the way of life for our ancestors … And we have felt that mining, rather than being a benefit for our communities, for our environment, ends up being a total change in the way of life of the people in the communities. Clearly our aspirations are not to have the greatest or newest technology, but to pass on to future generations what we have received from past generations …mining would totally destroy what we have been able to conserve up until today in our communities.

The grass roots campaign was initially focused on local awareness raising but pressure grew at the national level and in 2008 El Salvador's then President, Antonio Saca, declared that the government would oppose the granting of mining permits. The administrative pause on mining was continued by Saca's successors, Mauricio Funes and Salvador Sánchez Cerén. Pacific Rim Mining Corp., the Canadian owners of the El Dorado project, pursued arbitration against the Republic of El Salvador in the International Centre for Settlement of Investment Disputes claiming losses of US$77 million.[12] The outcome of the claim is pending.

Vidalina took her campaign to Canada as a representative of the National Roundtable Against Metallic Mining in El Salvador, and then to Australia, home of the new owners of El Dorado when the project changed hands. MiningWatch Canada and other organisations supported Vidalina's Canadian tour to raise awareness. In Australia she was supported by the Australian Unions, Mineral Policy Institute and Oxfam Australia, among others. The campaign is seeking legislation to ban all metallic mining in El Salvador. I asked Vidalina what makes her most proud when she reflects on her activism. Her answer was simple: that she has been true to herself. That she has lived a life respectful of her ancestors. 'Mother Nature, that's what fills me with love during this struggle.'

MiningWatch Canada is a mining advocacy organisation that campaigns and brokers for change. The organisation has assisted scores of people like Vidalina to raise awareness about how Canadian companies operate overseas and to lobby government, international institutions, investors and companies for reform. We met Catherine Coumans, Research Coordinator and Asia Pacific Program Coordinator of MiningWatch Canada, in Chapter 3. I asked Catherine about how they approach their advocacy work:

> We're very flexible and opportunistic, and we're very strategic. We'll push and push and push on a certain issue and if it doesn't budge and some little crack opens up somewhere else we'll go, oh look, this little crack's opened up and we'll rush over there and we'll push and push and push there and suddenly boom, we get a bit of a breakthrough ... We're very plugged in, we know what's going on at the UN, we know what's going on at the national government level, we know what's going on with the corporations, we know what's going on at the ICMM and we're constantly aware of all these connections and the languages being used and the framing of things ... When we're involved with communities on the ground, we're extremely aware of when a particular issue that's arising within a particular community is the right thing for us to bring forward because this is going to provide the kind of timely example that will accelerate change. So we're very acute at figuring out what those issues are, and then we just plug away at things, we literally just plug away at things and we try to bring as many people on board as we can.

Exploiting the cracks is an effective way to move mountains but there is more to the MiningWatch approach than campaigning. 'The thing that I always really love,' said Catherine, 'is when finally, people who thought they were extremely far from the centres of power, who felt that they were extremely unlikely to be heard, or have any influence over their own situation, suddenly find out that they do and they can.' Catherine has organised international visits and brokered new networks for many people impacted by mining. People whose authority comes from real experience.

Brokers network people, but they also connect people with knowledge. They link the producers of knowledge with the users and it is through these connections that new decisions are made. Knowledge brokering is not the exclusive domain of civil-society, or even outside change-agents. Knowledge brokering inside organisations helps professionals to share experiences and improve practice, but brokering tends to be most effective when the broker is a trusted outsider. Academics and international institutions commonly play the role of a broker. The World Bank Institute and the African Development Bank, for example, created a community of practice called GOXI to broker knowledge about governance in the extractive industries.

The third type of outside change-agent are those that engage with the industry. These people may come from professional civil society organisations, like Birdlife International, WWF or the Nature Conservancy; sustainability consulting firms, like Banarra, Synergy, On Common Ground and Monkey Forest; or they may be applied academics, like myself. They gain exposure to the challenges faced by the industry and the internal constraints, and use their knowledge of the corporate environment to propose and trial alternatives and support the corporate idealists and managers working inside mining companies. Like campaigners and brokers, engagers are critical of industry practice, but they channel this critique into constructive solutions.

Academics that are engaged with the mining industry are motivated to make an impact with their work. Professor Chris Moran, the Director of the Sustainable Minerals Institute, at the University of Queensland, has said that his aim is to create an academic institute who's 'hand prints are apparent on an observable reduction in the footprint of the industry'. Professor David Boger, whom we met in Chapter 3, spent his career applying the discoveries that he made in the field of rheology, to new technologies to reduce the footprint of mine tailings. The Mining and Environment Research Network (MERN) was a large network of academic institutions that was active in the 1990s. MERN generated momentum for the study of sustainable development in the mining industry in the lead up to the MMSD.[13] In my own research on mining, I have tried to identify the problems and situations where academic research can make a difference to outcomes on the ground. In one study we looked at 30 multi-stakeholder groups that have formed to address the cumulative impacts of mining. We found that trust played an important role in the functioning of these groups and that one of the best ways to foster trust in these environments was for the groups to share food together. This finding would never make an impact in the academic literature but it was highly practical for the groups that were trying to work collaboratively together to address the impacts of mining.[14]

Applied academics also engage with governments and produce advocacy research for civil society. Michael Ross is a Professor at The University of California, Los Angeles. We met Michael in Chapter 6. Michael worked with Oxfam America to produce a seminal research report on mining and poverty in 2001. 'I was aware at the time when I produced it that it was also an advocacy piece,' he said. The academic thoroughness of the work lent credibility to the Oxfam campaign, and Oxfam's reach as an organisation amplified the impact of Michael's academic writing. 'If I had produced it just by myself it would never have received the light of day.' Michael drew from his earlier experiences with Greenpeace and his work as a Congressional Aide in the United States House of

Representatives to develop sense of social change, and how it worked, as well as to develop the skills to present material in a way that was more digestible to the public and more likely to get traction.

I asked Michael about whether he needs to justify to his colleagues the applied research and change advocacy that has been part of his academic career. 'If it was all that I did than I don't think I would be regarded with any great respect from my colleagues,' he said. 'I have to show that I can produce work that has academic merit as well and stands on its own among my peers, in addition to this other work.'

Academic work needn't be applied to have an impact. Professor Anthony Bebbington, Professor of Geography at Clark University, undertakes research on social movements, rural development and cultural change. Tony sees mining as an entry point for the study of wider phenomena. He sees a distinction between being applied and being relevant. 'Applied research is research that is applied to a particular problem and is trying to generate results to address that problem,' said Tony. 'Relevant research is research where you try and do it in a way that what you do and what you say will seem relevant to a whole range of social and political actors who are addressing the problems.'

The managers, corporate idealists, engagers, brokers and campaigners that are moving the mining industry in the direction of sustainable development do so within a complex and interactive web of agency. In the following section we look at the sometimes supportive, and sometimes antagonistic, relationships between these different agents.

The theatre of agency

Within the governance ecosystem of mining, the change-agents working on the outside, and those working on the inside, form a symbiotic relationship. On the outside, advocates use campaigning to highlight poor industry practice and to propose alternative ways of operating that are beyond the industry's current aspirations. Brokers bring people together to share experiences and knowledge in a safe environment. Engagers work with corporate idealists and managers inside companies to devise solutions to sustainability challenges and to help industry match on the ground practice with its often lofty rhetoric. Engagers also assist with improvements in corporate policy to inch the aspirations of industry forward.

The demands for change from the outside create internal space for the insiders to deliver on that change. Engagers have the advantage of understanding industry constraints, where campaigners may propose unworkable solutions. The campaigners who's trade is advocacy are not limited to only imagine a world that is politically acceptable within a company, but one that is possible in a world that is equitable and sustainable (see Figures 11 and 12).

Government policy-makers and the professionals within international institutions also play important roles in setting acceptable standards. Government regulation works by setting a regulatory bar to enforce a standard of acceptable industry practice and then deploys suasive and market-based instruments to

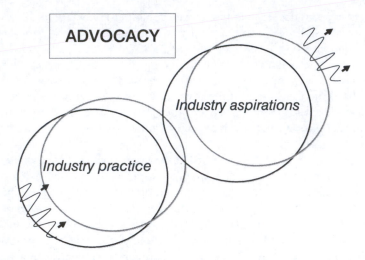

Figure 11 Diagram representing the focus areas for advocacy in bridging industry practice with industry aspirations toward sustainable development

Advocacy targets poor practice and weaknesses in the stated aspirations or policy of industry, with the aim to shift the industry towards stronger sustainability positions. Advocacy promotes an alternative future and encourages industry to adopt policy that better reflects this vision.

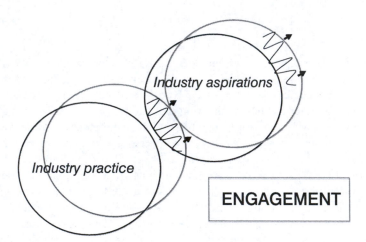

Figure 12 Diagram representing the focus areas for engagement in bridging industry practice with industry aspirations toward sustainable development

Engagement targets the mismatch between practice and stated aspirations and works with industry to deliver sustainability improvements. Engagement also works to reform and incrementally improve corporate sustainability policy.

incentivise performance above current practice and to encourage more ambitious industry aspirations.

While the relationships between change-agents can be symbiotic, they also have the potential to be downright parasitic. Tension, friction and misunderstanding can sour relationships, and undermine success. Corporate idealists often view advocates as impractical and relentlessly negative. Campaigners often think the insiders working on sustainable development issues, who more often than not used to be outsiders, are sell-outs that have traded their integrity for a corporate pay cheque, and a platinum frequent flyer status. While they may be relatively 'poor', campaigners think of themselves as passionate, and noble. Corporate idealists think campaigners must keep themselves warm at night with their self-righteous attitude. Sometimes the friction between different types of change-agents is plain silly. But by appreciating the different models of change sophisticated change-agents can understand the symbiotic relationships that can exist between people positioned both inside and out, and use the tensions between these models to be more effective.

In my work I have experienced lost friendships, because of my choice to engage with the mining sector. I also recall a time when I was active in Friends of the Earth, known for its grass-roots style of advocacy, and we jeered a colleague because he had chosen to join the more 'corporate' Greenpeace! It is natural to develop an allegiance to our colleagues and the model of change implicit in the way we work.

It is part of positioning one self in the world.

WWF has been one of the most successful engagement focused NGOs. Within the environmental movement WWF has been widely criticised for their brand of practical idealism working directly with companies to foster change. As we have seen in the early chapters of this book their record of delivery in the mining sector is impressive, but it represents a different culture than that of activist or campaigning NGOs. Knowing your niche can help a change-agent to not blur the boundaries too far. For example, there are huge risks for activist NGOs, who have a reputation for being a 'bulldog', to come 'inside the tent' and 'hop into bed' with the 'enemy'. But it shouldn't stop them from liaising closely with the NGOs comfortable with engagement, and performing in a bit of theatre. Corporate partnerships take years to mature and require constructive participation. Critical advocacy organisations might play a more meaningful role outside these partnerships, exerting influence by maintaining public pressure and strategising with the engaged civil society groups working on the inside.

Multi-stakeholder partnerships also require patience and present dilemmas for campaigning organisations if the pace of change is slow. In Chapter 5 we saw that Global Witness invested a lot in the creation of the Kimberley Process Certification Scheme, but pulled out after it felt the scheme was no longer delivering on its potential. Annie Dunnebacke, Deputy Campaigns Director of Global Witness, shared with me the reasoning. The questions we were asking were, 'At what point do you feel like by staying in you can still drive change and reform, and give something more meaning than it currently has? [And] at what point do you need to step away because, actually, your participation is (a) lending credibility to something that shouldn't have credibility [and (b)] undermining your own credibility?' she said.

These are very legitimate questions that are commonly raised during engagement with powerful institutions. There are no guarantees that reform will not give way to recidivism. Years of hard work can be erased quickly when the climate turns. For example, in the pockets of the mining industry where sustainability thinking is nurtured, large retrenchments of staff have accompanied the most recent industry downturn. Engaging the broader workforce in the change process can help to shield the business from such a loss, but such a large loss of the sustainability professionals that incubate change is bound to have an impact on corporate culture and corporate performance.

The change-agents engaging with companies must also appreciate the ethical and power dynamics that can potentially undermine their work, and make them vulnerable to being used. People and institutions under pressure became practised at deflecting demands for deeper reform. I was reminded of this when I attended a human rights conference in Phnom Penh, Cambodia. Cambodia is an economy dependent on international aid and with a history of serious human rights abuses. For thirty years Cambodia's wily Prime Minister, Hun Sen, has courted international aid but not bowed to its conditions. This art is also practised by his Ministers, but sometimes with less finesse. A Minister of Hun Sen's government opened the conference that I was attending. He spoke little about the topic but did share with the audience, and more specifically the Australian Ambassador, who was in the room, his unsuccessful attempts to spirit a kangaroo from Australia into Cambodia for his private zoo. To perplexed stares and nervous giggles the Minister reassured his crowd of humanitarians that kangaroo's were much easier to source from Thailand.

The scepticism, even cynicism, of the sustainability professionals that engage with the industry is fuelled by very real instances of 'greenwashing'. Front groups backed by industry funds can mask poor corporate performance, feign reform where no such reform exists, or manufacture 'grassroots' organisations who defend the status quo (a practice sometimes called 'astro-turfing'). This scepticism, however, is sometimes expressed in very personal ways. It can be incredibly destructive, hollowing out the middle ground and promoting adversarial relationships. Campaigners can sometimes too easily dismiss the first signs of reform as not enough, not appreciating that the first steps are the hardest to make and can create better conditions for future change. Campaigners may also not appreciate that for engagers sometimes working with the worst performer is the best strategy, as long as the company is open to new ways of doing things.

Experienced change-agents embrace the performance in agency. They seize the moment to take advantage of a good crisis and they prepare the ground to be ready for when a crisis hits. In the final section we return to the MMSD, look at how far the industry has come, and discuss what the future might hold for the sustainable development agenda.

Conclusion: The mines are they a-changin'?

It was mid-1998, nearly 20 years ago, when Hugh Morgan, Doug Yearly and Robert Wilson started to discuss the possibility of an initiative to examine sustainable development in the mining industry. These conversations led to the Global Mining Initiative, the Mining Minerals and Sustainable Development Project and its final report, *Breaking New Ground*, and the International Council for Mining on Metals, an industry association established to implement MMSD's agenda for change. In this book we have looked back on the history of many initiatives that have aimed to advance different areas of sustainability. In this final section I will reflect on whether the mining industry has indeed changed – first, by comparing the record of the post-MMSD period with the recommendations of *Breaking New Ground*; second, by considering the breadth and depth of change, the extent to which change has extended across the sector and been embedded within companies; and third, by questioning the longevity of change, and whether sustainable development is still a relevant discourse, capable of driving the next wave of reform.

There is no escaping the fact that for many of the issues addressed in detail by the MMSD, tangible improvements have been painfully slow. Reading *Breaking New Ground* today I am still struck by its relevance. The issues raised by civil society and affected communities today are the same issues that were recorded then. This is a testament to the team that lead the MMSD process and the quality of debate that it fostered, but it is also an indication that challenges remain.

Breaking New Ground synthesised the findings of the MMSD dialogue into a set of recommendations for the industry that we first looked at in Chapter 1 (Table 1 is repeated here as Table 8 for convenience). Returning to these recommendations again, in light of the previous chapters, we can see that a remarkable number have been achieved in the decade since the dialogue. The development of corporate policies and management systems; the adoption of the ICMM's Sustainable Development Framework to ensure industry implementation; the creation of project level grievance-handling and dispute resolution mechanisms; adoption of the principle of free, prior and informed consent from indigenous peoples; wider use of agreement-making with affected communities and indigenous peoples; the establishment of a register of all payments by mining companies to governments; the harmonisation of reporting requirements; and action on protected areas with the IUCN. All of these recommendations have been substantially fulfilled. National industry codes of conduct have not materialised outside of a handful of countries like Canada, South Africa, Mongolia and Australia.[15] Industry-wide grievance-handling mechanisms have remained elusive and government regulation of the industry has been patchy at best. But as a list of achievements it reads very well.

So what should we make of the fact that many of the challenges still remain, even while many of the solutions put forward by MMSD have been met?

Table 8 Summary of actions to support sustainable development in the minerals industry from the Mining, Minerals and Sustainable Development project

Summary of actions recommended by Breaking New Ground	
• Greater research and education to better understand the implications of mining and minerals production on sustainable development. • Development of corporate policies and management systems to embed sustainable development commitments. • Adoption of a global declaration by the minerals industry and a protocol to ensure industry-wide implementation (including independent auditing). • Development of national industry codes of conduct. • Drafting of a collective statement of principles by civil society outlining their expectations. • Improved government policy and regulation, including the avoidance of riverine disposal of tailings, and the wider adoption of financial surety to ensure rehabilitation after mine closure. • Better integration within impact assessment • Integrated planning for the closure of operations.	• Creation of project level and industry wide grievance handling and dispute resolution mechanisms. • Respect for the principle of free prior and informed consent from Indigenous Peoples. • Wider use of agreement making processes with communities and indigenous peoples. • Establishment of an international and public register of all payments by mining companies to governments at all levels to address corruption. • Harmonization of reporting guidelines. • Development of clear criteria between the mining industry and key actors like the IUCN on mining and protected areas. • Establishment of a global financial facility to remediate abandoned mines and a global initiative to address mining legacies. • Creation of an ongoing multi-stakeholder forum on mining, minerals and sustainable development.

Source: IIED and WBCSD, 2002, *Breaking New Ground*

One answer is that after a slow start many of the recommendations were only achieved relatively recently and it will take time for them to have an impact. Acceptance of FPIC by the industry only occurred in 2013, for example, and the first country to be found compliant by the EITI was only in 2009. Another answer is that the recommendations made by the MMSD were just the first down payment, on a much longer process of reform. Many of the problems the mining industry faces are complex, even wicked, and a list of recommendations, no matter how good they are, will fall short of representing transformational change. The issues may still be relevant but the proposed solutions now need updating. A further reason is that the expectations of society are also in flux. Professor Tony Hodge, former President of Friends of the Earth Canada, coordinator of MMSD North America, and now President of the ICMM, reflected on this issue during our interview:

> There is no doubt there has been massive change in the industry over the past 20 years. Things are happening today, that 20 years ago simply would never

have happened. Change is spectacular. Further, we are now beginning to recognise that there are bigger issues that provide an important overarching context – and this background context is also changing. So the question is not did MMSD do its work, did it come up with a recipe for change, is the industry changing, is it real? That's a way too superficial take on things, because there are phenomena changing in society – outside the industry – that are equally, perhaps more important than the change inside. So it's a moveable feast and the long-run waves of social change may be the key to understanding. The question is, what today, is the relationship between action within the mining industry and the evolution of society around the mining industry, and will that lead to an approach collectively? Will that lead to an approach moving forward that brings a sense of alignment between the values that are being expressed in society by the action of society and the values that are being expressed in the industry as reflected by the actions of the industry?

In the contemporary context the bridging of societal values and the values of the industry will take deep changes in corporate culture. Keith Slack, Global Program Manager of Oxfam America's Extractive Industries team, believes that there are still significant cultural hurdles that companies will need to overcome if they are to live up to their rhetoric:

> These are almost existential challenges that companies are going to have to face now as they ... re-envision themselves as not just extractors and entities that are set up to make a profit, but ones that are actually making a long-term contribution to sustainable development, which many of the more progressive-minded international companies say they want to do.

Turning to the extent to which change has been embedded within companies and extended across the sector, the results are mixed. George Littlewood, former Vice President of External Affairs for CRA and one of the nine *sherpas* of the Global Mining Initiative, put it this way:

> I would have hoped that through the MMSD process that [the earlier cultural change at Rio Tinto] would not only have been reinforced but also adopted on a much broader basis. But I think it lost its momentum ... ICMM is doing a very good job but you wish the industry itself had embedded the GMI learnings more deeply and widely.

Breaking New Ground found that 'some good companies are improving, but the bad are inexcusable, and the past record is even worse'.[16] As a statement, it is hard to dispute that this is not also true of today. A core group of companies have moved someway along the process, but a much wider group of companies remain only partially engaged. In the pockets of the industry where the sustainability professionals reside the sophistication of their discussions is incredible. But a fundamental challenge is that progress on the hard issues, those closest to the core activities of mining, like mine waste, have been the slowest to move.

One important difference between the time period of the MMSD and the present is that the business case for action on sustainable development is now much clearer. *Breaking New Ground* found that, 'Most companies [we]re struggling to establish a clear business case for pursuing [sustainable development].'[17] As we saw in Chapter 5, local community advocacy and conflict has been the biggest driver of corporate recognition of the business case for sustainable and equitable development. Demands for change expressed as blockades have a way of making executives take notice.

Professor Caroline Digby, former Research Manager of the MMSD and Director of the Centre for Sustainability in Mining and Industry at the University of Witwatersrand, reflected on this issue of whether the business case was now understood and whether sustainability had been embedded within companies:

> If we look at change from MMSD to now, I think there has been all that focus on developing standards, guidelines and toolkits. If any site implemented even 50% of any of that stuff, we'd all be delighted. I think that most companies have very little idea about how that plays out on the ground in the specific cultural settings and political settings [in which they work]. That will need to be focused on. Now for me, that then raises the question about who the real change-agents will be, because that's about leadership on the ground, that's about the mine manager really believing this is core business. So there is a whole band of people that haven't actually been touched by this agenda.

I am quite frequently surprised when I meet mining executives about how many have never heard of the MMSD or even the ICMM. I sometimes think that this might be a measure of success, that sustainability issues are now so normal that it is possible to run an environment or exploration department, or a even a whole mining operation without an awareness of the deep sustainable development controversies faced by the industry and how the industry has tried to collectively respond to them. Mostly, though, I think that awareness of the MMSD, ICMM and the recent history of sustainability reform are fundamental for employees in the mining sector, and that the time that has elapsed since the MMSD may have contributed to collective industry amnesia. One corporate mining professional that I spoke to put it this way:

> There was a generational change of CEOs about six years ago, and actually we're seeing exactly the same thing now. I think it's probably fair to say that some of those new CEOs didn't have the same understanding or commitment. And some of the companies that weren't around the table at MMSD, and subsequently have become very big, possibly haven't been through some of the experiences that some of the bigger, longer-established companies have been through, which was, in a sense, what took them to the table at MMSD.

Professor Caroline Digby has also sensed some repetition in the conversations about sustainable development that may be a product of the time that has elapsed since MMSD:

> I guess I have been doing this for 25 years, at least. And particularly in the last six months, I have been in a number of different fora where to me it has not moved at all, really. It's still talking about the same issues, it's still asking the same questions, it's still believing that it's the first time this conversation has been had, or had, at this depth or gravity, and therefore are we really going to be able to change things now? I think badging this as sustainability in the mining industry is never going to work, because it is always seen as something for a group of champions who happen to be greenies, environmentalists, social justice advocates, or whatever. And actually to get real change this is going to have to be much more embedded in business. The language around sustainability is just going to have to go.

There is now a need for a renewed agenda for change. The MMSD process served the industry well. It spurred a wave of reform, debate, dialogue and reflection that has contributed to improvements in the lives of many people and the quality of the global environment. A renewed agenda, perhaps in the form of a MMSD +20, would rekindle and widen the reach of sustainable development issues and foster a new generation of change-makers to deliver the necessary reform. I believe that sustainable development is the right frame of reference, but whatever the chosen discourse, the focus of dialogue must be on how to embed change in core business activities and decisions. Planning for such a process would need to start soon, and could usefully be linked to efforts to tailor the United Nations Sustainable Development Goals to the specific challenges of the sector.

In this book we have seen the best and the worst of the mining industry. Remarkable progress has been juxtaposed with unacceptable behaviour and recidivism. The change-agents, working on the inside and out, who have shared their stories with me, truly do move mountains. There is a much to be optimistic about, yet there is also much still to do. As for whether the mines are a-changin', I am tempted to say 'that the answer is blowin' in the wind', but we have seen that some things have changed, for some mines, in some places. Sometimes reform has lasted changes in leadership or changes in circumstance; other times reforms were abandoned at the first opportunity. Mostly, the period since the MMSD can be described as a period where progress towards sustainable development has been made, thanks to the dedication of a remarkably diverse range of mountain movers.

Notes

1 Russell, G. (1980), 'Brazil: The treasure of Serra Pelada.' *Time*, 116(10): 43.
2 For more on the importance of governance in shaping natural resource development outcomes see: World Bank (2004), *Striking a Better Balance*. Final Report of the Extractive Industries Review. Washington, DC. Vol. 1; International Finance Corporation (IFC) (2006), Performance Standard 1. Social and Environmental

Assessment and Management Systems. International Finance Corporation. 30 April; International Council on Mining and Metals (ICMM) (2011), 'Mining: Partnerships for development toolkit,' London; Cheshire, L., Everingham, J.A. and C. Pattenden (2011), 'Examining corporate-sector involvement in the governance of selected mining-intensive regions in Australia.' *Australian Geographer*, 42(2): 123–138; Porter, M., Franks, D.M. and J.E. Everingham (2013), 'Cultivating collaboration: Lessons from initiatives to understand and manage cumulative impacts in Australian resource regions.' *Resources Policy*, 38(4): 657–669.

3   Sagebien, J. and N.M. Lindsay (eds) (2011), *Governance Ecosystems: CSR in the Latin American mining sector*. US and UK: Palgrave Macmillan, p. 13.

4   Campbell, B. (2003), 'Factoring in governance is not enough. Mining codes in Africa, policy reform and corporate responsibility.' *Minerals & Energy – Raw Materials Report*, 18(3): 2–13; Sarrasin, B. (2006), 'The mining industry and the regulatory framework in Madagascar: Some developmental and environmental issues.' *Journal of Cleaner Production*, 14, 388–396; van Duzer, J.A., Simons, P. and G. Mayeda (2013), *Integrating Sustainable Development into International Investment Agreements: A guide for developing countries*. London: Commonwealth Secretariat.

5   Otto, James M. (1992), 'Criteria for assessing mineral investment conditions.' *Mineral Investment Conditions in Selected Countries of the Asia-Pacific Region*. ST/ESCAP/1197, United Nations, New York; Otto's finding have been supported by subsequent authors including: Tole, L. and G. Koop (2011), 'Do environmental regulations affect the location decisions of multinational gold mining firms?' *Journal of Economic Geography*, 11(1), 151–177; and, Vivoda, V. (2011), 'Determinants of foreign direct investment in the mining sector in Asia: A comparison between China and India.' *Resources Policy*, 36(1): 49–59; Lisa Sachs and colleagues from the Columbia Centre on Sustainable Investment found that changes to fiscal regimes were not a deterrent to foreign mining investment as had been claimed by the industry: Sachs, L.E., Toledano, P., Mandelbaum, J. and J. Otto (2013), 'Impacts of fiscal reforms on country attractiveness: Learning from the facts.' In P. Sauvant (ed.), *Yearbook on International Investment Law and Policy*, Chapter 8, pp. 345–386. New York: Oxford University Press.

6   The Intergovernmental Forum on Mining, Minerals, Metals and Sustainable Development was announced by South Africa and Canada at the Rio +10 Summit in Johannesburg. The goal was to create an ongoing forum for government-to-government discussion about mining and sustainable development.

7   Jung, A. (2008), '10 years of fatal transactions.' Online resource: http://www.medico.de/media/input-referat-10-years-of-fatal-transactions.pdf Accessed: 1 July 2014.

8   For more on horizontal and vertical diffusion see: Le Meur, P.Y., Horowitz, L.S. and T. Mennesson (2013), '"Horizontal" and "vertical" diffusion: The cumulative influence of Impact and Benefit Agreements (IBAs) on mining policy-production in New Caledonia.' *Resources Policy*, 38(4): 648–656.

9   Bader, C. (2014), *The Evolution of a Corporate Idealist: When girl meets oil*. Brookline, MA: Bibliomotion, pp. xx–xxi.

10 For more on the role of corporate sustainability professionals inside mining companies see: Kemp, D. (2010), 'Community relations in the global mining industry: Exploring the internal dimensions of externally orientated work.' *Corporate Social Responsibility and Environmental Management*, 17(1): 1–14.

11 Wand, P. and B. Harvey (2012), 'The sky did not fall in! Rio Tinto after Mabo.' In T. Bauman and L. Glick, *The Limits of Change: Mabo and native title 20 years on*. Canberra: AIATSIS, pp. 289–309.

12 Pacific Rim Mining Corp. (2009), 'Notice of Arbitration.' Pac Rim Cayman LLC v. Republic of El Salvador. 30 April. Online resource: http://www.italaw.com/sites/default/files/case-documents/ita0591_0.pdf Accessed: 26 January 2015.

13 The Mining and Environment Research Network (MERN) was a collaboration of more than 60 academic institutions focused on mining. MERN was coordinated by Alyson Warhurst at the University of Bath, but was originally established in 1991 by researchers at the University of São Paulo and the Centre for Mineral Technology (Centro de Tecnología Mineral) in Brazil; the Institute for Research on Public Health (Instituto de Salud Popular) and the Catholic University of Peru (Pontificia Universidad de la Católica del Perú) in Lima, Peru; the Centre for Studies in Mining and Development (Centro de Estudios Mineria y Desarrollo) in La Paz, Bolivia; and the Centre for Studies of Copper and Mining (Centra de Estudios del Cobre y de la Mineria) in Santiago, Chile. See: Warhurst, A. (ed.) (1999), *Mining and the Environment: Case studies from the Americas*. Ottawa, Canada: International Development Research Centre.

14 For a published account of our work on cumulative impacts and governance in Australian resource regions see: Porter et al. (2013), 'Cultivating collaboration.'

15 In Canada, the Mining Association of Canada developed the 'Towards Sustainable Mining' framework; in South Africa the Department of Minerals & Energy led the 'Sustainable Development through Mining' programme and the 'Broad-based Socio-Economic Empowerment Charter for the South African Mining Industry'; in Mongolia, government, industry, civil society and academia worked together to develop the 'Responsible Mining Initiative'; and in Australia The Minerals Council of Australia developed the 'Enduring Value' framework.

16 IIED and WBCSD (2002), *Breaking New Ground*, p. xxiv.

17 IIED and WBCSD (2002), *Breaking New Ground*, p. xviii.

Bibliography

Accountability Counsel et al. (2010). 'Comments on IFC's consultation drafts of the IFC Sustainability Policy and Performance Standards and Disclosure Policy.' 27 August, 38p. Online resource: http://www.ciel.org/Publications/CSO_Submission_IFC_27Aug10.pdf Accessed: 21 September 2014.

African National Congress (ANC) (2012). 'Maximising the developmental impact of the People's mineral assets: State intervention in the minerals sector.' March.

African Union (2009). 'Africa mining vision.' February. Online resource: http://pages.au.int/sites/default/files/Africa%20Mining%20Vision%20english_0.pdf Accessed: 7 February 2015.

Agreements, Treaties and Negotiated Settlements Project (ATNS) (2011). 'Rio Tinto Alcan Gove Traditional Owners Agreement.' Online resource: http://www.atns.net.au/agreement.asp?EntityID=5599 Accessed: 8 August 2014.

Akam, S. (2012). 'Sierra Leone diamond firm: From war booty to IPO.' Reuters. 4 April. Online resource: http://www.reuters.com/article/2012/04/04/us-sierraleone-diamonds-idUSBRE83311520120404 Accessed: 4 July 2014.

American Petroleum Institute (API) (2012). 'API files court challenge against costly, anti-competitive SEC rule.' October. Online resource: http://www.api.org/news-and-media/news/newsitems/2012/oct-2012/api-files-court-challenge-against-costly-sec-rule Accessed: 21 January 2015.

American Petroleum Institute (API) (2013). 'API lauds court win ending SEC's anti-competitive disclosure rule.' July. Online resource: http://www.api.org/news-and-media/news/newsitems/2013/july-2013/api-lauds-court-win-ending-sec-anti-competitive-disclosure-rule Accessed: 21 January 2015.

Anglo American (2003). 'SEAT: Socio–Economic Assessment Toolbox.' London.

Anglo American (2007). 'SEAT: Socio–Economic Assessment Toolbox.' Version 2. London.

Anglo American (2012). 'SEAT Toolbox: Socio–Economic Assessment Toolbox.' Version 3. London. Online resource: http://www.angloamerican.com/~/media/Files/A/Anglo-American-PLC-V2/documents/communities/seat-toolbox-v3.pdf Accessed: 7 February 2015.

Arbeláez-Ruiz, D. and D.M. Franks (2014). 'Getting to the table: How a new generation of organisations is improving dialogue and recording conflict over mining in Latin America.' *Americas Quarterly*, 8(2): 111–113.

Ashe, K. 2012. 'Elevated mercury concentrations in humans of Madre de Dios, Peru.' *PLoS ONE*, 7(3): e33305.

Asner, G., Llactayo, W., Tupayachi, R. and E. Ráez Luna (2013). 'Elevated rates of gold mining in the Amazon revealed through high-resolution monitoring.' *Proceedings of the National Academy of Sciences*, 110(46): 18454–18459.

Atkins, D. and S. Wildau (2008). *Participatory Water Monitoring: A guide for preventing and managing conflict*. Advisory note. Compliance Advisor Ombudsman. Washington, USA.

Australian Government (2008). 'Bark Petition (transcript) tabled in the House of Representatives 14 and 28 August, 1963.' Online resource: http://australia.gov.au/about-australia/australian-story/bark-petition-1963 Accessed: 8 August 2014.

Auty, R. (1993). *Sustaining Development in Mineral Economies: The resource curse thesis*. London and New York: Routledge.

Ax, J. (2014). 'Frenchman gets two years in U.S. prison for role in Guinea mine scandal.' *Reuters*. 25 July. Online resource: http://www.reuters.com/article/2014/07/25/us-usa-guinea-mining-idUSKBN0FU23S20140725 Accessed: 20 January 2015.

Azam, S. and Q. Li (2010). 'Tailings dam failures: A review of the last one hundred years.' *Geotechnical News*, December, 50–53.

Bader, C. (2014). *The Evolution of a Corporate Idealist: When girl meets oil*. Brookline, MA: Bibliomotion.

Balleny, L. (2013). 'Miners less resistant to transparency than big oil.' *Thomson Reuters Foundation*. 1 August. Online resource: http://www.trust.org/item/20130801110131-vi1ez/ Accessed: 21 January 2015.

Barrett, D., Sonter, L., Almarza, A., Franks, D.M., Moran, C.J., Cohen, T. and C. Hedemann (2010). 'Quantitative approach to improving the business of biodiversity investment.' Final report. Centre for Water in the Minerals Industry, University of Queensland. Australian Coal Association Research Program. Project Number: C17030.

Bateman, P. (2010). 'Cyanide management: Ten years since Baia Mare.' *Mining Environmental Management*, July: 13–15. Online resource: http://www.euromines.org/sites/default/files/publications/cyanide-management-ten-years-baia-mare-—-july-2010.pdf Accessed: 22 December 2014.

Bertone, T. (2013). 'Pope Francis' greeting to mining industry representatives for Day of Reflection.' 7 September. Online resource: http://www.zenit.org/en/articles/pope-francis-greeting-to-mining-industry-representatives-for-day-of-reflection Accessed: 9 January 2015.

Bieri, F. (2010). *From Blood Diamonds to the Kimberley Process: How NGOs cleaned up the global diamond industry*. Surrey: Ashgate.

Billon, P. (2001). 'The political ecology of war: Natural resources and armed conflicts.' *Political Geography*, 20(5): 561–584.

Billon, P. (2006). 'Fatal Transactions: Conflict diamonds and the (anti)terrorist consumer.' *Antipode*, 38(4): 778–801.

Blair, T. (2003). Speech by Tony Blair, UK Prime Minister. Extractive Industries Transparency Initiative, London Conference, 17 June. Online resource: http://collections.europarchive.org/tna/20070701080507/http://www.dfid.gov.uk/pubs/files/eitidraftreportspeech.pdf Accessed: 19 January 2015.

Boege, V. and D.M. Franks(2012). 'Reopening and developing mines in post-conflict settings: The challenge of company–community relations.' In P. Lujala and S.A. Rustad (eds), *High-Value Natural Resources and Post-Conflict Peacebuilding*. Milton Park and New York: Earthscan, pp. 87–120.

Boger, D. (2013). 'Rheology of slurries and environmental impacts in the mining industry.' *Annual Review of Chemical and Biomolecular Engineering*, 4: 239–257.

Boger, D.V. (2009). 'Rheology and the resource industries.' *Chemical Engineering Science*, 64(22): 4525–4536.

Bone, A. (2012). 'The Kimberly Process Certification Scheme: The primary safeguard for the diamond industry.' In P. Lujala and S.A. Rustad (eds), *High-Value Natural Resources and Post-Conflict Peacebuilding*. Earthscan, London, pp. 189–194.

Brooks, W.E., Sandoval, E., Yepez, M.A. and H. Howard (2007). *Peru Mercury Inventory 2006*. Reston, VA: US Geological Survey.

Browne, J. (2010). *Beyond Business: An inspirational memoir from a visionary leader*. London: Phoenix. 310p.

Brundtland, G.H. (1987). 'Our common future: Chairman's foreword.' In *Report of the World Commission on Environment and Development: Our Common Future*. United Nations, A/42/427.

Brunnschweiler, C.N. and E.H. Bulte (2008). 'Linking natural resources to slow growth and more conflict.' *Science*, 320(5876): 616–617.

Bulaong Jnr., O. (2004). 'A case study on Marcopper Mining Corporation and the tragedy of 1996.' Institute for Ethical Business Worldwide, University of Notre Dame, Consortium Case. April. Online resource: http://www.ethicalbusiness.nd.edu/researchScholarship/Consortium%20cases/Marcopper_CaseApril2.pdf Accessed: 4 January 2015.

Buxton, A. (2012). MMSD +10: Reflecting on a decade of mining and sustainable development. International Institute for Environment and Development, London. June.

Buxton, A. (2013). 'Responding to the challenge of artisanal and small-scale mining. How can knowledge networks help?' London: International Institute for Environment and Development.

Campbell, B. (2003). 'Factoring in governance is not enough. Mining codes in Africa, policy reform and corporate responsibility.' *Minerals & Energy – Raw Materials Report*, 18(3): 2–13.

Campbell, N. (2010). Testimony to the Special Court for Sierra Leone. Online resource: https://www.youtube.com/watch?v=bItA7VstArE Accessed: 1 July 2014.

Carr, R.S., Nipper, M. and G. Plumlee (2003). 'Survey of marine contamination from mining-related activities on Marinduque Island, Philippines: Porewater toxicity and chemistry.' *Aquatic Ecosystem Health & Management*, 6(4): 369–379.

Cheshire, L., Everingham, J.A. and C. Pattenden (2011). 'Examining corporate-sector involvement in the governance of selected mining-intensive regions in Australia.' *Australian Geographer*, 42(2): 123–138.

Chevron Australia. (2005). 'Draft Environmental Impact Statement/Environmental Review and Management Programme for the Gorgon Development.' Chapter 14. *Social and Cultural Environment – Effects and Management*. September. Online resource: https://www.chevronaustralia.com/docs/default-source/default-document-library/chapter_14_social_and_cultural_environment_risks_and_management.pdf?sfvrsn=0 Accessed 13 May 2015.

Coll, S. (2000). 'The other war.' *Washington Post Magazine*, 9 January. Online resource: http://www.washingtonpost.com/wp-dyn/content/article/2006/11/28/AR2006112800682.html Accessed: 4 July 2014.

Collier, P. (2010). *The Plundered Planet: Why we must – and how we can – manage nature for global prosperity*. New York: Oxford University Press.

Collier, P. and A. Hoeffler (1999). 'Justice-seeking and loot-seeking in civil war.' The World Bank, Washington, DC, 17 February.

Collins, N. and L. Lawson (2014). 'Investigating approaches to working with artisanal and small-scale miners: A compendium of strategies and reports from the field.' International Mining for Development Centre. Online resource: http://im4dc.org/wp-content/uploads/2013/09/Collins-ASM-FR-Completed-Report.pdf Accessed: 13 May 2015

Comité Technique de Revue des Titres et Conventions Miniers (CTRTCM). (2014). 'Publication of the Report and Recommendation of the CTRTCM on the Licenses and Mining Convention Obtained by VBG.' 9 April. Conakry. Online resource: http://www.contratsminiersguinee.org/blog/publication-report-recommendation-VBG.html Accessed: 20 January 2015.

Commonwealth Department of the Environment (DoE) (2014). 'Australia's biodiversity conservation strategy – case studies.' Online resource: http://www.environment.gov.au/biodiversity/conservation/strategy/case-studies Accessed: 8 November 2014.

Cooney, J. (1997). 'Placer Dome: "We are responsible".' *The Catholic Register*. 28 April. p. 17.

Cooney, J. (2014). 'Interview with Rick Cluff.' CBC *The Early Edition*, British Columbia. 4 December. Online resource: http://www.cbc.ca/player/Radio/Local+Shows/British+Columbia/The+Early+Edition/Full+Episodes/ID/2625541410/ Accessed: 5 January 2015.

Cote, C.M., Cummings, J., Moran, C.J. and K. Ringwood (2012). 'Water accounting in mining and minerals processing.' In J. Godfrey and K. Chalmers (eds), *Water Accounting: International approaches to policy and decision-making*. Cheltenham, UK; Northampton, MA: Edward Elgar, pp. 91–105.

Coumans, C. (2002). 'Placer Dome case study: Marcopper Mines.' April. Online resource: http://www.miningwatch.ca/sites/www.miningwatch.ca/files/PD_Case_Study_Marcopper_0.pdf Accessed: 4 January 2015.

Courier Mail (1957). 'Bauxite will "open" Gulf, says Nicklin.' 17 December 1957, p. 3.

Courtenay, P.P. (1982). *Northern Australia: Patterns and problems of tropical development in an advanced country*. Melbourne: Longman Cheshire.

Credit Suisse (2012). 'Australian ESG/SRI. $21.4bn in ESG concerns on Australian stocks.' July. Online resource: https://plus.credit-suisse.com/u/F7o3dB

Danielson, L. (2006). 'Architecture for change: An account of the Mining, Minerals and Sustainable Development Project.' Global Public Policy Institute, Berlin, Germany.

Dashwood, H.S. (2014). *The Rise of Global Corporate Social Responsibility: Mining and the spread of global norms*, Cambridge: Cambridge University Press.

David, C.P. (2002). 'Heavy metal concentrations in marine sediments impacted by a mine-tailings spill, Marinduque Island, Philippines.' *Environmental Geology*, 42(8): 955–965.

Davis Jr., R.A., Welty, A.T., Borrego, J., Morales, J.A., Pendon, J.G. and J.G. Ryan (2000). 'Rio Tinto estuary (Spain): 5000 years of pollution.' *Environmental Geology*, 39(10): 1107–1116.

Davis, L. (1995). 'New Directions for CRA.' Speech to the Securities Institute of Australia, Melbourne/Sydney, March.

Davis, M.L. (2007). Sustainable Development Policy. Xstrata. December.

Davis, R. and D.M. Franks (2014). 'Costs of company–community conflict in the extractive sector.' Corporate Social Responsibility Initiative Report no. 66. Harvard Kennedy School, Cambridge, MA. Online resource: http://www.hks.harvard.edu/m-rcbg/CSRI/research/Costs%20of%20Conflict_Davis%20%20Franks.pdf Accessed: 7 February 2015.

Edraki, M., Baumgartl, T., Manlapig, E., Bradshaw, D., Franks, D.M. and C.J. Moran (2014). 'Designing mine tailings for better environmental, social and economic outcomes: A review of alternative approaches.' *Journal of Cleaner Production*. DOI: 10.1016/j.jclepro.2014.04.079.

Elmes, A., Yarlequé Ipanaqué, J.G., Rogan, J., Cuba, N. and A. Bebbington (2014). 'Mapping licit and illicit mining activity in the Madre de Dios region of Peru.' *Remote Sensing Letters*, 5(10): 882–891.

Epstein, E.J. (1982). *The Rise and Fall of Diamonds: The shattering of a brilliant illusion*. New York: Simon and Schuster.

Equator Principles (2014). 'About the Equator Principles.' Online resource: http://www.equator-principles.com/index.php/about-ep/about-ep Accessed: 23 June 2014.

Erskine, P. (2014). 'Ecological rehabilitation, past, present and future.' Keynote presentation to Best Practice Ecological Rehabilitation of Mined Lands 2014, 25 September Singleton.

Extractive Industries Transparency Initiative (EITI) (2014). 'Investors' statement on transparency in the extractives sector.' November. Online resource: https://eiti.org/files/Investors-November-2014.pdf Accessed: 20 January 2015.

Extractive Industries Transparency Initiative (EITI) (2014). 'Progress Report 2014: Making transparency matter.' Online resource: https://eiti.org/files/EITI_ProgressReport_2014_En_Web_Interactif_r.pdf Accessed: 20 January 2014.

Farah, D. (2004). *Blood From Stones: The secret financial network of terror*. New York: Broadway Books.

Ferguson, S. (2010). 'What's yours is mine.' *Four Corners*, Australian Broadcasting Corporation. 7 June. Online resource: http://www.abc.net.au/4corners/special_eds/20100607/mining/ Accessed: 5 February 2015.

Flynn A. (2014). 'Rio Tinto, Guinea seal deal on $US20 billion Simandou mine.' *The Australian*. 27 May. Online resource: http://www.theaustralian.com.au/business/mining-energy/rio-tinto-guinea-seal-deal-on-us20-billion-simandou-mine/story-e6frg9df-1226932660235 Accessed: 20 January 2015.

Franks, D.M. and P. Erskine (2012). 'Mine site rehabilitation in Sierra Leone – A rapid appraisal of selected sites.' Brisbane: Centre for Mined Land Rehabilitation and The University of Queensland, Brisbane.

Franks, D.M. and F. Vanclay (2013). 'Social Impact Management Plans: Innovation in corporate and public policy.' *Environmental Impact Assessment Review*, 43: 40–48.

Franks, D.M., Boger, D., Côte, C. and D. Mulligan (2011). 'Sustainable development principles for the disposal of mining and mineral processing wastes.' *Resources Policy*, 36(2): 114–122.

Franks, D.M., Brereton, D. and C.J. Moran (2013). 'The cumulative dimensions of impact in resource regions.' *Resources Policy*, 38(4): 640–647.

Franks, D.M., Brereton, D., and C.J. Moran (2010). 'Managing the cumulative impacts of coal mining on regional communities and environments in Australia.' *Impact Assessment and Project Appraisal*, 28(4): 299–312.

Franks, D.M., Davis, R., Bebbington, A.J., Ali, S.H., Kemp, D. and M. Scurrah (2014). 'Conflict translates environmental and social risk into business costs.' *Proceedings of the National Academy of Sciences*, 111(21): 7576–7581.

Franks, D.M., Fidler, C., Brereton, D., Vanclay, F. and P. Clark (2009). 'Leading practice strategies for addressing the social impacts of resource developments.' Centre for Social Responsibility in Mining, Sustainable Minerals Institute, The University of Queensland. Briefing paper for the Department of Employment, Economic Development and Innovation, Queensland Government. November. Brisbane. Online resource: https://www.csrm.uq.edu.au/publications?task=download&file=pub_link&id=287 Accessed: 7 February 2015.

Fraser, B. (2009). 'Peruvian gold rush threatens health and the environment.' *Environmental Science and Technology*, 43(19): 7162–7164.

Freestone, D. (2013). *The World Bank and Sustainable Development: Legal essays*. Leiden, The Netherlands: Martinus Nijhoff Publishers.

Gardner, E. (2012). 'Peru battles the golden curse of Madre de Dios.' *Nature*, 486(7403): 306–307.

General Accounting Office (2002). 'Significant Challenges Remain in Deterring Trade in Conflict Diamonds.' Statement of Loren Yager, Director, International Affairs and Trade, Testimony Before the Subcommittee on Oversight of Government Management, Restructuring and the District of Columbia, Committee on Governmental Affairs, U.S. Senate. 13 February. GAO-02-425T.

Gilbertson, B. (2002). BHP Billiton Statement at Global Mining Initiative Conference, 15 May 2002, Toronto. Online resource: http://www.bhpbilliton.com/home/investors/reports/Documents/BrianGilbertsonSpeechGMIConf.pdf Accessed: 23 June 2014.

Glaister, B.J. and G. Mudd (2010). 'The environmental costs of platinum–PGM mining and sustainability: Is the glass half-full or half-empty?' *Minerals Engineering*, 23(5): 438–450.

Global Mining Initiative (GMI) (undated). 'Chronology of Events of ICMM Significance.'

Global Witness (1998). 'A rough trade: The role of companies and governments in the Angolan conflict.' December. London, United Kingdom. 15p. Online resource: http://www.globalwitness.org/sites/default/files/pdfs/A_Rough_Trade.pdf   Accessed: 11 July 2014.

Global Witness (1999). 'A crude awakening: The role of the oil and banking industries in Angola's civil war and the plunder of state assets.' December. London. 22p.

Global Witness (1999). 'Campaign launched to stop billion dollar diamond trade from funding conflict in Africa.' Press release: 3 October. Online resource: http://www.africa.upenn.edu/Hornet/irin_10499.html Accessed: 1 July 2014.

Global Witness (2001). 'Campaign success: BP makes move for transparency in Angola.' Press release: 12 February. Online resource: http://www.globalwitness.org/library/campaign-success-bp-makes-move-transparency-angola Accessed: 19 January 2015.

Global Witness (2002). 'All the Presidents' men.' March. London.

Global Witness (2002). 'Publish what you pay.' Press release: 13 June. Online resource: http://www.globalwitness.org/library/publish-what-you-pay   Accessed: 19   January 2015.

Global Witness (2003). 'Conflict diamonds: Possibilities for the identification, certification and control of diamonds.' June.

Global Witness (2011). 'Global witness leaves Kimberley Process, calls for diamond trade to be held accountable.' Press release: 5 December. Online resource: http://www.globalwitness.org/library/global-witness-leaves-kimberley-process-calls-diamond-trade-be-held-accountable Accessed: 1 July 2014.

Global Witness (2014). 'FBI surveillance implicates diamond billionaire in plan to subvert US fraud probe.' 9 April. Online resource: http://www.globalwitness.org/sites/default/files/library/GW%20BSGR%20report%20-%2009.04.14.pdf   Accessed: 20 January 2015.

Global Witness (2014). 'The Kimberley Process.' Online resource: http://www.globalwitness.org/campaigns/conflict/conflict-diamonds/kimberley-process Accessed: 22 July 2014.

Gooch, C. (2011). 'Why we are leaving the Kimberley Process – A message from Global Witness Founding Director Chairman Gooch.' 5 December. Online resource: http://www.globalwitness.org/library/why-we-are-leaving-kimberley-process-message-global-witness-founding-director-charmian-gooch Accessed: 1 July 2014.

Graetz, G. (2015). 'Ranger Uranium Mine and the Mirarr (Part 1), 1970–2000: The risks of "riding roughshod".' *The Extractive Industries and Society*, 2(1): 132–141.

Grant, J. (2012). 'The Kimberly Process at ten: Reflections on a decade of efforts to end the trade in conflict diamonds.' In P. Lujala and S.A. Rustad (eds), *High-Value Natural Resources and Post-Conflict Peacebuilding*, London: Earthscan, pp. 159–179.

Groom, J. (2003). 'Mining and the environment: Challenges and opportunities.' Proceedings of the 19th World Mining Congress, 1–5 November 2003, New Delhi, pp. 111–122.

Hailu, D., Gankhuyag, U. and C. Kipgen (2014). 'How Does the Extractive Industry Promote Growth, Industrialization and Employment Generation?' Paper presented to the United Nations Development Programme and Government of Brazil, Dialogue on the Extractive Sector and Sustainable Development – Enhancing Public–Private–Community Cooperation in the context of the Post-2015 Agenda, Brasilia, Brazil, 3–5 December.

Hair, J., Dysart, B., Danielson, L. and A.O. Rubalcava (1997). 'Pangue Hydroelectric Project (Chile): An independent review of the International Finance Corporation's compliance with applicable World Bank Group environmental and social requirements.' April, Santiago, Chile.

Harvey, B. (2013). ComRel conversations. Interview with Bruce Harvey by Dr Deanna Kemp. Centre for Social Responsibility in Mining, University of Queensland. Online resource: https://www.csrm.uq.edu.au/docs/ComRel_Conversations_2_Bruce_Harvey_Transcript.pdf Accessed: 28 July 2014.

Henisz, W., Dorobantu, S. and L. Nartey (2013). 'Spinning gold: The financial returns to stakeholder engagement.' *Strategic Management Journal*, 35(12): 1727–1748.

Hentschel, T., Hruschk, F. and M. Priester (2002). 'Global report on artisanal & small-scale mining.' Report for the Mining, Minerals and Sustainable Development Project, no. 70. International Institute for Environment and Development and World Business Council for Sustainable Development. January, London.

Hidalgo, C., Peterson, K., Smith, D. and H. Foley (2014). 'Extracting with purpose: Creating shared value in the oil and gas and mining sectors' companies and communities.' Shared Value Initiative and FSG. October. Online resource: http://sharedvalue.org/resources/report-extracting-purpose

Hill, C., Leske J. and S. Lillywhite (2013). 'The right to decide: Company commitments and community consent.' CAER and Oxfam Australia, Belconnen, Australia.

Hilson, G. (2006). 'Abatement of mercury pollution in the small-scale gold mining industry: Restructuring the policy and research agendas.' *Science of the Total Environment*, 362(1–3): 1–14.

Hilson, G. and J. McQuilken (2014). 'Four decades of support for artisanal and small-scale mining in sub-Saharan Africa: A critical review.' *The Extractive Industries and Society*, 1(1): 104–118.

Hooke, R., Martín–Duque, J. and J. Pedraza (2012). 'Land transformation by humans: A review.' *GSA Today*, 22(12): 4–10.

Huissier de Justice (2014). Transcription de l'enregistrement audio des conversations entre M. Cilins et Mme Touré.' Online resource: https://s3.amazonaws.com/s3.documentcloud.org/documents/1105519/transcription-enregistrement-audio-frederic.pdf Accessed: 20 January 2015.

IndustriALL, Construction, Forestry, Mining and Energy Union, United Steelworkers, Earthworks and MiningWatch Canada (2013). 'More shine than substance: How the RJC certification fails to create responsible jewelry.' May.

Instituto Nacional de Estadísticas (2007). División Político-Administrativa y Censal. Santiago de Chile. Online resource: http://www.ine.cl/canales/chile_estadistico/territorio/division_politico_administrativa/pdf/DPA_COMPLETA.pdf Accessed: 4 June 2014.

Instituto Nacional de Estadísticas (2012). División Político-Administrativa y Censal. Santiago de Chile.

International Commission on Intervention and State Sovereignty (2001). 'The Responsibility to Protect.' November, International Development Research Centre, Ottawa, p. 4.

International Copper Study Group (2013). 'The World Copper Fact Book 2013.' Portugal.

International Council on Mining and Metals (ICMM) and International Union for Conservation of Nature (IUCN) (2014). 'Biodiversity performance review.' Executive summary. November. London.

International Council on Mining and Metals (ICMM) (2002). ICMM Toronto Declaration. 15 May. Online resource: http://www.icmm.com/document/31 Accessed: 13 June 2014.

International Council on Mining and Metals (ICMM) (2003). 'Mining and protected areas.' Position statement. September. London.

International Council on Mining and Metals (ICMM) (2006). 'The challenge of mineral wealth: Using resource endowments to foster sustainable development.' August. London.

International Council on Mining and Metals (ICMM) (2008). 'Mining and Indigenous Peoples Position Statement.' May. Online resource: http://www.icmm.com/document/293 Accessed: 21 September 2014.

International Council on Mining and Metals (ICMM) (2011). 'Mining: Partnerships for Development Toolkit.' London.

International Council on Mining and Metals (ICMM) (2012). 'Trends in the mining and metals industry. Mining's contribution to sustainable development.' October. London.

International Council on Mining and Metals (ICMM) (2012). 'Water management in mining: A selection of case studies.' May. London.

International Council on Mining and Metals (ICMM) (2013). 'Approaches to understanding development outcomes from mining.' July. London, 59p.

International Council on Mining and Metals (ICMM) (2013). 'Indigenous Peoples and Mining Position Statement.' May. 6p. Online resource: http://www.icmm.com/document/5433 Accessed: 21 September 2014.

International Council on Mining and Metals (ICMM) (2013). 'Mining's contribution to sustainable development.' Address by Mark Cutifani, CEO, Anglo Gold Ashanti (7 February), Mining Indaba, Cape Town. Online resource: https://www.youtube.com/watch?v=n__qA79cjtI & https://www.icmm.com/document/5043 Accessed: 9 January 2015.

International Council on Mining and Metals (ICMM) (2014). 'Benchmarking safety data: Progress of ICMM members.' Online resource: http://www.icmm.com/publications/safety-data Accessed: 21 August 2014.

International Council on Mining and Metals (ICMM) (2014). Our members. Online resource: http://www.icmm.com/members Accessed: 19 June 2014.

International Cyanide Management Institute (ICMI) (2014). 'Directory of signatory companies.' Online resource: http://www.cyanidecode.org/signatory-companies/directory-of-signatory-companies Accessed: 10 November 2014.

International Finance Corporation (IFC) (2006). 'IFC Performance Standards on Environmental and Social Sustainability.' April, Washington; International Finance Corporation (IFC; 2012). 'IFC Performance Standards on Environmental and Social Sustainability.' January, Washington.

International Finance Corporation (IFC) (2006). 'Performance Standard 7. Indigenous Peoples.' 30 April. Online resource: http://www.ifc.org/wps/wcm/connect/ a6b1b6804885565ab9bcfb6a6515bb18/PS_7_IndigenousPeoples.pdf?MOD=AJPER ES&attachment=true&id=1322818661604 Accessed: 21 September 2014.

International Finance Corporation (IFC) (2006). Performance Standard 1. Social and Environmental Assessment and Management Systems. International Finance Corporation. 30 April.

International Finance Corporation (IFC) (2007). 'Environmental, health and safety guidelines for mining.' December. 33p. Online resource: http://www.ifc.org/wps/ wcm/connect/1f4dc28048855af4879cd76a6515bb18/Final%2B-%2BMining.pdf?M OD=AJPERES&id=1323153264157 Accessed: 22 December 2014.

International Finance Corporation (IFC) (2007). 'Guidance Note 7. Indigenous Peoples.' 31 July. Online resource: http://www.ifc.org/wps/wcm/connect/707761004 885582bbf24ff6a6515bb18/2007%2BUpdated%2BGuidance%2BNote_7.pdf?MOD =AJPERES&attachment=true&id=1322818940215 Accessed: 21 September 2014.

International Finance Corporation (IFC) (2008). 'Lessons learned: Pangue hydroelectric. Summary.' Environment and Social Development Department. Online resource: http://www.ifc.org/wps/wcm/connect/85ce100048865954b8dafa6a6515bb18/ pangue_summary.pdf?MOD=AJPERES&CACHEID=85ce100048865954b8dafa6a6 515bb18 Accessed: 23 June 2014.

International Finance Corporation (IFC) (2010). 'Performance Standard 7 – Rev-0.1 Indigenous Peoples. Mark up of draft Policy and Performance Standards on Social and Environmental Sustainability (Against April 30, 2006 Version).' 14 April. 7p. Online resource: http://www.ifc.org/wps/wcm/connect/345b950049800a0ba8ebfa336 b93d75f/CODE_Progress%2BReport_AnnexB_PS7.pdf?MOD=AJPERES Accessed: 21 September 2014.

International Finance Corporation (IFC) (2010). 'Performance Standard 7 – V2. Indigenous Peoples. Draft sustainability framework – Tracked Changes (Against April 14, 2010 Version (V1).' 1 December. 7p. Online resource: http://www.ifc. org/wps/wcm/connect/1f59e880498007f6a1e7f3336b93d75f/Phase3_PS7_V1_Vs_ V2.pdf?MOD=AJPERES Accessed: 21 September 2014.

International Finance Corporation (IFC) (2010). 'Review and update of the Policy and Performance standards on Social and Environmental Sustainability and Policy on Disclosure of Information.' Indigenous Peoples Thematic Consultation Summary, 29 July. Washington, DC. Online resource: http://www.ifc.org/wps/wcm/ connect/6268c58049800a5baa5bfa336b93d75f/IFCConsultationIndigenousPeoples. pdf?MOD=AJPERES Accessed: 21 September 2014.

International Finance Corporation (IFC) (2012). 'Guidance Note 7. Indigenous Peoples.' 1 January 2012. Online resource: http://www.ifc.org/wps/wcm/connect/ 50eed180498009f9a89bfa336b93d75f/Updated_GN7-2012.pdf?MOD=AJPERES Accessed: 21 September 2014.

International Institute for Environment and Development (IIED) (2014). 'PDF downloads tracking: Breaking new ground'. Accessed: 23 June 2014.

International Institute on Environment and Development (IIED) and World Business Council for Sustainable Development (WBCSD; 2002). *Breaking New Ground: Mining minerals and sustainable development. The report of the MMSD project.* London: Earthscan.

International Labour Organization (1989). 'Convention concerning Indigenous and Tribal Peoples in independent countries.' No. 169. Online resource: http://

www.ilo.org/dyn/normlex/en/f?p=NORMLEXPUB:12100:0::NO:12100:P12100_INSTRUMENT_ID:312314:NO Accessed: 8 August 2014.

International Monetary Fund (IMF) (2012). 'Macroeconomic policy frameworks for resource-rich developing countries.' August, 55p. Online resource: http://www.imf.org/external/np/pp/eng/2012/082412.pdf Accessed: 9 February 2015.

International Tanker Owners Pollution Federation (ITOPF) (2013). 'Oil tanker spill statistics 2012.' London.

International Tanker Owners Pollution Federation (ITOPF) (2014). 'Oil tanker spill statistics 2013.' London.

IRIN (2009). 'Credibility of Kimberley Process on the line, say NGOs.' Online resource: http://m.irinnews.org/Report/84949/GLOBAL-Credibility-of-Kimberley-Process-on-the-line-say-NGOs#.U_PR4dkazCQ Accessed: 15 August 2014.

Johnson, K. (2001). 'Signing of the Western Cape communities co-existence agreement.' Comalco. 14 March 2001. Online resource: http://www.riotinto.com/documents/ReportsPublications/MDG_Western_Cape_Communities_Coexistence_Agreement.pdf Accessed: 22 August 2014; Keenan and Kemp (2012), 'Mining and local-level development.'

Jowitt, S.M., Mudd, G.M. and Z. Weng (2013). 'Hidden mineral deposits in cu-dominated porphyry-skarn systems: How resource reporting can occlude important mineralization types within mining camps.' *Economic Geology*, 108(5): 1185–1193.

Jung, A. (2008). '10 years of Fatal Transactions.' Online resource: http://www.medico.de/media/input-referat-10-years-of-fatal-transactions.pdf Accessed: 1 July 2014.

Kawamoto, K. (2012). 'Diamonds in war, diamonds for peace: Diamond sector management and kimberlite mining in Sierra Leone.' In P. Lujala and S.A. Rustad (eds), *High-Value Natural Resources and Post-Conflict Peacebuilding*. Milton Park and New York: Earthscan, pp. 121–145.

Keen, D. (2005). *Conflict and Collusion in Sierra Leone*. US and UK: Palgrave Macmillan.

Keenan, J.C. and D.L. Kemp (2014). 'Mining and local-level development: Examining the gender dimensions of agreements between companies and communities.' Centre for Social Responsibility in Mining, The University of Queensland, Brisbane, Australia.

Kellogg Innovation Network (KIN). (2014). 'Reinventing mining: Creating sustainable value introducing the Development Partner Framework.'

Kemp, D. (2010). 'Community relations in the global mining industry: Exploring the internal dimensions of externally orientated work.' *Corporate Social Responsibility and Environmental Management*, 17(1): 1–14.

Kemp, D. and J.R. Owen (2013). 'Community relations in mining: Core to business but not "core business".' *Resources Policy*, 38(4): 523–531.

Kemp, D., Owen, J.R., Gotzman, N. and C.J. Bond (2011). 'Just relations and company–community conflict in mining.' *Journal of Business Ethics*, 101(1): 93–109.

Kimberley Process Certification Scheme (2014). 'About: Kimberley process basics.' Online resource: http://www.kimberleyprocess.com/en/about Accessed: 21 July 2014.

Kimberley Process Certification Scheme (KPSC) (2002). 'Essential Elements of an International Scheme of Certification for Rough Diamonds, With a View to Breaking the Link Between Armed Conflict and the Trade in Rough Diamonds.' 20 March. Kimberley Process Working Document nr 1/2002.

Knight, D. (2002). 'Global groups seek action on mining industry.' Inter Press Service News Agency, 28 May. Online resource: http://www.ipsnews.net/2002/05/environment-global-groups-seek-action-on-mining-industry/ Accessed: 13 June 2014.

Koidu Holdings (2012). 'Company history timeline.' Online resource: http://www. koiduholdings.com/company-history.php Accessed: 4 July 2014.

Koori Mail (1993). 'Mabo style claim held to ransom by mining giant.' Wednesday 28 July, p. 1.

Kretschmer, T. (1998). 'De Beers and beyond: The history of the international diamond cartel.' London Business School Case. Online resource: http://pages.stern.nyu. edu/~lcabral/teaching/debeers3.pdf Accessed: 27 June 2014.

Langton, M. (2012). '2012 Boyer Lectures. Lecture 1 – Changing the paradigm: Mining companies, native title and Aboriginal Australians.' Sunday 18 November 2012. Online resource: http://www.abc.net.au/radionational/programs/boyerlectures/boyers-ep1/4305610 Accessed: 12 September 2014.

Le Meur, P.Y., Horowitz, L.S. and T. Mennesson (2013). '"Horizontal" and "vertical" diffusion: The cumulative influence of Impact and Benefit Agreements (IBAs) on mining policy-production in New Caledonia.' *Resources Policy*, 38(4): 648–656.

Levin, E. (2012). 'Understanding artisanal & smallscale mining in protected areas and critical ecosystems: A growing global phenomenon.' Presentation for ASM Protected and Critical Ecosystems London Roundtable. November.

Libby, R.T. (1989). *Hawke's Law: The politics of mining and Aboriginal land rights in Australia.* Nedlands: University of Western Australia Press.

Lujala, P. and S.A. Rustad (eds) (2012). *High-Value Natural Resources and Post-Conflict Peacebuilding.* Milton Park and New York: Earthscan. 688p.

Lynch, S. (2012). 'Business groups sue SEC over Dodd-Frank anti-bribery rule.' *Reuters*. October. Online resource: http://www.reuters.com/article/2012/10/11/us-sec-lawsuit-idUSBRE8991NL20121011 Accessed: 21 January 2015.

Macdonald, I. and K. Southall (2005). 'Mining Ombudsman case report: Marinduque Island.' Oxfam Australia. March. Fitzroy.

Maconachie, R. and G. Hilson (2011). 'Artisanal gold mining: A new frontier in post-conflict Sierra Leone?' *The Journal of Development Studies*, 47(4): 595–616.

Maconachie, R. and T. Binns (2007). '"Farming miners" or "mining farmers"?: Diamond mining and rural development in post-conflict Sierra Leone.' *Journal of Rural Studies*, 23(3): 367–380.

Manson, K. (2013). 'Battlefields, diamonds and the "hell" of the MBA.' *Financial Times*, 7 October. Online resource: http://www.ft.com/intl/cms/s/2/95a65f74-08b7-11e3-8b32-00144feabdc0.html#axzz36TQvDNpe Accessed: 4 July 2014.

Marcel, M. (1989). 'Privatización y finanzas públicas: el caso de Chile 1985–88.' In Colección Estudios Cieplan no. 26, June, pp. 5–60. Online resource: http://www. cieplan.org/media/publicaciones/archivos/88/Capitulo_1.pdf Accessed: 16 June 2014.

Marcopper Mining Corporation (MMC) (1996). 'So the people may know …' Marcopper flyer reproduced in Bulaong Jnr. (2004). Online resource: http://www.ethicalbusiness. nd.edu/researchScholarship/Consortium%20cases/Marcopper_CaseApril2.pdf Accessed: 4 January 2015.

Martinez, C. and D.M. Franks (2014). 'Does mining company-sponsored community development influence social licence to operate? Evidence from private and state-owned companies in Chile.' *Impact Assessment and Project Appraisal*, 32(4): 294–303.

McBryde, E. (2014). 'Gladstone mayor wary of mining exploitation.' *The Gladstone Observer*. 3 October. Online resource: http://www.gladstoneobserver.com.au/news/mayor-is-wary-of-mining-exploitation/2407590/ Accessed: 14 January 2015.

McNab, K., Keenan, J., Brereton, D., Kim, J., Kunanayagam, R. and T. Blathwayt (2012). 'Beyond voluntarism: The changing role of corporate social investment in the extractives sector.' Centre for Social Responsibility in Mining, The University of Queensland. Brisbane.

McNab, K., Onate, B., Brereton, D., Horberry, T., Lynas, D. and D.M. Franks (2013). 'Exploring the social dimensions of autonomous and remote operation mining: Applying social licence in design.' Prepared for CSIRO Minerals Down Under Flagship, Mineral Futures Collaboration Cluster, by the Centre for Social Responsibility in Mining and the Minerals Industry Safety and Health Centre, Sustainable Minerals Institute, The University of Queensland, Brisbane.

Mines and Communities (2001). 'The London Mining Declaration.' Online resource: http://www.minesandcommunities.org/article.php?a=8245 Accessed: 13 June 2014.

Mining Journal (2002). 'UK calls for transparency.' 6 September, 339 (8701). Online resource: http://www.infomine.com/news/mining.journal/Sep06-02.pdf Accessed: 15 January 2015.

MiningWatch Canada (2013). 'Barrick Ignores UN High Commissioner for Human Rights Recommendation regarding Papua New Guinea rapes.' Press release: 28 October. Online resource: http://www.miningwatch.ca/news/barrick-ignores-un-high-commissioner-human-rights-recommendation-regarding-papua-new-guinea-rap Accessed: 30 July 2014.

Mitchell, R. (1986). 'Historical aspects of Kimberlite petrology.' In R. Mitchell, *Kimberlites: Mineralogy, geochemistry and petrology*, New York: Springer, pp. 1–6.

Moburg, J. and E. Rich (2013). 'Beyond governments: Lessons on multi-stakeholder governance from the Extractive Industries Transparency Initiative (EITI).' Online resource: https://eiti.org/files/08_Moberg_Rich.pdf Accessed: 19 January 2015.

Moody, R. (1992). *The Gulliver File. Mines, People and Land: A global battleground*. London: Minewatch, p. 234.

Moody, R. (2002). 'Sustainable development unsustained: A critique of the MMSD project.' Nostromo Research and Society of St Columban, April, London.

Moran, R. (2001). 'More cyanide uncertainties: Lessons from the Baia Mare, Romania, spill – water quality and politics.' Mineral Policy Centre Issue Paper no. 3. Online resource: http://www.earthworksaction.org/files/publications/mcu_final.pdf Accessed: 9 November 2014.

Morgan, R. (2002). 'Communicating change.' International Council on Mining and Metals Newsletter, 1(3): 5.

Morris, M. and J. Linnegar (2004). *Every Step of the Way: The journey to freedom in South Africa*. Cape Town, South Africa: Human Sciences Research Council Press.

Mudd, G.M. (2007). 'Global trends in gold mining: Towards quantifying environmental and resource sustainability?' *Resources Policy*, 32(1–2): 42–56.

Mudd, G.M. (2009). 'Historical trends in base metal mining: Backcasting to understand the sustainability of mining.' *Proceedings of the 48th Annual Conference of Metallurgists*, Canadian Metallurgical Society, Sudbury, Canada, August 2009, pp. 273–284.

Mudd, G.M. (2009). 'The sustainability of mining in Australia: Key production trends and their environmental implications for the future.' Research report no. RR5, Department of Civil Engineering, Monash University and Mineral Policy Institute, Revised – April 2009.

Mudd, G.M. (2010). 'The environmental sustainability of mining in Australia: Key mega-trends and looming constraints.' *Resources Policy*, 35: 98–115.

Mudd, G.M. (2012). 'Sustainability reporting and the platinum group metals: A global mining industry leader?' *Platinum Metals Review*, 56(1): 2–19.

Mudd, G.M. (2014). 'The future of Yellowcake: A global assessment of uranium resources and mining.' *Science of the Total Environment*, 472: 590–607.

Mudd, G.M. and D.V. Boger (2013). 'The ever growing case for paste and thickened tailings: Towards more sustainable mine waste management.' *AusIMM Bulletin*, April: 56–59.

Mudd, G.M. and S.M. Jowitt (2014). 'A detailed assessment of global nickel resource trends and endowments.' *Economic Geology*, 109(7): 1813–1841.

Mudd, G.M. and C.P. Roche (2014). 'Mining in Morobe, Papua New Guinea – Impacts, assurance and self-determination.' Proceedings of Life-of-Mine 2014 Conference, Australasian Institute of Mining and Metallurgy, July 2014, Brisbane, pp. 313–335.

Mudd, G.M., Weng, Z. and S.M. Jowitt (2013). 'A detailed assessment of global cu reserve and resource trends and worldwide cu endowments.' *Economic Geology*, 108(5): 1163–1183.

Mudder, T. and M. Botz (2004). 'Cyanide and society: A critical review.' *The European Journal of Mineral Processing and Environmental Protection*, 4(1): 62–74.

Mudder, T., Botz, M. and K. Hagelstein (2006). 'Cyanide science and society.' Unpublished manuscript. Wyoming: TIMES Ltd.

Museum of Australian Democracy (2005). 'Yirrkala bark petitions 1963.' Online resource: http://foundingdocs.gov.au/item-did-104.html Accessed: 8 August 2014.

Natural Resource Governance Institute (NRGI). (2014). 'Natural Resource Charter.' 2nd edn.

Natural Value Initiative (NVI) (2011). 'Tread lightly: Biodiversity and ecosystem services risk and opportunity management within the extractive industry.' October. Online resource: http://www.naturalvalueinitiative.org/download/documents/Publications/NVI%20Extractive%20Report_Tread%20lightly_LR.pdf Accessed 13 May 2015

Northey, S., Haque, N. and G. Mudd (2013). 'Using sustainability reporting to assess the environmental footprint of copper mining.' *Journal of Cleaner Production*, 40: 118–128.

Organisation for Economic Co-operation and Development (OECD) (2013). 'Net official development assistance from DAC and other donors in 2012.' Online resource: http://www.oecd.org/development/stats/ODA2012.pdf Accessed: 7 February 2015.

Otto, James M. (1992). 'Criteria for Assessing Mineral Investment Conditions.' *Mineral Investment Conditions in Selected Countries of the Asia-Pacific Region*. ST/ESCAP/1197, United Nations, New York.

Pachas C., V.H. (2013). 'A vision for ecological gold mining in Peru.' ASM-PACE blog. 19 July. Online resource: http://www.asm-pace.org/blog/item/9-peru-madre-dios-artisanal-mining-biodiversity.html Accessed: 3 November 2014.

Pacific Rim Mining Corp. (2009). 'Notice of Arbitration.' Pac Rim Cayman LLC v. Republic of El Salvador. 30 April. Online resource: http://www.italaw.com/sites/default/files/case-documents/ita0591_0.pdf Accessed: 26 January 2015.

Payer, C. (1974). *The Debt Trap: The IMF and the Third World*. Penguin, Harmondsworth.

Payer, C. (1982). *The World Bank: A critical analysis*. New York: Monthly Review Press.

Placer Dome (2005). 'Fact sheet.' August. Online resource: http://web.archive.org/web/20051125012929/http://www.placerdome.com/__shared/assets/August_2005_Investor_Fact_Sheet2856.pdf Accessed: 4 January 2015.

Porter, M., Franks, D.M. and J.E. Everingham (2013). 'Cultivating collaboration: Lessons from initiatives to understand and manage cumulative impacts in Australian resource regions.' *Resources Policy*, 38(4): 657–669.

Project Underground and MiningWatch Canada (2002). 'STD toolkit: Philippines case studies.'

Publish What You Pay (PWYP). (2011). 'About us.' Online resource: http://www. publishwhatyoupay.org/about Accessed: 20 January 2015.

Publish What You Pay United States (PWYP US) (2014). 'Transparency on the move: Payment disclosure by the world's largest oil, gas & mining companies.' March. Online resource: http://pwypusa.org/sites/default/files/Company%20Coverage%20Fact%20 Sheet_Final.pdf Accessed: 21 January 2015.

Queensland Department of Infrastructure and Planning (QDIP) (2010). 'Social impact assessment. Guideline to preparing a social impact management plan.' September.

Queensland Department of Tourism Regional Development and Industry (QDTRDI) (2008). 'Sustainable Resource Communities Policy. Social impact assessment in the mining and petroleum industries.' Brisbane, September.

Radden Keefe, P. (2013). 'Buried Secrets: How an Isaraeli billionaire wrested control of one of Africa's biggest prizes.' *The New Yorker*. 8 July.

Regional Environmental Centre for Central and Eastern Europe (REC) (2000). 'The cyanide spill at Baia Mare, Romania: Before, during and after.' Szentendre, Hungary. Online resource: http://archive.rec.org/REC/Publications/CyanideSpill/ENGCyanide. pdf Accessed: 22 December 2014.

Reguly, E. (2013). 'Industry's reckoning: Why are world's top miners at the Vatican?' *The Globe and Mail*. 9 September.

Responsible Jewellery Council (RJC) (2013). RJC Response to 'More shine than substance' Report. June. Online resource: http://www.responsiblejewellery.com/ files/RJC-Response-to-More-Shine-than-Substance-Report-130613.pdf Accessed: 7 January 2015.

Rio Tinto (2010). History. Online resource: http://www.riotinto.com/aboutus/history-4705. aspx Accessed: 8 August 2014.

Roberts, B. (1976). *Kimberley, Turbulent City*. Cape Town: David Philip & Kimberley Historical Society.

Roberts, J. (1978). *From Massacres to Mining: The colonization of Aboriginal Australia*. London: Colonialism and Indigenous Minorities Research and Action, and War on Want.

Roberts, J. (1981). *Massacres to Mining: The colonization of Aboriginal Australia*. Melbourne: Dove Communications.

Roberts, R.G., Jones, R. and M.A. Smith (1990). 'Thermoluminescence dating of a 50,000-year-old human occupation site in Northern Australia.' *Nature*, 345(10 May): 153–156.

Roche, M. (2012). 'Queensland's resources outlook.' CEDA Resources Outlook, Queensland Resources Council. 30 October.

Ross, M. (1999). 'The political economy of the resource curse.' *World Politics*, 51(2): 297–322.

Ross, M. (2013). 'EITI 2.0.' Keynote address. International Mining for Development Conference, 20 May, Sydney. Transcript. Online resource: http://www. resourcegovernance.org/news/blog/eiti-20 Accessed: 17 January 2015.

Ross, M. (2001). 'Extractive sectors and the poor: An Oxfam America report.' October. Boston: Oxfam America.

Rotberg, R.I. (1988). *The Founder: Cecil Rhodes and the pursuit of power*. New York: Oxford University Press.

Ruggie, J. (2014). 'The past as prologue? A moment of truth for UN Business and Human Rights Treaty.' Institute for Human Rights and Business, 14 June. Online resource: http://www.ihrb.org/commentary/past-as-prologue.html Accessed: 29 September 2014.

Russell, G. (1980). 'Brazil: The treasure of Serra Pelada.' *Time*, 116(10): 43.

Sachs, J. and A. Warner (1995). 'Natural resource abundance and economic growth.' Development Discussion Paper, no. 517a. Cambridge, MA: Harvard Institute for International Development.

Sachs, J. and A. Warner (1997). 'Natural resource abundance and economic growth.' Centre for International Development and Harvard Institute for International Development. Cambridge, MA: Harvard University, November.

Sachs, L.E., Toledano, P., Mandelbaum, J. and J. Otto (2013). 'Impacts of Fiscal Reforms on Country Attractiveness: Learning from the facts.' In P. Sauvant (ed.), *Yearbook on International Investment Law and Policy*, Chapter 8, 345–386. New York: Oxford University Press.

Sagebien, J. and N.M. Lindsay (eds) (2011). *Governance Ecosystems: CSR in the Latin American Mining Sector*. US and UK: Palgrave Macmillan.

Sarrasin, B. (2006). 'The mining industry and the regulatory framework in Madagascar: Some developmental and environmental issues.' *Journal of Cleaner Production*, 14, 388–396.

Sierra Leone Truth and Reconciliation Commission (SLTRC) (2004). *Witness to Truth: Report of the Sierra Leone Truth and Reconciliation Commission*. Accra, Ghana.

Simons, P. and A. Macklin (2013). *The Governance Gap: Extractive industries, human rights, and the home state advantage*. London: Routledge.

Smillie, I., Gberie, L. and R. Hazleton (2000). 'The heart of the matter: Sierra Leone, diamonds and human security.' Partnership Africa Canada. January. Ottawa, Canada.

Smith, G. (2014). Participants in the Voluntary Principles Initiative gather for discussions on outreach and implementation and welcome five new participants and one new observer. Press statement, 28 March. Online resource: http://www.voluntaryprinciples.org/wp-content/uploads/2014/03/Press-Release-March-28-2014.pdf Accessed: 26 September 2014.

Sonter, L., Barrett, D., Soares-Filho, B. and C.J. Moran (2014). 'Global demand for steel drives extensive land-use change in Brazil's Iron Quadrangle.' *Global Environmental Change*, 26: 63–72.

Sonter, L., Moran, C.J. and D. Barrett (2013). 'Modelling the impact of revegetation on regional water quality: A collective approach to manage the cumulative impacts of mining in the Bowen Basin, Australia.' *Resources Policy*, 38(4): 670–677.

Special Court for Sierra Leone (SCSL) (2010). 'Transcript.' The Prosecutor of the special court v. Charles Ghankay Taylor. SCSL-2003-01-T. 10 August 2010.

Swenson J., Carter C., Domec J.-C. and C. Delgado (2011). 'Gold Mining in the Peruvian Amazon: Global prices, deforestation, and mercury imports.' *PLoS ONE* 6(4): e18875.

Taylor, M. (2013). 'Indigenous people and the resource extraction industry: Towards public, transparent and human rights compliance standards.' Compliance Advisor Ombudsman (CAO). Presentation to the ATNS Symposium, University of Melbourne, 25 June 2013. Online resource: http://atns.net.au/symposium/Day%20One/Dame%20Meg%20Taylor%20ATNS%20Symposium%2025%20June%202013.pdf Accessed: 28 July 2014.

Telmer K. and M. Veiga (2009). 'World emissions of mercury from small scale and artisanal gold mining.' In R. Mason and N. Pirrone N (eds), *Mercury Fate and Transport in the Global Atmosphere: Emissions, Measurements and Models*. New York: Springer, pp. 131–172.

Thomas, A. (1997). *Rhodes: The race for Africa*. London Bridge.

Thomson, I. and R. Boutilier (2011). 'Social license to operate.' In P. Darling, *SME Mining Engineering Handbook*, 3rd edn. Chapter 17.2. pp. 1779–1796.

Tickner, R. (2001). *Taking a Stand: Land rights to reconciliation*. Allen & Unwin, Crows Nest, 376p.

Tole, L. and G. Koop (2011). 'Do environmental regulations affect the location decisions of multinational gold mining firms?' *Journal of Economic Geography*, 11(1): 151–177.

Tremblay, G. and C. Hogan (2012). 'Canada's national orphaned and abandoned mines initiative.' Natural Resources Canada. Presentation to the Managing Mining Legacies Forum, 16–17 July. Online resource: https://www.cmlr.uq.edu.au/Portals/0/MMLF/Canada's%20National%20Orphaned%20and%20Abandoned%20Mines%20Initiative%20(NOAMI).pdf Accessed: 9 November 2014.

Unger, C., Lechner, A., Glennn V., Edraki, M. and D. Mulligan (2012). 'Mapping and prioritising rehabilitation of abandoned mines in Australia.' Proceedings of the Life of Mine Conference, Online resource: https://www.cmlr.uq.edu.au/Portals/0/MMLF/LOM%20Paper%20Unger%20et%20al%20July%202012.pdf Accessed: 9 November 2014.

United Kingdom Prime Minister's Office (2013). '2013 Lough Erne G8 Leaders' Communiqué.' Online resource: https://www.gov.uk/government/uploads/system/uploads/attachment_data/file/207771/Lough_Erne_2013_G8_Leaders_Communique.pdf Accessed: 21 January 2015.

United Nations (2008). 'United Nations Declaration on the Rights of Indigenous Peoples.' A/61/L.67 and Add.1, 15p. Online resource: http://www.un.org/esa/socdev/unpfii/documents/DRIPS_en.pdf Accessed: 5 February 2015.

United Nations (2012). The Future We Want. Resolution adopted by the General Assembly on 27 July 2012. A/RES/66/288: p. 44.

United Nations (2014). 'Open Working Group proposal for Sustainable Development Goals.' Full report of the Open Working Group of the General Assembly on Sustainable Development Goals. A/68/970.

United Nations Conference on Trade and Development (UNCTAD) (2011). 'World Investment Report 2011: Non-equity modes of international production and development.' Geneva.

United Nations Development Programme (2006). 'Evaluation of UNDP Assistance to Conflict-affected Countries: Case study – Sierra Leone.' Evaluation Office. New York.

United Nations Development Programme (UNDP) (2012). 'Strategy note. UNDP's strategy for supporting sustainable and equitable management of the extractive sector for human development.' December. New York.

United Nations Economic Commission for Africa (UNECA) and African Development Bank (AfDB) (2007). 'The 2007 Big Table. Managing Africa's natural resources for growth and poverty reduction.' Summary report. 1 February.

United Nations Economic Commission for Africa (UNECA) and African Union (2011). 'Minerals and Africa's Development.' The International Study Group Report on Africa's Mineral Regimes. Addis Ababa, Ethiopia. 210p.

United Nations Environment Programme (UNEP) and International Council on Metals and the Environment (ICME) (2000). 'A workshop on industry codes of practice: Cyanide management.' 25–26 May Ecole des Mines, Paris, France. Online resource: http://commdev.org/files/1807_file_cyanide_report.pdf Accessed: 22 December 2014.

United Nations Environment Programme (UNEP) and Office for the Co-ordination of Humanitarian Affairs (OCHA) (2000). 'Spill of liquid and suspended waste at the

Aurul SA retreatment plant in Baia Mare.' Cyanide Spill at Baia Mare Romania Assessment Mission 23 February – 6 March. Geneva.

United Nations Environment Programme (UNEP) (1997). 'Compendium of summaries of judicial decisions in environment related cases: Chile – Environmental protection, mining operations.' Pedro Flores y Otros v. Corporacion del Cobre, CODELCO, Division Salvador. Recurso de Proteccion, Copiapo. Supreme Court of Chile, ROL.12.753.FS.641 (1998). SACEP, UNEP, NORAD Publication Series on Environmental Law and Policy. no. 3. Online resource: http://www.unescap.org/drpad/vc/document/compendium/ch1.htm Accessed: 20 February 2007.

United Nations Environment Programme (UNEP) (2009). 'From conflict to peacebuilding: The role of natural resources and the environment.' Expert Advisory Group on Environment Conflict and Peacebuilding. Nairobi. 44p.

United Nations Environment Programme (UNEP) (2010). 'Sierra Leone: Environment, conflict and peacebuilding assessment.' Technical Report, February, Geneva.

United Nations Environment Programme World Conservation Monitoring Centre (UNEP-WCMC) (2013). 'Identifying potential overlap between extractive industries (mining, oil and gas) and natural World Heritage sites.' December.

United Nations Office of the High Commissioner for Human Rights (2011). 'Guiding principles on business and human rights: Implementing the United Nations "Protect, respect and remedy" framework.' New York and Geneva. HR/PUB/11/04. 35p. Online resource: http://www.ohchr.org/Documents/Publications/GuidingPrinciplesBusinessHR_EN.pdf?v=1392752313000/_/jcr:system/jcr:versionstorage/12/52/13/125213a0-e4bc-4a15-bb96-9930bb8fb6a1/1.3/jcr:frozennode Accessed: 5 February 2015.

United Nations Security Council (UNSC) (2000). 'Report of the Panel of Experts appointed pursuant to Security Council resolution 1306 (2000), paragraph 19, in relation to Sierra Leone.' S/2000/1195. December.

United Nations Sustainable Development Solutions Network (2013). 'Harnessing natural resources for sustainable development: Challenges and solutions.' Good Governance of Extractive and Land Resources Thematic Group, United Nations Sustainable Development Solutions Network. Technical report for the post-2015 development agenda. September. Online resource: http://unsdsn.org/wp-content/uploads/2014/02/TG10-Final-Report.pdf Accessed: 11 July 2014.

United States District Court for the District of Columbia (US DCDC) (2013). 'American Petroleum Institute et al., v. Securities and Exchange Commission and Oxfam America.' Civil Action no. 12–1668. 30p.

United States Geological Survey (USGS) (1996). 'The mineral industry of the Philippines.' Online resource: http://minerals.usgs.gov/minerals/pubs/country/1996/9326096.pdf Accessed: 4 January 2015.

United States Geological Survey (USGS) (2000). 'An overview of mining-related environmental and human health issues, Marinduque Island, Philippines: Observations from a joint U.S. Geological Survey – Armed Forces Institute of Pathology Reconnaissance Field Evaluation.' 12–19 May 2000, U.S. Geological Survey Open-File Report 00-397.

United States Geological Survey (USGS) (2014). 'Copper. Mineral commodity summaries.' February. pp. 48–49.

Uongozi Institute (2013). 'Tanzania Natural Resource Charter expert panel launched.' Online resource: http://www.uongozi.or.tz/news_detail.php?news=1873 Accessed: 21 January 2015.

van Duzer, J.A., Simons, P. and G. Mayeda (2013). *Integrating Sustainable Development into International Investment Agreements: A guide for developing countries*. London: Commonwealth Secretariat.

van Oranje, M. and H. Parham (2009). 'Publishing What We Learned: An assessment of the Publish What You Pay Coalition.' Online resource: https://eiti.org/files/ Publishing%20What%20We%20Learned.pdf Accessed: 13 May 2015.

Villegas, C., Weinberg, R., Levin, E. and K. Hund (2012). 'Artisanal and small-scale mining in protected areas and critical ecosystems programme (ASM-PACE)' A Global Solutions Study, September. Online resource: http://www.asm-pace.org/images/ documents/GSS.pdf Accessed: 13 May 2015.

Vivoda, V. (2011). 'Determinants of foreign direct investment in the mining sector in Asia: A comparison between China and India.' *Resources Policy*, 36(1): 49–59.

Voluntary Principles on Security and Human Rights (2000). 'Statement by the Governments of the United States of America and the United Kingdom.' Online resource: https://www.unglobalcompact.org/issues/conflict_prevention/meetings_and_ workshops/volsupport.html Accessed: 26 September 2014.

Voluntary Principles on Security and Human Rights (2013). 'Participation criteria.' Online resource: http://www.voluntaryprinciples.org/wp-content/uploads/2013/03/ VPs_Participation_Criteria_Final_-_127000_v1_FHE-DC.pdf Accessed: 26 September 2014.

Wade, R. (1997). 'Greening the bank: The struggle over the environment, 1970–1995.' In D. Kapur, J.P. Lewis and R. Webb (eds) *The World Bank: Its first half century* (vol. 2). Washington, DC: The Brookings Institution, pp. 611–734.

Wand, P. and B. Harvey (2012). 'The sky did not fall in! Rio Tinto after Mabo.' In T. Bauman and L. Glick, *The Limits of Change: Mabo and native title 20 years on*. Canberra: AIATSIS, pp. 289–309.

Wand, P. and B. Harvey (2012). 'The sky did not fall in! Rio Tinto after Mabo.' Extended unpublished manuscript.

Warhurst, A. (ed.) (1999). *Mining and the Environment: Case studies from the Americas*. Ottawa, Canada: International Development Research Centre.

Wharton, G. (1996). 'The day they burned Mapoon: A study of the closure of a Queensland Presbyterian Mission.' BA (Hons) thesis, University of Queensland.

Whitmore, A. (2006). 'The emperor's new clothes: Sustainable mining?' *Journal of Cleaner Production*, 14: 309–314.

Willemsen-Diaz, A. (2009). 'How Indigenous Peoples' rights reached the UN.' In C. Charters and R. Stavenhagen (eds), *Making the Declaration Work: The United Nations Declaration on the Rights of Indigenous Peoples*. International Work Group for Indigenous Affairs, Document no. 127. Copenhagen, pp. 16–31.

Williams, G.F. (1905). *The Diamond Mines of South Africa*. New York, B.F. Buck & company. Online resource: https://openlibrary.org/books/OL7219289M/The_diamond_mines_ of_South_Africa Accessed: 27 June 2014.

Wilson, A. and M. Cervantes (2014). 'Fraser Institute Annual Survey of Mining Companies 2013.' The Fraser Institute, Vancouver, Canada. Online resource: http:// www.fraserinstitute.org/uploadedFiles/fraser-ca/Content/research-news/research/ publications/mining-survey-2013.pdf Accessed: 28 July 2014.

Wilson, E. and E. Blackmore (2013). 'Dispute or dialogue: Community perspectives on company-led grievance mechanisms.' London: International Institute for Environment and Development.

Woodward, A.E. (1973). *Aboriginal Land Rights Commission First Report*. Canberra: Australian Government Publishing Service, July.

Woodward, A.E. (1974). *Aboriginal Land Rights Commission Second Report*. Canberra: The Government Printer of Australia. Parliamentary Paper no. 69, April.

World Bank (2004). *Striking a Better Balance* (vol. 1). Final Report of the Extractive Industries Review. Washington, DC.

World Bank (2014). 'Sierra Leone.' Online resource: http://www.worldbank.org/en/country/sierraleone Accessed: 22 July 2014.

World Commission on Dams (2000). *Dams and Development: A new framework for decision-making*. The report of the World Commission on Dams. November. London: Earthscan

World Information Service on Energy (2014). 'Chronology of major tailings dam failures, 1960–2014.' Online resource: http://www.wise-uranium.org/mdaf.html Accessed: 7 November 2014.

Wright, C. (2012). 'The Kimberly Process Certification Scheme: A model negotiation.' In P. Lujala and S.A. Rustad (eds), *High-Value Natural Resources and Post-Conflict Peacebuilding*. London: Earthscan, pp. 181–187.

Yothu Yindi Foundation (2014). 'Mining training centre to generate economic development for Yolngu people.' Press release: 2 August 2014. Online resource: http://www.yyf.com.au/news/detail.aspx?SubjectID=1&ArticleID=38 Accessed: 5 August 2014.

Index